Number Five: Texas A&M Southwestern Studies

ROBERT A. CALVERT *and* LARRY D. HILL
General Editors

TEXAS BAPTIST LEADERSHIP
AND SOCIAL CHRISTIANITY, 1900–1980

Texas Baptist Leadership and Social Christianity, 1900–1980

BY
JOHN W. STOREY

TEXAS A&M UNIVERSITY PRESS

College Station

Library of Congress Cataloging-in-Publication Data

Storey, John W. (John Woodrow), 1939–
    Texas Baptist leadership and social Christianity,
1900–1980.
    (Texas A & M southwestern studies ; no. 5)
    Bibliography: p.
    Includes index.
    1. Baptists—Texas—History—20th century.   2. Church
and social problems—Baptists—History—20th century.
3. Christian Life Commission.   4. Texas—Church
history.   I. Title.   II. Series.
BX6248.T4S86   1986   286'.1764   85-20747
ISBN 0-89096-251-0 **(cloth)**
ISBN 1-58544-070-1 (pbk.)

Manufactured in the United States of America
First Paperback Edition

For
Gail, Lisa, and Cynthia

Contents

Illustrations

Acknowledgments

IN a way, this study began a long time ago, when I was an under-graduate and an active member of the Baptist Student Union at Lamar State College in Beaumont, Texas. Having been reared in a rather conservative Baptist environment, I had little if any grasp of the social dimensions of the gospel until entering Lamar. There, in the early 1960s, I became aware of Professor T. B. Maston. His life and career drew my attention to social Christianity. Here was a fellow Texas Baptist with a social con-science. His courageous stand in those years on the racial issue was particularly inspiring. Some years later, upon learning that Professor Maston was quite conservative theologically, I began to question the traditional interpretation of the social gospel. If the social gospel was the response of theologically liberal Chris-tians to problems spawned by rapid urban and industrial growth in the North, as suggested by many scholars, how did one ac-count for a person such as Maston, a southerner, a theological conservative, and a Southern Baptist? This book is an attempt to answer that question.

Numerous individuals and institutions assisted me, and it is a pleasure to acknowledge their help. Professor Maston, now retired from Southwestern Baptist Theological Seminary; pro-fessors Andy Anderson and Wesley Norton, both of the Lamar University History Department; and Professor Rufus B. Spain, a former mentor at Baylor University, read the manuscript and offered many suggestions. Of course, I accept all responsibility for any shortcomings in the study. Generous grants from the Lamar University Research Council facilitated my travels about the state; a timely leave awarded by the university's Faculty Sen-ate enabled me to devote an entire summer to writing. I'd also like to thank Kent Keith, director of the Texas Collection, Baylor

University; Ben Rogers, archivist of the Fleming Library, Southwestern Baptist Seminary, Fort Worth; and Lou Milstead, secretary of the Christian Life Commission, Dallas, who were extremely helpful in locating and selecting photographs. Mrs. Laquita Stidham, the departmental secretary, deciphered my scrawl and made the manuscript presentable.

TEXAS BAPTIST LEADERSHIP
AND SOCIAL CHRISTIANITY, 1900–1980

Introduction

As a movement, the "social gospel" emerged in the late nine-teenth century and reached its peak in the optimistic years pre-ceding World War I. Responding to social ills spawned by in-dustrialization and urbanization and to the effects of scientific thought on traditional Protestantism, the social gospel "involved a criticism of conventional Protestantism, a progressive theology and social philosophy, and an active program of propagandism and reform." Because of its urban origins and liberal credo, his-torians, assuming that the rural and conservative South was inhospitable to a practical application of the scriptures, have generally slighted the former Confederacy when dealing with the social gospel. For instance, in *The Rise of the Social Gospel*, an influential pioneering study first published around 1940, C. Howard Hopkins dismissed the South with only a passing reference to the Southern Sociological Conference. Similarly, in *Origins of the New South* (1951), C. Vann Woodward, an emi-nent southern historian, wrote that American Christianity was characterized in the late nineteenth century by trends toward church unity, acceptance of a more liberal theology, and increased emphasis on a social application of the gospel. "Yet," concluded Woodward, "one searches vainly for important manifestations of any one of these three tendencies in the annals of Southern Christendom." Another prominent historian, Carl Degler, more recently insisted that the social gospel, while arousing many Prot-estant churches of the North, "scarcely touched the South."[1]

Recent scholarship, however, has challenged the traditional interpretation. Although historians were slow to follow his lead,

[1] C. Howard Hopkins, *The Rise of the Social Gospel in American Protestantism, 1865–1915* (1940; reprint, New Haven: Yale University Press, 1967), pp. 3, 278–79; C. Vann Woodward, *Origins of the New South, 1877–1913* (1951; reprint, Baton Rouge:

Hunter Dickinson Farish in 1938 noted that the Methodist Episcopal Church, South, increasingly saw "the importance of bringing its influence to bear on practical affairs." Scholarship since the 1960s documents this suggestive observation. In *Southern White Protestantism* (1964), Kenneth K. Bailey concluded that the three major Protestant denominations of the South "had all officially espoused broad social reform objectives" by the early twentieth century. Rufus B. Spain's study, *At Ease in Zion* (1967), modeled closely after the Farish book, specifically traced the social concerns of Southern Baptists in the postbellum era. Another church historian, John Lee Eighmy, in *Churches in Cultural Captivity* (1972), the most comprehensive work to date on the social aspects of Southern Baptist life, recounted the social attitudes of Southern Baptists from the 1840s to the early 1970s. Works such as these prompted even Hopkins recently to moderate his original thesis. In 1976, writing in collaboration with Ronald C. White, Jr., he broadened the geographical boundaries of the social gospel to include the rural South. And in *The Social Gospel in the South: The Woman's Home Mission Movement*, John Patrick McDowell further illuminated social religion below the Potomac.[2]

Louisiana State University Press, 1964), p. 450; Carl Degler, *Place over Time: The Continuity of Southern Distinctiveness* (Baton Rouge: Louisiana State University Press, 1977), pp. 22–23. Other notable studies, which for the most part ignore the South, are Donald B. Meyer, *The Protestant Search for Political Realism, 1919–1941* (Berkeley: University of California Press, 1960), p. 45; Robert Moats Miller, *American Protestantism and Social Issues, 1919–1939* (Chapel Hill: University of North Carolina Press, 1958), pp. 298–313; and Henry F. May, *Protestant Churches and Industrial America* (New York: Harper Torchbook, 1967).

[2] Farish, *The Circuit Rider Dismounts: A Social History of Southern Methodism, 1865–1900* (Richmond, Va.: Dietz Press, 1938), p. 98; Bailey, *Southern White Protestantism in the Twentieth Century* (1964; reprint, Gloucester, Mass.: Peter Smith, 1968), pp. 38–43; Spain, *At Ease in Zion: A Social History of Southern Baptists, 1865–1900* (Nashville: Vanderbilt University Press, 1967); Eighmy, *Churches in Cultural Captivity: A History of the Social Attitudes of Southern Baptists* (Knoxville: University of Tennessee Press, 1972); Ronald C. White, Jr., and C. Howard Hopkins, *The Social Gospel: Religion and Reform in Changing America* (Philadelphia: Temple University Press, 1976), pp. 80–96; McDowell, *The Social Gospel in the South: The Woman's Home Mission Movement in the Methodist Episcopal Church, South, 1886–1939* (Baton Rouge: Louisiana State University Press, 1982); Wayne Flynt, "One in the Spirit, Many in the Flesh: Southern Evangelicals," *Varieties of Southern Evangelicalism*, ed. David E. Harrell, Jr. (Macon, Ga.: Mercer University Press, 1981), pp. 40–44.

In view of current scholarly findings, what is the need for yet another study of the social attitudes and policies of southern Protestants—specifically, Texas Baptists? There are three compelling reasons. To begin with, Eighmy's study, though perhaps the best work to date on Baptists and society, is misleading in its contention that the social attitudes of Southern Baptists since the late nineteenth century developed mainly in response to the social gospel movement of the North.[3] To be sure, the more prominent advocates of practical religion in Texas were familiar with the literature of the leading social gospel thinkers. Longtime Waco pastor Joseph Martin Dawson; Thomas Buford Maston, who was a distinguished ethics professor at Southwestern Baptist Theological Seminary in Fort Worth; and Acker C. Miller, the first director of the Christian Life Commission of Texas, readily acknowledged an indebtedness to such figures as Washington Gladden, Josiah Strong, and Walter Rauschenbusch.[4]

Similar to ministers of the social gospel movement,[5] moreover, Texas Baptists, when unable to provide explicit biblical sanctions for specific programs, insisted that the tone and nature of Jesus' ministry were sufficient. "He did not devote Himself directly to the correction of evils through governmental processes," Dawson wrote in 1914, "but He did enunciate principles which had in them sufficient dynamite to blow into atoms every corrupt principle incorporated in the government of His time and of all time." The Social Service Committee of the Baptist General Convention of Texas put it more directly. Proclaiming in 1917 that "Jesus was the great sociologist," the committee declared that, in the absence of the spoken word, the attitude and spirit of Jesus furnished adequate basis for supporting civil

[3] Eighmy, *Churches in Cultural Captivity*, p. x.

[4] See Oral Memoirs of T. B. Maston, Waco, 1973, Baylor University Program of Oral History, pp. 24–25, 110; Oral Memoirs of Joseph M. Dawson, Waco, 1973, Baylor University Program of Oral History, pp. 138–39; and Oral Memoirs of Acker C. Miller, Waco, 1973, Baylor University Program of Oral History, pp. 25–26. All citations from Oral Memoirs are taken from typed transcripts of tape-recorded interviews (Archives, Texas Collection, Baylor University, Waco, Texas). See also Thomas B. Maston, interview with author, Fort Worth, Mar. 16, 1979, p. 9. All citations from this interview are taken from a typed transcript of taped conversations.

[5] Hopkins, *Rise of the Social Gospel*, pp. 207–14.

reform, child welfare, improvement of labor conditions, social centers, and settlement houses.[6]

Socially alert Texas Baptists, then, were influenced by the social gospel movement. It not only sharpened their awareness and understanding of social issues, but also provided them a rationale for social involvement based on the spirit of Jesus' ministry. Nevertheless, it is an overstatement to suggest, as Eighmy does, that Baptist concern for society was primarily a response to outside influences. The preachments of the social gospel, for instance, had nothing to do with Baptist support of orphanages, hospitals, insane asylums, educational institutions, and prohibition. In these areas, Baptist concern for the well-being of society was independent of and, in some cases, pre-dated the social gospel movement.

Second, there were fundamental differences between socially alert Baptist churchmen in Texas and northern disciples of the social gospel. Whereas the social gospel that emerged from the urban-industrial milieu of the North was characterized by a rather liberal theological outlook,[7] the advocates of practical religion in Texas remained wedded to a conservative theology that stressed original sin, the transcendence of God, and skepticism of human progress and reason. Hence, such important Texans as Dawson and Maston were out of step with the theology of the social gospel movement. Although both men were affected by the social gospel and appreciated the practical endeavors of its exponents, they, like other Baptist progressives, studiously eschewed the theological liberalism of their northern counterparts. These Texas Baptists saw no contradiction between theological conservatism and social activism.

Moreover, whereas leading social gospel thinkers of the North generally proposed social and institutional solutions to

[6] *Baptist Standard* (Dallas), Sept. 24, 1914, p. 3; Baptist General Convention of Texas, *Proceedings*, 1917, pp. 63–64 (cited hereafter as BGCT, Proceedings).

[7] Theological liberalism and conservatism are not easily defined, for there is significant variety within each category. Broadly, however, *liberalism* as used here denotes a certain degree of optimism about human progress, faith in reason, a deemphasis of original sin, and belief in the immanence of god. According to Hopkins, *Rise of the Social Gospel*, pp. 302–22, the theology of the social gospel was characterized by such emphases.

such issues as inadequate wages or child labor, even the most socially conscious Texas Baptists remained firmly committed, at least until the Great Depression, to individual salvation as the cure for social inequities. In 1914, for instance, Dawson was convinced that "the reformation of society must be preceded by getting the individual saved from sin." The Waco cleric did not alter this view until compelled to do so by the privation of the 1930s. In *Christ and Social Change*, he announced that injuries caused by institutions could not be corrected by merely saving individuals. The system itself had to be restructured. Still, Maston, whose career was devoted to awakening Baptists to the broader aspects of the gospel, wrote in 1968 that he hoped Southern Baptists would "not swing too far in the direction of social action" and thus "lose the evangelistic spirit that has helped make us what we are."[8]

This explains why Texas Baptist progressives preferred Walter Rauschenbusch over other social gospel ministers, for he too stressed the need for individual regeneration.[9] Despite an affinity for Rauschenbusch, however, socially attuned Texas Baptists, because of their conservative theological underpinnings, were not in the mainstream of the social gospel movement. Consequently, using the term *social gospel* to discuss Texas Baptists is inappropriate, inasmuch as it usually connotes a social activism buttressed by a liberal interpretation of scripture. Since the social awareness of Texas Baptists came about within a conservative theological mold and necessitated no significant theological shifts, the terms *social Christianity* or *applied Christianity* more accurately describe the efforts of Texas churchmen to bring the gospel to bear upon society.

Third, such a study is in order because the activities of Texas Baptists, despite their being the largest body in the Southern Baptist convention, have not been adequately explored. Eighmy emphasized the accomplishments of Jesse B. Weather-

[8] *Baptist Standard*, July 30, 1914, p. 13; Joseph M. Dawson, *Christ and Social Change* (Boston: Judson Press, 1937), pp. 116–23; and Thomas B. Maston to Jimmy Allen, Sept. 13, 1968, Maston Collection, Treasure Room, Fleming Library, Southwestern Baptist Seminary, Fort Worth, Texas.

[9] See Oral Memoirs, Maston, p. 25; Oral Memoirs, Dawson, p. 139.

spoon, a noted ethics professor at Southern Baptist Theological Seminary in Louisville, Kentucky, and the Poteats of North Carolina. Texans of national stature such as Dawson, one of the foremost advocates of social Christianity in the early twentieth century, and Maston, the most influential advocate of practical religion among Southern Baptists in the last forty years, were scarcely mentioned.[10]

Surprisingly, even Texas Baptist church historians have given little attention to the social efforts of the Baptist General Convention. *A History of Texas Baptists* (1923) by James M. Carroll, a prominent Texas Baptist whose brother founded Southwestern Seminary, is a useful record of organizational developments from the 1820s to the 1920s, especially regarding state conventions, colleges, and newspapers. But Carroll did not deal specifically with social matters. Joseph M. Dawson, in *A Century with Texas Baptists* (1947), examined the relationship between prohibition and the heightened social vision of Southern Baptists but stopped short of the far-reaching developments following World War II. And in a more recent work, *The Blossoming Desert: A Concise History of Texas Baptists* (1970), Robert A. Baker, a church historian at Southwestern Seminary, gave scant coverage to the Christian Life Commission of Texas, although its objectives and leaders were cited.[11]

This historiographical shortcoming is all the more noticeable in light of the fact that Texas Baptists have wielded considerable influence in social matters at the national level, particularly since World War II. After retiring from the First Baptist Church, Waco, Dawson served as the first full-time director of the Baptist Joint Committee on Public Affairs in Washington, D.C., from 1946 to 1953. Concerned primarily with issues of church and state, this was the only agency at the time in which the major Baptist bodies of the nation cooperated. James Dunn,

[10] Eighmy, *Churches in Cultural Captivity*, pp. 84–88, 132–35, 150–55, 181, 184–85, 204–205.

[11] James M. Carroll, *A History of Texas Baptists* (Dallas: Baptist Standard Publishing Co., 1923); Joseph M. Dawson, *A Century with Texas Baptists* (Nashville: Broadman Press, 1947), pp. 44–46; Robert A. Baker, *The Blossoming Desert, A Concise History of Texas Baptists* (Waco: Word Books, 1970).

another socially conscious Texas churchman, currently holds this position. In addition to holding other important positions within the national convention, Maston presided over the Southern Baptist Advisory Council on Work with Negroes, which was created in the wake of the Supreme Court's 1954 *Brown* decision. Since 1953, Texans Acker C. Miller and Foy Valentine have directed the Christian Life Commission of the Southern Baptist Convention, an agency dedicated to a practical application of the gospel. Another Texan, Jimmy Allen, is president of the national convention's Radio and Television Commission in Fort Worth. These Texans have exerted a positive influence on the national convention, for Texas Baptists have generally been progressive in applying the gospel to society. In 1950, for instance, Texas Baptists were the first to establish a Christian Life Commission, and in the 1950s and 1960s, albeit not without some protest and conflict, they adjusted more readily to altered racial patterns than fellow Baptists elsewhere in the South.[12]

But why should Texas Baptists be any more progressive than Southern Baptists elsewhere? Church historians Spain and Eighmy attributed the South's resistance to change to the rural background of the region, with its emphasis on traditional cultural values.[13] Since 1900, however, Texas has experienced steady urban growth, which accelerated dramatically after World War II. By 1950 Texas had become the most urbanized state in the South and one of the more urbanized areas of the nation, with 62.7 percent of its population residing in cities. Ten years later the state's urban population had increased to 75 percent. Such growth has often been dramatic. During the 1950s alone Houston's population increased by more than 50 percent.[14] In 1960

---

[12]John W. Storey, "Texas Baptist Leadership, the Social Gospel, and Race, 1954–1968," *Southwestern Historical Quarterly* 83, no. 1 (July, 1979): 35–46. For an account of the racial troubles in Georgia see Oral Memoirs of John Jeter Hunt, Jr., Waco, 1978, Baylor University Program of Oral History, pp. 222–49.

[13]Eighmy, *Churches in Cultural Captivity*, p. 55; Spain, *At Ease in Zion*, p. 211.

[14]*Dallas Morning News Texas Almanac and State Industrial Guide, 1970–1971 Tour Texas Edition* (Dallas: A. H. Belo Corp., 1969), pp. 165, 172–73. Prior to 1950, the Texas Almanac defined urban as an incorporated area with a population of 2,500 or more. Everything else was rural. Since 1950, all persons living in incorporated or unincorporated areas of 2,500 or more have been classed as urban.

Houston and Dallas, respectively, were the sixteenth and twentieth largest Standard Metropolitan Statistical Areas of the United States.[15] So, if Eighmy and Spain were correct, one logically could assume that the progressiveness of Texas Baptists, particularly since World War II, was due largely to the urban character of the state.

Though plausible, urbanization alone is an insufficient answer, for Texas Baptists remained disproportionately rural until recently. In 1980 only 52 percent of the congregations within the General Convention were classified as urban.[16] Moreover, figures showing that Texas has become overwhelmingly urban are somewhat deceptive. The U.S. Census Bureau defines as urban any community with a population of twenty-five hundred or more. Consequently, many Texans who are classified as urban live in small communities of three thousand to fifteen thousand that have more in common with the rural parts of the state than with the sprawling metropolitan areas of Houston, Dallas–Fort Worth, San Antonio, or El Paso. Furthermore, many of the post–World War II migrants to the large urban centers came either from the Texas countryside or the rural South, thus bringing with them traditional values resistant to change. So although there has been a dramatic shift in Texas from the countryside to the city, it does not automatically follow that there was an equally dramatic shift in social attitudes.

The progressive character of the Baptist General Convention of Texas, especially its leadership, was due to a combination of factors, of which urbanization was only a part. The principal institutions of the General Convention were never implacably opposed to social Christianity. There are at least four bases of influence among Texas Baptists: the editorship of the *Baptist Standard* (Dallas), which has a substantially wider circulation than any other Southern Baptist weekly;[17] pastorates of the large

---

[15] Blaine A. Brownell, *The Urban South in the Twentieth Century* (Saint Charles, Mo.: Forum Press, 1974), p. 16.

[16] W. E. Norman, statistician, BGCT, to author, May 18, 1981.

[17] *Encyclopedia of Southern Baptists*, (Nashville: Broadman Press, 1958), III, 1599, 1645, 1938. See also Oral Memoirs of E. S. James, Waco, 1973, Baylor University Program of Oral History, pp. 214–15.

urban congregations, such as those in Dallas, San Antonio, Fort Worth, and Houston; full-time executive positions within the bureaucracy of the General Convention in Dallas, such as the directorship of the Christian Life Commission; and the professoriate at Southwestern Seminary, who train future denominational leaders. Editors of the *Baptist Standard*, professors at Southwestern Seminary, key executive figures within the Dallas hierarchy, and respected pastors have generally been sympathetic, although not always fully committed, to a social application of the scriptures.[18]

Although primarily concerned about personal evangelism, the founder of Southwestern Seminary, Benajah Harvey Carroll, for instance, was amenable to social Christianity. Consequently, shortly after the seminary was moved from Waco to Fort Worth in 1910, several members of the faculty offered courses on the subject.[19] Likewise, in 1950, when Texas Baptists created the Christian Life Commission, they gave it a substantially larger budget than the Southern Baptist Convention had given the Social Service Commission, which had been in existence since 1913. Whereas the budget for the Social Service Commission was only $12,500 in 1951,[20] the new Christian Life Commission of Texas was allotted $21,500.[21] And in 1960 the national agency was allocated only $35,000,[22] while the Texas commission was allowed $54,408.58.[23] Such figures confirm the recollection of Acker C. Miller, who noted that "Texas Baptists were very generous in providing money for this work."[24] Indeed, monetarily at least, Texas Baptists were more supportive of social Christianity

[18] Prominent urban ministers who resisted social Christianity were J. Frank Norris, First Baptist Church of Fort Worth, and W. A. Criswell, First Baptist Church of Dallas, the largest Baptist congregation in the world.

[19] Oral Memoirs, Dawson, pp. 140–41; Dawson, *Century with Texas Baptists*, pp. 44–46; Oral Memoirs, Maston, pp. 23–25, 108–10.

[20] Davis C. Hill, "Southern Baptist Thought and Action in Race Relations, 1940–1950," (Th.D., diss., Southern Baptist Theological Seminary, 1952), p. 200.

[21] *Christian Life Commission, Baptist General Convention of Texas, 1950–1970* (Dallas: Christian Life Commission of Texas, n.d.), p. 5.

[22] *Annual* of the Southern Baptist Convention (Nashville, 1960), p. 274 (cited hereafter as *Annual*, SBC).

[23] BGCT, *Proceedings*, 1960, p. 77.

[24] Oral Memoirs, Miller, p. 88.

than the Southern Baptist Convention leadership in Nashville.[25] So from early in this century Texas churchmen who encouraged a practical application of the gospel usually could count on some institutional support, or at least did not have to contend with strong institutional opposition.

Education has also contributed to the progressiveness of Texas Baptist leadership. The advocates of social Christianity in Texas generally recognized the value of schooling, often pursuing it at some personal sacrifice. Joseph Dawson borrowed money to attend Baylor University in 1898. Acker C. Miller in 1917 chose Southern Seminary in Louisville over Southwestern. The Fort Worth school was near his home, but Miller wanted to leave the area to gain another perspective on life. Besides, said Miller, professors at Southwestern "were teaching the books that the Louisville men were writing."[26] In the 1920s and 1930s Thomas Maston attended several institutions, continually striving to broaden his vision.[27] As these men acknowledged, educational experiences sharpened their understanding of applied Christianity. Moreover, as a professor at Southwestern Seminary, Maston was in a position to influence the social thought of a new generation of Baptist leaders. Since World War II, for instance, Foy Valentine, Jimmy Allen, and James Dunn, who successively directed the Christian Life Commission of Texas from 1953 to 1980, have obtained doctoral degrees at the Fort Worth seminary, each majoring in ethics under Maston.[28]

Geography, too, has perhaps contributed to the advancement of social Christianity in Texas. Although this point should not be overemphasized, Texas, despite its being a part of the former Confederacy, was also a western state, not as bound by the culture of the Old South. As historian Numan V. Bartley observed, polls taken in the mid-1950s showed considerably more resistance to racial change in the deep southern states

[25] Oral Memoirs of Foy Dan Valentine, Waco, 1975–1976, Baylor University Program of Oral History, Interview 4, pp. 2–4, 7.

[26] Oral Memoirs, Miller, pp. 20–24. See also Oral Memoirs, Dawson, p. 14.

[27] John W. Storey, "Thomas Buford Maston and the Growth of Social Christianity among Texas Baptists," *East Texas Historical Journal* 19, no. 2 (1981): 30–31.

[28] Ibid., pp. 38–39.

from Georgia to Louisiana than in the peripheral areas of Tennessee and Texas.[29] Certainly, many important Texas Baptist leaders had little attachment to the Old South and thus proved to be flexible on race and other social issues. Even within Texas, the leaders of social Christianity, with a few notable exceptions, came from central and west Texas, not from the more "southern" region of east Texas. Dawson grew up near Waxahachie and held important pastorates at Temple and Waco. Maston, who was reared in east Tennessee, in 1920 came as a student to Fort Worth, where he remained during a long and distinguished career. Miller, born on a horse ranch near San Angelo, held pastorates in central Texas until going to work for the Baptist General Convention in Dallas in 1941.

Central or west Texas origins, of course, neither predisposed one toward a social application of the gospel nor freed one of racial prejudice. Nevertheless, as many Baptist spokesmen from these areas grew up unfettered by the weight of inherited biases, they could more easily accept racial justice when confronted with the issue. Ewing S. James, who became editor of the *Baptist Standard* in late 1954, was a case in point. The Baptist journalist was reared and educated in the early 1900s in western Oklahoma and thereafter held pastorates in small west Texas communities. Until the 1954 *Brown* decision, James had never given much thought to racial matters. But afterward he "began to look the matter straight in the face" and "decided a person couldn't . . . be a segregationist and be the kind of Christian . . . [he] ought to be." The editor subsequently threw his "influence . . . on the side of desegregation because . . . it appeared to be right in the sight of God."[30]

Jimmy Allen and James Dunn had similar experiences. Unlike James, however, both men were reared in a major metropolitan area of central Texas and in their youth harbored strong antiblack sentiments. Allen, growing to maturity in Dallas in the 1940s, frequently engaged blacks in fistfights. "There was," he said, "a great degree of racism and race hatred in my back-

[29] Bartley, *The Rise of Massive Resistance: Race and Politics in the South during the 1950's* (Baton Rouge: Louisiana State University Press, 1969), pp. 13–14.
[30] Oral Memoirs, James, pp. 89–90, 161.

ground." His father was a paternalistic segregationist and his grandmother Allen "didn't think a Negro had a soul." Likewise, Dunn, reared in the 1940s and 1950s on the edge of a black community in southeast Fort Worth, had little sympathy for racial justice. But like James, both men altered their attitudes and behavior when faced with the contradiction between Christian ideals and racial intolerance. In 1944, for instance, at a Young Men's Mission Conference in Ridgecrest, North Carolina, Clarence Jordan of Americus, Georgia, one of the featured speakers, forced Allen to see the discrepancy between his racial attitudes and Christian faith. In Dunn's case, it was Ralph Phelps, Jr., a Maston protégé, who challenged him to apply his faith in all areas, including race.[31]

The importance of geography was evident to Foy Valentine, who was director of the Christian Life Commission of Texas when the 1954 *Brown* decision was rendered. According to Valentine, race was not as troublesome an issue in Texas as elsewhere. East Texas, he elaborated, "which culturally reflected the racism of the Deep South," stoutly resisted racial change, but elsewhere in the state there was not "that much of a crisis over race."[32] Valentine's observation has validity, for although many Texas Baptist leaders questioned the wisdom of the 1954 desegregation ruling, they held attitudes on race less strongly than other values. For instance, they generally advised restraint and discouraged efforts to establish private schools. Although not in accord with the Supreme Court's decision, David H. Gardner, then editor of the *Baptist Standard*, urged compliance as an alternative to any actions that would be detrimental to the public schools. "The idea of abolishing our public school system is unthinkable," he wrote, for "such a course would . . . doom many of the youths of today and the future to live in ignorance, and [thus] imperil the nation."[33]

[31] Oral Memoirs of Jimmy Raymond Allen, Waco, 1973, Baylor University Program of Oral History, pp. 18, 32–34; James Dunn, interview with author, Dallas, May 23, 1979, pp. 1, 6–8. All citations from this interview are taken from a typed transcript of taped conversations.

[32] Oral Memoirs, Valentine, Interview 1, pp. 10, 51, 53; Interview 3, p. 8.

[33] *Baptist Standard*, June 10, 1954, p. 2; see also Aug. 16, 1945, p. 3, and Oct. 7,

Ultimately, however, the exponents of social Christianity in Texas were successful because they shared the theological conservatism of fellow churchmen. The commitment of Dawson, Maston, and other Texas progressives to conservative theology and personal evangelism enabled them to encourage a social application of the gospel without being discredited as liberals. Had they been perceived as unsound theologically, neither Dawson nor Maston could have wielded much influence within the Baptist General Convention. Similarly, in the 1950s, when the Christian Life Commission of Texas embarked on a comprehensive campaign to educate Texas Baptists on social responsibility, it astutely anchored its case in the Bible, distributing statewide a series of pamphlets entitled *The Bible Speaks*. The commission sought to show that the Bible provided ample basis for church involvement in matters of race, economics, politics, and international affairs.

Although theological conservatism did not prevent Texas Baptists from coming to grips with social issues, it nonetheless colored their approach to politics. From Dawson to the current leadership of the Texas Christian Life Commission, advocates of social Christianity have generally advised a cautious, conservative political strategy. As Maston wrote in 1943, Christians could promote social change so long as it was accomplished by evolution instead of revolution.[34] Moreover, the emphasis on individual salvation made socially alert Texas Baptists slow to perceive the corporate nature of sin. The remedy for social ills was not legislative coercion but a change of heart. Jesus came to save the individual, Dawson reassured his Temple congregation in 1914, and "the apprehension of this fundamental fact will do more than all the programs and legislative measures ever concocted by wisacres [sic] and agitators." Likewise, in a 1932 series entitled "Social Teachings of the Bible," Maston insisted that the best way to reform society was "to remake the man. . . . The

---

1948, p. 4. See also Oral Memoirs of R. A. Springer, Waco, 1971, Baylor University Program of Oral History, p. 89.

[34] Maston Collection, vol. 11, "The Christian as Citizen," Sunday school lesson, p. 166.

only way to build a heaven on earth," he said, was "to create a heaven in the hearts of men."[35] Only gradually did Texas Baptists grasp the corporate nature of evil.

If Texas Baptists leaders by the early twentieth century were beginning to see the social dimensions of their faith, to what extent was the vision shared by the rank and file? The hate mail received by Maston, primarily regarding race, indicates that many fellow Texans neither understood nor sympathized with the seminarian. Yet, because of the structure of the Baptist General Convention of Texas, the positions of denominational leaders no doubt reflect more closely the sentiments of fellow Baptists than the pronouncements emanating from Methodist conferences or Presbyterian synods reflect their constituents. Like the Southern Baptist Convention, the Texas convention is composed of locally autonomous and democratically run congregations. Because the state convention does exert influence but cannot impose its will at the local level,[36] its resolutions on controversial issues reflect what a majority of messengers from communities across the state are willing to accept. Hence, the creation and continued support of the Christian Life Commission suggests that Texas Baptists as a body have matured considerably in their grasp of social Christianity since 1900, when prohibition alone dominated Baptist concern. For Texas Baptists, however, the battle for prohibition had unforeseen consequences. It expanded their grasp of social problems and catapulted them into the political process, as preachers and lay persons alike embraced political means in pursuit of moral objectives.

[35] *Baptist Standard*, Sept. 24, 1914, p. 3; Maston Collection, vol. 3, Baptist Training Union Programs, p. 30.
[36] See Oral Memoirs, Allen, p. 93.

1

Preachers, Politics, and Prohibition, 1900–1919

SUPPORT of national prohibition during the first two decades of the twentieth century had a dual effect on Texas Baptists. It involved them in the political process, thereby generating a debate on separation of church and state; and it awakened many of them to the broader dimensions of their faith, causing them to see that the gospel was social as well as personal. The political activism spawned by prohibition spilled over into other areas. And unlike the 1920s, when numbers of Baptists were outspokenly hostile to anything that smacked of social redemption, churchmen in these years were basically untroubled by any conflict between personal evangelism and the pursuit of worthy social objectives. Joseph M. Dawson exemplifies the point. He easily coupled personal evangelism and social justice, including racial equity. Such concern for society, moreover, went beyond a few prominent individuals. By 1915 it had been institutionalized, as the Baptist General Convention of Texas established the Civic Righteousness and Social Service committees to focus denominational attention on a wide array of social matters. Prohibition, of course, remained the paramount concern.

The interest of Texas Baptists in prohibition, dating from the early years of the Republic, gained momentum in the 1880s. Denominational leaders figured prominently in the first statewide attempt to end the liquor traffic by constitutional amendment in 1887. Again, in 1911 Baptists pushed vigorously, albeit unsuccessfully, for statewide prohibition, and in 1913 they endorsed the national Webb-Kenyon measure, which forbade the interstate shipment of liquor into dry areas.[1] In the crusade

---

[1]Zane Allen Mason, *Frontiersmen of the Faith: A History of the Baptist Pioneer Work in Texas, 1865–1885.* (San Antonio: Naylor, 1970), pp. 69–70; Harlan J. Matthews et al., *Centennial Story of Texas Baptists* (Dallas: Baptist General Convention of Texas,

against alcohol Texas Baptists were little different from their counterparts elsewhere.[2] They used essentially the same arguments, adopted similar tactics, and doggedly pursued the same goal. Alcohol was blamed for virtually all ills, from individual degradation to broken homes to low productivity in the marketplace to imperiled democracy, and authorities from the ranks of medicine, science, education, and politics who opposed the vile beverage were quoted profusely; the usual methods of battling John Barleycorn were persistent pressure on state and federal legislators and local option elections, culminating in statewide and, eventually, national prohibition. The anticipated objective was a sober republic dedicated to total abstinence.[3]

One Baptist leader who doggedly fought for prohibition was James B. Cranfill. Born on a farm in Parker County in 1858, he was typical of many Texas Baptists. As a young man in rural north central Texas, Cranfill played the fiddle, smoked, danced, and indulged a weakness for cards. He was not a prohibitionist.

1936), pp. 11, 54, 239; Frances Hazmark, "The Southern Religious Press and the Social Gospel Movement, 1910–1915" (M.A. thesis, Lamar University, 1979), pp. 17–20.

[2] Admittedly, interpretations of prohibition vary widely. On the one hand, Richard Hofstadter, *The Age of Reform: From Bryan to F.D.R.* (New York: Vintage Books, 1955), p. 288, and Andrew Sinclair, *Prohibition: The Era of Excess* (Boston: Little, Brown, 1962), pp. 23–24, harshly denounce the prohibitionists as rural evangelical fanatics and, citing Sinclair, use such terms as "hysteria," "sadism," "persecution," and "a thirst for power" to describe the movement. On the other hand, James H. Timberlake, *Prohibition and the Progressive Movement, 1900–1920* (Cambridge: Harvard University Press, 1963), pp. 2–4, 20–33; Joseph R. Gusfield, *Symbolic Crusade: Status Politics and the American Temperance Movement* (Urbana: University of Illinois Press, 1963), pp. 6–7; Paul C. Conley and Andrew A. Sorenson, *The Staggering Steeple: The Story of Alcoholism and the Churches* (Philadelphia: United Church Press, 1971); Jack S. Blocker, Jr. *Retreat from Reform: The Prohibition Movement in the United States, 1890–1913* (London: Greenwood Press, 1976), pp. 4–5, 12–13; and Norman H. Clark, *Deliver Us from Evil: An Interpretation of American Prohibition* (New York: Norton, 1976), pp. 10–13, offer a more balanced view of national prohibition and depict the movement in more positive terms. Two fine state studies in this latter vein are Paul E. Isaac, *Prohibition and Politics: Turbulent Decades in Tennessee, 1885–1920* (Knoxville: University of Tennessee Press, 1965), pp. 21–27, and Jimmie Lewis Franklin, *Born Sober: Prohibition in Oklahoma, 1907–1959* (Norman: University of Oklahoma Press, 1971), pp. 6–9. My work supports the judgment of scholars such as Timberlake.

[3] Sinclair, *Prohibition*, pp. 46–53; Baptist General Convention of Texas, *Proceedings*, 1886, p. 9; 1892, p. 52; 1900, p. 57; 1906, p. 86; 1908, p. 91; 1910, p. 107; 1911, pp. 15–16; 1913, pp. 149–50; 1916, pp. 41–44; and 1919, pp. 160–62 (cited hereafter as BGCT, *Proceedings*).

But in 1882 the young Texan became a Missionary Baptist and promptly turned from his waywardness. Cranfill thereafter became a model of sobriety, a determined foe of liquor, and a prominent figure in the National Prohibition party. In 1892 he was that party's vice-presidential nominee.[4] That same year he became the co-owner and editor of the *Texas Baptist Standard* of Waco, a position through which Cranfill exercised considerable influence among Southern Baptists of Texas.

In 1900 editor Cranfill verbalized the sentiment of many fellow Baptists. "We believe that the American saloon is the greatest curse our country has to bear," wrote he in an editorial endorsement of national and state Prohibition party candidates, "and so believing shall stand for every movement that seeks its overthrow." The Baptist journalist even went so far as to endorse the hatchet-wielding methods of Mrs. Carrie Nation in Kansas, insisting that violence sometimes was necessary. "It often seems that the only way to annihilate the saloon is to meet lawlessness with lawlessness," he explained, "and if women take the lead, so be it."[5]

Although Texas Baptists obviously agreed with their editor on this point,[6] at least a few had reservations. George S. Tumlin, pastor of the Broadway Baptist Church, Fort Worth, sharply rebuked the *Standard* for inconsistency. As the Baptist journal had taken "a bold stand" against lynching, Tumlin could not understand its approval of "the same spirit in Kansas." Mob violence of any kind, the pastor asserted, bred disrespect for the law.[7] Undaunted, Cranfill retorted that Mrs. Nation's behavior was justified by the refusal of state officials to uphold prohibition statutes. The *Baptist Standard*, to be sure, did not endorse mob violence, but the liquor traffic was a demon that had to be destroyed. "A mad dog running wild," Cranfill reasoned, "has no rights that any man is bound to respect." Though conceding that "we all must be good," the journalist concluded that in the

[4] *Blocker, Retreat from Reform*, pp. 19–22.

[5] *Baptist Standard*, Sept. 20, 1900, p. 4; Jan. 24, 1901, p. 4.

[6] See ibid., Feb. 21, 1901, p. 13; Apr. 18, 1901, p. 2; and San Marcos Baptist Association, *Minutes*, 1901, p. 9.

[7] *Baptist Standard*, Mar. 28, 1901, p. 1.

crusade against alcohol there was "no obligation on us to be goody-good."[8] Texas Baptists took Cranfill to heart—they were never "goody-good" in dealing with John Barleycorn.

Exponents of Richard Hofstadter's view that prohibition was nothing more than a "rural-evangelical virus" would likely show-case Cranfill's enthusiasm, as well as that of other Texas Baptists, as proof of the thesis.[9] That would be a mistake, for prohibition was a positive reform supported not only by rural fundamentalists but also by millions of urbanites drawn from business, labor, and the legal, medical, and teaching professions, numerous Catholic societies, the Federal Council of Churches, the Southern Sociological Congress, and such leading social gospel ministers as Charles Stelzle and Walter Rauschenbusch.[10]

As was true of evangelicals elsewhere, moreover, the prohibition movement contributed to the growing social awareness of Southern Baptists in Texas.[11] When Benajah Harvey Carroll joined the cause of prohibition in 1887, for instance, he glimpsed the broader application of the scriptures and attempted "to build thereafter a church with a social conscience." Although continuing to stress personal evangelism, Carroll subsequently "felt a deeper concern for matters of public and community meaning."[12] Prohibition, furthermore, was the vehicle linking Texas churchmen to the social gospel movement of the North. Of course, prohibition and the social gospel were separate movements, and many Baptists who crusaded against alcohol did not necessarily support other social gospel objectives. Still, the two movements often coalesced as Protestants in both causes en-

[8] Ibid., Feb. 7, 1901, p. 4.

[9] Hofstadter, Age of Reform, p. 188. See also Sinclair, Prohibition, pp. 23–24, 46.

[10] See Timberlake, Prohibition and the Progressive Movement, pp. 2–4, 20–33; Gusfield, Symbolic Crusade, pp. 6–7; Blocker, Retreat from Reform, pp. 4–5, 12–13; Clark, Deliver Us from Evil, pp. 10–13; Ronald C. White, Jr., and C. Howard Hopkins, The Social Gospel: Religion and Reform in Changing America (Philadelphia: Temple University Press, 1976), pp. 86–87, 205–206; and Lewis L. Gould, Progressives and Prohibitionists: Texas Democrats in the Wilson Era (Austin: University of Texas Press, 1973), pp. 42–43.

[11] Timberlake, Prohibition and the Progressive Movement, pp. 5–10, 20–25.

[12] Joseph M. Dawson, A Century with Texas Baptists (Nashville: Broadman Press, 1947), pp. 44–46.

gaged in a cooperative effort to accomplish specific ends through the political process.[13] So in the battle against liquor Texas Baptists identified themselves with one of the goals of the social gospel and readily turned to politics to achieve their objective.

Involvement in the political process invariably led Texas Baptists into a symbiotic association with such groups as the National Prohibition party, Anti-Saloon League, and Women's Christian Temperance Union. These secular organizations looked to local congregations for contributions, votes, and, often, leadership; the churches, in turn, viewed these agencies as vehicles through which the attack on liquor could be channeled. Despite the unity of purpose, however, the prohibitionists often squabbled among themselves over means. This was especially true of the Prohibition party, organized in 1869, and the Anti-Saloon League, founded in 1893. The two groups were fundamentally different. Whereas the Prohibitionists wanted to organize a mass following, seize the reins of power, and then implement, in addition to prohibition, a broad program of reforms ranging from female suffrage to government control of the railroads, the league devoted itself singlemindedly to slaying the saloon. Whereas the Prohibitionists strove to capture the machinery of government, the league sought instead to bend government to its will on the liquor issue. Whereas the Prohibitionists, in order to wrest power from the Democrats or Republicans, needed a plurality in a field of three or a majority in a two-person contest, the league, a nonpartisan organization, could exercise considerable political influence by simply controlling enough votes to swing an election one way or the other. And whereas the Prohibitionists failed, the league became an immensely successful reform lobby. The Prohibitionists reached their peak in the early 1890s and declined steadily thereafter, although they continued tenaciously to claim leadership of the prohibition movement. That claim was increasingly challenged by the league,

[13] Henry F. May, *Protestant Churches and Industrial America* (New York: Harper Torchbook, 1967), pp. 127–35; John Lee Eighmy, *Churches in Cultural Captivity: A History of the Social Attitudes of Southern Baptists* (Knoxville: University of Tennessee Press, 1972), p. 80.

which, despite setbacks, gained momentum and eventually prevailed.[14]

To a certain extent Texas Baptists mirrored this tension within the prohibition movement. James B. Cranfill, who had voted Prohibitionist in every state and federal election since 1884, remained convinced that the party offered the best hope for defeating the liquor traffic. The Anti-Saloon League was only "a half-way house," he argued, and its nonpartisanship was inconceivable. As the Baptist journalist remarked: "I have never been able to see how a man who at heart opposes the liquor traffic could . . . maintain a non-partisan position."[15] But by the early twentieth century Cranfill, who relinquished control of the *Baptist Standard* in 1904, was out of step with other prominent denominational leaders. Indeed, many Texas Baptists were attracted to the league by the very feature Cranfill found so incomprehensible—its nonpartisanship. For Protestants who were reluctant to engage directly in the affairs of state, the league, by virtue of its nonalignment, offered an opportunity for church members, as citizens, to influence political decisions without seeming actually to engage in politics.[16] This was important to many Texas Baptists, as the report of the Committee on the Liquor Traffic to the Baptist General Convention made clear in 1914. "We cordially endorse the Anti-Saloon League," the report read, "with the conviction that its management will conduct its operations on purely non-partisan and non-factional lines." The committee explained that such a course would prevent pastors and churches from being "embarrassed by entangling alliances."[17]

Because the Anti-Saloon League was not firmly planted in

[14] Blocker, *Retreat from Reform*, pp. 206–10, 221–27; Jack S. Blocker, Jr., "The Modernity of Prohibitionists: An Analysis of Leadership Structure and Background," *Alcohol, Reform and Society: The Liquor Issue in Social Context*, ed. Jack S. Blocker, Jr. (London: Greenwood Press, 1979), p. 151; and Sinclair, *Prohibition*, pp. 65, 84–86.

[15] *Baptist Standard*, Mar. 3, 1910, p. 10; see also July 24, 1902, p. 1.

[16] Timberlake, *Prohibition and the Progressive Movement*, pp. 19–20.

[17] BGCT, *Proceedings*, 1914, p. 136. See also Southeast Texas Baptist Association, *Minutes*, 1911, p. 22; Dallas County Missionary Baptist Association, *Minutes*, 1907, p. 23; San Antonio Baptist Association, *Minutes*, 1912, pp. 26–27; and Limestone County Baptist Association, *Minutes*, 1911, p. 7.

Texas until 1907, its task was not so much to arouse as to harness the already existing prohibition sentiment. From the outset the league found eager and willing allies among Texas Baptists. In August, 1907, George W. Carroll, a successful Beaumont businessman and civic leader; James B. Gambrell; and other prominent Baptist leaders endorsed the league. One reason for past failures in the war against alcohol was the "desultory and haphazard way" the battles had been waged. The Anti-Saloon League, wrote Gambrell and Carroll, would give cohesion and direction to the attack.[18] The Baptist General Convention agreed. In 1908 the convention, without mentioning the league by name, pledged "its aid and support to all organizations and movements engaged in promoting the interest of State-wide prohibition"; in 1909, for the first time, it specifically endorsed "the plan and purposes of the organization known as the Anti-Saloon League"; the following year it encouraged its membership to open "its churches on proper occasions to the Anti-Saloon League of Texas"; and in December, 1912, it sent two delegates to the Anti-Saloon League Conference in Washington, D.C. Noticeably, from 1909 to 1917 the only time the convention failed to applaud the league was 1911, the year Prohibitionist James B. Cranfill was chairman of the Committee on the Liquor Traffic.[19]

Perhaps the most striking illustration of the closeness between Texas Baptists and the Anti-Saloon League was the readiness of prominent churchmen to fill key positions in the secular organization. To a much greater extent than the Prohibition party, the league drew its leaders from the clergy.[20] This was certainly so in Texas, where noted Baptists directed the league's activities from 1907 to 1918. Benjamin F. Riley, an Alabamian who came to Texas in 1900 as minister of the First Baptist Church, Houston, resigned his pastorate in 1907 to become the full-time president of the newly formed Texas league. A highly respected member of the Baptist community, Riley served as

[18] *Baptist Standard*, Aug. 22, 1907, p. 1. See also Union Baptist Association, *Minutes*, 1907, pp. 28–30.
[19] BGCT, *Proceedings*, 1908, p. 94; 1909, p. 78; 1910, p. 107; 1912, p. 118; 1911, pp. 14–16.
[20] Blocker, *Alcohol, Reform and Society*, pp. 160–62.

chairman of the General Convention's Committee on the Liquor Traffic in 1908. The following year he assumed leadership of the Southern Negro Anti-Saloon League, whose headquarters were transferred from Dallas to Birmingham, Alabama, in June, 1909.[21] But Riley's departure did not interrupt the connection between the league and Texas Baptists. J. H. Gambrell, an important denominational worker who was overshadowed by his more illustrious brother James B. Gambrell, served as the league's superintendent from 1910 to 1915. In 1912 the General Convention not only praised Superintendent Gambrell for his work in the prohibition movement but also selected him, along with Arthur J. Barton, to attend the Anti-Saloon League Conference coming up in December in Washington, D.C.[22] It was Barton who replaced Gambrell in 1915 as superintendent of the Texas league, a post he retained until October, 1918, by which time the state had become dry. Barton rose to national prominence in both the church and the temperance movement. He was chairman of the Southern Baptist Convention's Standing Committee on Temperance, later absorbed by the Social Service Commission, from 1910 to 1942, and he served on the national executive committee of the Anti-Saloon League from 1913 to 1934, the last ten years as its chairman.[23]

With such prominent denominational spokesmen serving in roles of leadership, the league probably did not seem secular to some Baptists. The prohibition organization looked like an extension of the church,[24] and local Baptists across the state gave it their enthusiastic support. Congregations in the areas of Beaumont, Houston, San Antonio, Waco, Austin, Fort Worth, Dallas, Nacogdoches, and elsewhere responded warmly, urging members not only to pray for but also to give time and money to the league.[25] In 1913 the Dallas County Missionary Baptist As-

[21] BGCT, *Proceedings*, 1908, p. 94; *Baptist Standard*, May 6, 1909, p. 3.
[22] BGCT, *Proceedings*, 1912, pp. 88, 118.
[23] *Encyclopedia of Southern Baptists* (Nashville: Broadman Press, 1958), I, 146.
[24] See Gould, *Progressives and Prohibitionists*, p. 48.
[25] See Van Zandt County Missionary Baptist Association, *Minutes*, 1912, pp. 23–24; 1914, p. 10; Southeast Texas Baptist Association, *Minutes*, 1911, p. 22; Austin Baptist Association, *Minutes*, 1912, pp. 40–41; Tarrant County Baptist Association, *Minutes*,

sociation bespoke the sentiments of many churchmen, declaring that it "ought to [be] . . . a matter of religious, a[s] well as patriotic duty, to liberally contribute money to the funds of the Anti-Saloon League."[26] Actually, Texas Baptists and the league needed and used one another. The league relied heavily on the support of the local churches, and Baptists soon recognized that the league was the most effective nonpartisan instrument for drying out the nation.[27]

So arm-in-arm with the Anti-Saloon League, Texas Baptists in 1908 began a relentless push for a statewide referendum on alcohol. The task was formidable. Because of the state constitution's local-option clause, Baptists and their new allies in the Anti-Saloon League had first to persuade the Democratic party and then a two-thirds majority in the legislature to hold a statewide prohibition election. In 1908 a slim majority of Democratic voters asked for such an election, but state lawmakers in 1909 failed to comply. So by a more substantial margin in 1910, the Democratic electorate again called for a statewide vote on prohibition. This time the legislature acquiesced, and the date was set for July 22, 1911. Having labored diligently in these previous campaigns,[28] Baptists now made ready for the final victory.

In the months prior to the crucial referendum, Baptist leaders seemed indefatigable. They implored the faithful to pay their poll taxes or obtain exemptions and cast their ballots against the liquor crowd. Blacks, about 17 percent of the total population, were specifically addressed with these instructions.[29] Without much subtlety, the *Baptist Standard* even raised the racist specter of rape, editorializing that "saloons brutalize and

1910, p. 16; 1911, p. 28; 1912, p. 38; Limestone County Baptist Association, *Minutes*, 1907, p. 15; 1908, pp. 22–23; 1909, pp. 12–13; 1918, p. 22.

[26] Dallas County Baptist Association, *Minutes*, 1913, p. 22.

[27] BGCT, *Proceedings*, 1915, pp. 127–28; 1916, p. 44; Dallas County Missionary Baptist Association, *Minutes*, 1907, p. 23; and San Antonio Baptist Association, *Minutes*, 1912, pp. 26–27.

[28] BGCT, *Proceedings*, 1908, p. 94; 1910, p. 107. See also *Baptist Standard*, Jan. 23, 1908, p. 1; Mar. 12, 1908, p. 5; Apr. 2, 1908, p. 1; Aug. 25, 1910, pp. 1, 9; Oct. 15, 1910, pp. 1–2; Gould, *Progressives and Prohibitionists*, pp. 44–48.

[29] *Dallas Morning News Texas Almanac and State Industrial Guide, 1970–1971 Tour Texas Edition* (Dallas: A. H. Belo Corp., 1969), p. 175.

profligate blacks and white women suffer from their outrages."[30]
Despite such efforts, the drys eventually lost by fewer than six
thousand votes. Baptist leaders proved to be sore losers. "There
is not a sane man in the state that does not believe that the
prohibition amendment last July was adopted by a substantial
majority," reported the Committee on the Liquor Traffic in October, 1911, and "that we were cheated out of that election by
the liquor traffic and its minions." In a spirit of righteous indig-
nation Texas Baptists resolved to have the issue "speedily . . .
re-submitted to the voters of our state,"[31] and they looked to the
Anti-Saloon League for direction "in pressing the battle to complete and uncompromising victory."[32]

Given their long-standing commitment to separation of
church and state, Baptist involvement in the political process, even through nonpartisan organizations, invariably led to
charges that the denomination's behavior in support of prohibition violated a premise of Baptist life. Some national politicians,
nettled by the intrusion of ministers into the affairs of state,
even suggested retaliating by restricting the privileges of the
church, particularly regarding taxation.[33] Sensitive to such
threats and criticism, Baptist leaders readily joined the debate
and swiftly disposed of the issue. Separation of church and state
had never meant that preachers and laymen should sit idle while
critical moral battles were being waged. The influential editor of
the *Baptist Standard*, James B. Gambrell, a former Confederate
soldier who had come to Texas from Mississippi in the 1890s, put
it bluntly: "A preacher who can hold his peace while the saloon,
in combination with politicians and others, is pulling countless
numbers down to ruin is not rightly regarded a gospel preacher
at all." Such a man, said Gambrell in descriptive language, "is

[30] *Baptist Standard*, Jan. 5, 1911, p. 8. See also Jan. 19, 1911, p. 13; Mar. 23, 1911,
p. 8; Apr. 13, 1911, pp. 5, 32; July 13, 1911, p. 1; and Hazmark, "Southern Religious
Press," pp. 17–20.
[31] BGCT, *Proceedings*, 1911, pp. 15–16.
[32] Ibid., 1912, p. 89. Actually, prohibitionists often fared poorly in statewide refer-
endums. Between 1909 and 1913 eight states, including Texas, rejected dry amendments. By contrast, four of the six that had gone dry between 1907 and 1909 had done so
by legislative action. See Blocker, *Retreat from Reform*, p. 216.
[33] Sinclair, *Prohibition*, p. 71.

a mollie-coddle and a milksop, and whatever dignity he has is of that pale pea green variety, that will not stand wind nor weather."[34] In Gambrell's view, separation of church and state was not transgressed when preachers challenged "the unholy union of saloon and state."[35]

This sentiment was shared by other Baptist leaders, including the controversial J. Frank Norris, editor and owner of the *Baptist Standard* from 1908 to 1909, who insisted that preachers, like everyone else, had "political as well as pulpit rights."[36] And during the first two decades of this century individual Texas Baptists exercised those rights by endorsing prohibition candidates, encouraging church members to vote "right" on the issues, and canvassing the state in behalf of the cause.[37] If such activity "was meddling in politics," declared one preacher, "then I am . . . a political preacher."[38]

Churchmen usually justified political activism on the grounds of good citizenship, the presumed moral nature of government, and the biblical example. To Texas Baptists, good citizenship entailed being informed on public issues and participating, at least to the extent of voting, in the affairs of government. Actually, there was nothing novel in this, for leaders at Baylor University had carefully cultivated a public-spirited policy for years. Rufus C. Burleson, a pioneer Texas minister and educator who was president of Baylor at Waco from 1886 to 1897, had always impressed upon students the importance of good citizenship and good government. He not only invited state leaders to speak at the Waco campus but also frequently took students to Austin to see the capitol and learn about governmental matters.[39]

Nonetheless, emphasis on Christian citizenship definitely accelerated as the drive for prohibition gained momentum. Almost weekly the *Baptist Standard* carried long articles and

[34] *Baptist Standard*, Aug. 25, 1910, pp. 1, 9.

[35] Ibid., Jan. 23, 1908, p. 1.

[36] Ibid., Feb. 18, 1909, p. 1.

[37] Ibid., Mar. 3, 1910, pp. 10–11; July 20, 1911, p. 1; July 9, 1914, p. 2; July 16, 1914, p. 1. See also Oral Memoirs of Joseph M. Dawson, Waco, 1973, Baylor University Program of Oral History, p. 35.

[38] *Baptist Standard*, July 9, 1914, p. 2.

[39] Oral Memoirs, Dawson, pp. 29–30.

speeches by prominent denominational figures exhorting the faithful to fulfill civic obligations. A November, 1909, address to the Dallas Baptist Pastors' and Laymen's Conference by Pat Neff, a Baylor graduate during the Burleson years who later became governor of Texas and president of his alma mater, was typical. In that florid nineteenth-century style of oratory for which he was famous, Neff, then county attorney of McLennan County, grandiloquently described the Christian citizen. "Crowned with the glories of war and decked with the flowers of peace, robed in the mantle of religious freedom, holding in one hand the constitution of his country and in the other the Bible of his God," the Christian citizen "stands today before the world the biggest, and the best, the noblest and the divinest gift this earth holds up to its maker." Service, the Baptist lawyer continued, was a prerequisite of citizenship. No one, he said, had the right to separate himself from the world and "to be absorbed and satisfied" with himself, for "the Bible standard of success and greatness is service." In Neff's opinion, "every Christian ought to be a politician to the extent of taking an active interest in every public or political question that touches the morals or the material prosperity of the people." It was criminal, he thought, "to be silent when your country needs your voice."[40] Though less dramatically, numerous other church leaders agreed. George W. Truett, pastor of the large First Baptist congregation of Dallas, put it succinctly. "Preachers are citizens, along with their neighbors, and have civic duties which may not be absolved."[41] James B. Gambrell was even more direct: "I hold that it is the duty of every Christian to go into politics and stay in."[42]

Such calls to civic duty were usually coupled to explanations that government was moral in both origin and function. Sounding somewhat like Thomas Hobbes, Arthur J. Barton, who held important positions in both the Baptist General Convention of Texas and the Southern Baptist Convention, told an assembly of Texas Baptist laymen in 1913 that "all government"

[40] *Baptist Standard*, Feb. 10, 1910, pp. 2, 8.
[41] Ibid., May 11, 1920, p. 12. See also Mar. 26, 1908, p. 2; May 29, 1913, pp. 4–5; and June 5, 1913, p. 10.
[42] Ibid., Apr. 2, 1908, p. 1.

rested "fundamentally upon morals," inasmuch as imperfect beings had to live together; they thus formed government "for the
restraint of the selfishness and evil in the strong and for the protection of the weak." Similarly, James B. Gambrell believed "the
elimination of moral questions from politics" would be "like taking the soul out of the body." To Gambrell, government and morals were inextricable, and so there was no reason why church
and state could not "co-operate for the promotion of public
morality."[43]

It remained for Neff, however, to put the matter in a loftier
context. In his speech to the Dallas pastors and laymen he had
emphasized that governments were "moral institutions," the
purposes of which were to enable "man . . . to fulfill the purpose
of his existence, and to work out the divinity of history." Like
nineteenth-century historian George Bancroft, Neff believed
that the hand of God was clearly discernible in American history. "The man who does not see the handiwork of Providence in
. . . this American Republic is a man who has never looked for
it," he declared, adding that "a divine purpose runs like a silken
thread throughout the warp and woof of American history."
Given the divine origins and moral purposes of government,
Neff believed the responsibilities of citizenship were incumbent
upon all Americans.[44]

As in other matters, Texas Baptists ultimately rested their
case on the Bible, noting that Moses, the ancient prophets, and
Jesus all had set examples for political activism. Moses conveyed
God's law to mankind; the prophets served as God's watchmen
over religious, social, and political affairs, rebuking civil authorities who transgressed the law; and Jesus disturbed the social and
political tranquillity.[45] According to one pastor, the Bible showed
that preachers had always been "aggressive agitators." Individuals who decried preachers in politics should examine the
scriptures.[46]

[43]Ibid., May 29, 1913, pp. 4–5; Mar. 18, 1909, p. 1. See also Aug. 25, 1910, pp. 1,
9; Oct. 13, 1910, p. 2; and May 29, 1913, pp. 4–5.
[44]Ibid., Feb. 10, 1910, p. 2.
[45]Ibid., Feb. 10, 1910, p. 8; Oct. 13, 1910, p. 2; July 9, 1914, p. 2.
[46]Ibid., July 9, 1914, p. 2.

Although Texas Baptists easily justified and readily engaged in state politics in the early twentieth century, some preachers nonetheless had questions concerning the proper extent of ministerial involvement. Joseph M. Dawson, though always active in public affairs, remarked that "participation in politics raised a question in my mind as to what a pastor could do in respect to government." As Dawson readily admitted, political activism sometimes rankled church members. In the 1910 Democratic primary, for instance, Dawson, then pastor of the First Baptist Church, Hillsboro, openly supported prohibitionist Cone Johnson. A popular doctor was irritated by this, Dawson recalled, and consequently always brought his wife to church, "but he himself refused to enter," sitting outside "reading the papers in rigid protest against my sermonic utterances." And in the early 1920s, when Dawson was pastor of the First Baptist Church, Waco, his active involvement in the gubernatorial campaigns of Pat Neff alienated some of his deacons.[47]

Nevertheless, in support of prohibition Texas Baptists did enter the political arena early in this century, and, as was true of evangelical Protestants elsewhere,[48] that activism led many of them to grasp the wider dimensions of the Christian faith. As reflected in the 1908 report on the liquor traffic to the General Convention, concern for temperance awakened Baptists to a broad range of social issues. Read by Benjamin F. Riley, the report observed that liquor was "so interlaced . . . into commerce, politics, society, and the administration of law" that it influenced business, colored legislation, undermined the social fabric, muzzled the courts, and infringed upon the church.[49] Baptists of this persuasion increasingly suggested that the church should expand its vision to include society as well as the individual.

[47] Oral Memoirs, Dawson, pp. 35, 39.
[48] Timberlake, *Prohibition and the Progressive Movement*, pp. 6–7. The actions of Texas Baptists do not bear out the claim that prohibition was a substitute for all other social concerns, as argued by Liston Pope, *Millhands and Preachers* (New Haven: Yale University Press, 1940), p. 29, and Norman A. Yance, *Religion Southern Style, Southern Baptists and Society in Historical Perspective*, Perspectives in Religious Studies, Special Studies Series, no. 4, (Danville, Va.: Association of Baptist Professors of Religion, 1978), p. 7.
[49] BGCT, *Proceedings*, 1908, p. 91.

Historian Wayne Flynt's observation with regard to Protestants in Alabama is applicable to Texas Baptists. Those churchmen who became involved in politics because of prohibition often remained active in behalf of other social endeavors.[50]

Significantly, during the first two decades of this century Texas Baptists had no difficulty accepting a social application of the scriptures. Although personal evangelism was always paramount, churchmen readily acknowledged that salvation carried a commitment to service. As a contributor to the *Baptist Standard* stated in 1902: "We hear a great deal today about a 'social gospel,' and I am glad of the conception, and of the favour which it receives. Only let us remember that the gospel is social second, and individual first."[51] Another contributor, who declared that the life of Jesus was sufficient basis for social involvement, detailed social issues to which the church had already or was currently addressing itself—free public schools, orphanages, juvenile courts, legislation to correct laboring conditions in manufacturing plants and to restrict the employment of women and children in factories, and the improvement of low-income housing in the larger cities.[52]

In 1918 Charles T. Alexander, a respected Texas Baptist and frequent contributor to the *Standard*, envisioned the institutionalization of social activism at the local congregational level. "The time is coming," he believed, "when the wide-awake church will . . . have what we may call a sociological department" to handle an array of services. Characteristically, however, Alexander cautioned that the church "must not forget that its supreme message is to the individual and not to humanity en masse," and "it must not forget that its supreme message is for the life to come and not for . . . this transitory life."[53] Evangelism, then, continued to be the major thrust of Texas Baptist life, but recognition of the social aspects of the gospel was growing.

Texas Baptists, moreover, did not as yet automatically as-

[50] Wayne Flynt, "Alabama," *Religion in the Southern States, A Historical Study,* ed. Samuel S. Hill (Macon, Ga.: Mercer University Press, 1983), pp. 18–20.
[51] *Baptist Standard,* Feb. 6, 1902, p. 6.
[52] Ibid., Nov. 2, 1911, p. 7.
[53] Ibid., Nov. 21, 1918, p. 20.

sociate social Christianity with theological liberalism, against which they were ever vigilant.[54] Although concerned lest social Christianity lead to liberalism, Texas churchmen saw no contradiction as such between social involvement and theological conservatism. The associate editor of the *Baptist Standard*, Eugene Coke Routh, a native Texan who was educated at the University of Texas (B.A., 1897), was typical. In 1913, although fearful that social Christianity *could* lead to a repudiation of "the heart of Christianity"—the deity of Jesus and the inspiration of scripture—he nonetheless endorsed a practical application of Christian ideals. "We must be conservative enough in doctrine to take our stand with these men of the first century," wrote the journalist, but progressive "in methods and in Christian service." Acknowledging that "a great deal" currently was "being said about social service," Routh asserted that there was "nothing new about it," for Jesus himself provided "examples of social service" in the parable of the good Samaritan and in acts of compassion toward the needy. Hence, contemporary Christians interested "in carrying out Christ's program" should build hospitals, orphanages, and Christian schools and should address themselves to white slavery, low wages, child labor, and bad housing conditions.[55] As Routh saw it, there was no reason why Texas Baptists could not remain true to their conservative faith while coming to grips with social problems.

As was common among Texas Baptists, however, the journalist concluded that social ills were symptoms of a deeper malady—individual sin. Social service was useful because it called

[54] See Oral Memoirs of T. B. Maston, Waco, 1973, Baylor University Program of Oral History, p. 25; *Baptist Standard*, Aug. 12, 1909, pp. 2–3; Mar. 17, 1910, p. 6; and Jan. 9, 1913, p. 10. See also James J. Thompson, Jr., *Tried as by Fire: Southern Baptists and the Religious Controversies of the 1920s* (Macon, Ga.: Mercer University Press, 1982), pp. 34–37, a fine study detailing Southern Baptist hostility to the social gospel in the 1920s. Among other things, Thompson traces the conflict to a growing awareness in the 1920s of the "liberal tone" of the social gospel. My own research suggests that many Texas Baptist leaders were well aware of the liberal underpinnings of the social gospel before World War I but were able in those pre-war years to separate political activism from liberal theology and thereby to support social endeavors. Because of internal tension generated in large measure by J. Frank Norris of Fort Worth, it became much more difficult for Texas Baptists to accomplish this in the 1920s.

[55] *Baptist Standard*, Jan. 2, 1913, pp. 5, 13; Mar. 20, 1913, p. 2.

attention "to the terrible symptoms of a disease," but "social service alone" would "never reach the seat of the trouble." According to Routh, evangelical religion was "the hope, the one cure of all these evils." Consequently, if society wanted to deal with causes rather than symptoms, it needed "the evangelistic, rather than the social, service of the churches."[56]

Herein was a basic distinction between the social Christianity of Texas Baptists and the social gospel movement of the North. Turning Routh upside down, the social gospel ministers such as Washington Gladden and Walter Rauschenbusch were convinced that such intense individualism obscured the perception of corporate evil and predisposed traditional Protestantism to flay symptoms rather than grappling with causes of social problems. Whereas Routh and other Texas Baptists saw society as atomistic individuals and thus assumed that the ultimate cause of social ills was personal sin, the social gospel ministers looked upon society as a whole and were convinced that social maladies were rooted, at least partially, in institutional conditions. Hence, whereas churchmen such as Routh sought to convert individual sinners in the hope of improving society, the social gospel sought to reform social conditions that debased the individual. To Baptists such as Routh, the individual was the ultimate concern; to the social gospel preachers, individual salvation could not be separated from social regeneration.[57]

Even the most progressive disciple of social Christianity among Texas Baptists, Joseph M. Dawson, ultimately reduced issues to the need for individual salvation. Born in June, 1879, in the cotton belt about twelve miles west of Waxahachie, Dawson grew up in Italy, Texas. With financial assistance from a local resident, he entered Baylor University in October, 1898. Interested in journalism, Dawson founded and was first editor of the school newspaper, the *Lariat*. Later, he served briefly as editor of the *Baptist Standard*, until a conflict with owner J. Frank Norris caused him to leave. While attending Baylor, Dawson

[56] Ibid., Mar. 20, 1913, p. 2.

[57] See Henry Steele Commager, *The American Mind: An Interpretation of American Thought and Character Since the 1880s* (New Haven: Yale University Press, 1950), pp. 170–77.

held pastorates in several small neighboring communities. After graduation in 1904 he served at Lampasas (1905–1906); the First Baptist Church, Hillsboro, (1908–12); the First Baptist Church, Temple, (1912–15); and the First Baptist Church, Waco, (1915–46).[58]

In 1914 Dawson preached to his Temple congregation perhaps the first formal series of sermons by a Texas Baptist on the social applications of the gospel.[59] At the request of editor Routh, the four sermons were printed in the *Standard* and thus had an impact well beyond Dawson's local congregation. Preparation for these sermons indicated Dawson's familiarity with the leading figures of the social gospel movement. He read the works of Washington Gladden, Josiah Strong, Charles Reynolds Brown, and Walter Rauschenbusch. The latter, who stressed personal as well as social regeneration, was Dawson's favorite. "I procured all his books and read them," he later recalled.[60]

The Texas clergyman addressed himself to a variety of specific social issues—child labor, exploitation of immigrants and women, labor conditions, capitalism, and women's rights. Some church members found the sermons unpalatable, pointing out that Jesus had lived within an oppressive social order without ever advocating specific social reforms. Dawson readily conceded the point but hastily added that the nature and tone of Christ's ministry provided ample basis for social activism. The New Testament concept of human dignity and value, for instance, was "revolutionary" and "capable of infinite application." This precept alone, Dawson contended, should arouse Baptists to the needs of child laborers who were denied education and burdened with oppressive conditions; of those immigrants who

[58] Oral Memoirs, Dawson, pp. 13–14, 86–90, 117–18; James Leo Garrett, Jr., "Joseph Martin Dawson: Pastor, Author, Denominational Leader, Social Activist," *Baptist History and Heritage* 14 (Oct., 1979): 7–15.

[59] In his Oral Memoirs, p. 138, Dawson says the sermons were preached in 1912. Because the *Baptist Standard* published them in 1914, however, they probably were not delivered until then. Much of the succeeding material on Dawson has been published in John W. Storey, "Joseph Martin Dawson: An Assessment of a Texas Baptist Activist," *Journal of Texas Baptist History* 2 (1982): 13–24.

[60] Oral Memoirs, Dawson, pp. 138–39.

were "sought as cheap laborers and herded like sheep to the polls to vote for corrupt measures"; of women exploited through prostitution; of the unfortunate victims of the saloon; and of "the masses of submerged industrial classes, who in a Christless economic order, are doomed to poverty and all the ills incident thereto."[61]

Turning specifically to labor, Dawson maintained that the principle of human dignity, if faithfully applied, would produce sweeping results. Working conditions would be improved, thereby protecting labor "against needless exposure to peril by machinery"; hours of toil would be reduced, providing "sufficient leisure" to "lift the laboring man above the daily grind of a brute"; and wages would be increased, thus ensuring that workers had "proper housing, provisions, and all else needful to sane and healthful living."[62]

These were progressive pronouncements for a Texas Baptist in 1914. Yet in many respects the Temple pastor was quite conventional. His position on women's rights would hardly have satisfied such feminists as Susan B. Anthony or Charlotte Perkins Gilman. For the most part, Dawson believed women had already achieved economic independence. "Nearly all the callings open to man have been invaded by women," declared he, "and some of them she has all but monopolized." The teaching profession, Dawson thought, was a case in point. Actually, the cleric had reservations about women in the marketplace. Competition with men would lower wages, and the home would be imperiled. On suffrage, Dawson stated the case for and against but refused to commit himself. Of one thing he was certain, however. "In no sphere does woman shine so radiantly as in religious service."[63] Although feminists could take little comfort in his stance on women's rights, Dawson was not far out of step with the leading figures of the social gospel movement in the North. Rauschenbusch supported suffrage but otherwise felt that the

[61] *Baptist Standard*, Sept. 24, 1914, p. 3; July 30, 1914, pp. 12–13.
[62] Ibid., Sept. 24, 1914, p. 3.
[63] Ibid., Oct. 15, 1914, p. 3. Dawson's wife, who was an able speaker, became widely known for her talks at religious gatherings.

role of women should be confined to families, and preferably large ones.[64]

On economic issues, however, the Texan, while no doubt closely reflecting the sentiment of fellow Baptists, was more conservative than the social gospel ministers. That Dawson saw the needs of labor was evident in his 1914 sermon "Christ and the Laboring Man." But unlike Washington Gladden,[65] whom he read, Dawson disclosed little sympathy for unionization or the strike. Indeed, he objected to the use of force, arguing that economic rights would "not be obtained by coercion,—by that agitation which incites hatred,—but in the promotion of understanding and fraternity." Glibly, the pastor assured fellow Baptists that "the spirit of Jesus," if "applied in all our industrial relations," would "speedily" solve "many problems."[66]

With regard to the leaders of industry, Dawson was far less critical of the prevailing economic order than was Rauschenbusch, who doubted that one could be a Christian and a capitalist at the same time.[67] Although Jesus directed some of his sharpest remarks at the rich, it was "perfectly certain" to Dawson "that Jesus made no crude attack on capital nor prohibited private property." Moreover, he was equally certain that the destruction of private property "would tend to destroy the individuality of men, and would take away one of the most powerful incentives to progress."[68]

But Dawson hastily added that wealth carried with it responsibilities. Like other ministers, he emphasized stewardship. Indeed, quite pragmatically, the Baptist preacher maintained that "the strongest bulwark against socialism" was "the stewardship of wealth," warning that the present social order would likely be destroyed if the rich failed to behave responsibly. So if not for the sake of justice, then for the sake of self-interest, one should use wealth "as a means of public service."

[64] White and Hopkins, Social Gospel, p. 288.

[65] C. Howard Hopkins, The Rise of the Social Gospel in American Protestantism, 1865–1915 (1951; reprint, New Haven: Yale University Press, 1967), pp. 28–31, 89.

[66] Baptist Standard, Sept. 24, 1914, pp. 3, 10.

[67] Hopkins, Rise of the Social Gospel, pp. 221–24.

[68] Baptist Standard, Oct. 1, 1914, p. 3.

Significantly, at a time when most workers made only one or two dollars a day, Dawson believed Henry Ford had already set an example by raising the minimum wage at his plant to five dollars a day.[69] Hence, the Texan's conception of stewardship resembled more closely that of Gladden than of steel tycoon Andrew Carnegie. Wages, not libraries, were the test of stewardship.

The factor most sharply differentiating the socially conscious Dawson from the social gospel ministers of the North was his emphasis upon individualism. Like other Texas churchmen, he ultimately reduced social ills to individual solutions. His 1914 sermons on social Christianity, for instance, usually closed with a call for personal regeneration. What laborers needed, he remarked, was "not a new job, but a new personality. By divine grace and saving power, Jesus came to give new existence to men, not primarily to rehabilitate the conditions of their toil." Along with other Baptists, Dawson believed "the reformation of society must be preceded by getting the individual saved from sin."[70]

Although this emphasis placed Dawson outside the mainstream of the social gospel movement, it linked him inseparably to fellow Baptists, for whom personal evangelism was the primary concern. Furthermore, Dawson's "soundness" on this issue probably made it easier for his Temple congregation and *Baptist Standard* readers to accept his pronouncements on social issues. Had the pastor been out of step on this point, his effectiveness as a spokesman for social Christianity among Texas Baptists probably would have been undermined. Sharing as he did with fellow Baptists a firm commitment to personal regeneration, however, Dawson could prod them to see the broader aspects of faith. Still, such individualism caused Dawson to rely essentially on moral suasion for the accomplishment of socially desirable goals. As yet, he did not see that the attainment of social justice sometimes required more than saving individual sinners.

Significantly, this concern for social Christianity went beyond such individuals as Dawson. There were institutional expressions of interest. The crusade for prohibition had awakened

[69] Ibid.
[70] Ibid., Sept. 24, 1914, p. 3; July 30, 1914, pp. 12–13.

many Baptists to the realization that liquor was intertwined with a variety of other issues. Consequently, in 1915 the General Convention established two separate but overlapping standing committees—the Civic Righteousness and Social Service committees. The Civic Righteousness Committee initially concerned itself exclusively with prohibition, whereas the Social Service Committee grappled with a broader range of matters.[71]

As the latter committee explained, "social and service" included everything related to human existence, religious and secular, "because, truly speaking, the secular side of life is inseparable from the moral and the religious." Hence, it was the duty of the church "to correct the wrongs of individuals and of all forms and conditions of society, whether they be in political, church, social, amusement, business relations, or whatever or wherever they be found." Stressing a practical application of the gospel, the Social Service Committee concluded that Texans should be concerned about disputes between landowners and farm tenants; conflicts between labor and capital, liquor, prostitution; and "this age craze for amusements and 'athletics.'"[72] This practical thrust of the gospel was continually reaffirmed, as the committee in subsequent reports added settlement houses, prison reform, and child welfare to its list of concerns.[73] And if anyone had reservations about such endeavors, the 1917 report reassured fellow Baptists, exuberantly proclaiming that "Jesus [himself] was the great sociologist."[74]

This declaration did not signal an abandonment of the individual. The Social Service Committee always stressed the primacy of personal salvation but also pointedly reminded fellow Baptists that the gospel went beyond evangelism. In 1917, for instance, the committee agreed that changing hearts was more important than altering the environment but added that "the

[71] BGCT, *Proceedings*, 1915, pp. 26, 126. Some local Baptist associations had already established social service committees. See Union Baptist Association, *Minutes*, 1913, p. 38; 1914, pp. 26–27; and San Antonio Baptist Association, *Minutes*, 1913, pp. 30–31.
[72] BGCT, *Proceedings*, 1915, pp. 26–27, 126–28.
[73] See ibid., 1916, pp. 27–29; 1917, pp. 63–64.
[74] Ibid., 1917, p. 63.

obligation to change the environment that is unholy is as binding as the command to preach the gospel." And in 1918 Wallace Bassett, an important denominational leader who was just beginning his forty-eight-year pastorate at Cliff Temple Baptist Church in Dallas, further explained the committee's position. Individual salvation was of fundamental importance, but, he added: "While Jesus never taught sociology, or social service as such, . . . his recognized teachings about man, society, the family, the state, wealth, the child, charity and love make obligatory on us the giving to his words as broad an application as the needs of men." The Dallas pastor concluded that "we do not need a new theology for social service. We only need to use his words as he intended we should use them." [75]

Although the Social Service Committee did not follow up these reports with specific social programs, its work nevertheless was an important development in the social consciousness of Texas Baptists. It became the vehicle through which socially alert churchmen could convey their concerns to fellow Baptists across the state. Furthermore, reports of the Social Service Committee, though not binding on locally autonomous congregations, carried the weight of moral suasion and thereby provided local pastors of like mind with a degree of institutional support for social endeavors. Moreover, given the democratic nature of Baptist polity, reports adopted by the Baptist General Convention reflected rather closely the prevailing sentiment. So Texas Baptists, it would seem, were responsive to a social application of the gospel by the mid-teens.

Bassett's report of 1918, however, was the high-water mark. Because the social consciousness of many Texas Baptists did not extend much beyond prohibition, achievement of this objective satisfied their aspirations for a social application of the gospel. The reaction of Baptists in the Houston area was common. As soon as the Texas legislature slew John Barleycorn in 1918, the Union Association turned its attention to the "evils" of dancing, movies, "fishing parties, auto joy riding, Sunday excursions,

[75] Ibid., 1917, pp. 63–64; 1918, p. 30; see also 1916, pp. 27–29; 1917, pp. 63–64.

Sunday baseball and many others."[76] And in 1919, when fundamentalist J. Frank Norris presented the report of the Social Service Committee to the General Convention, he sounded the call
for a fervent evangelism.[77] As the 1920s began, support for social
Christianity was already ebbing.

[76] Union Baptist Association, *Minutes*, 1918, p. 27. See also Southeast Texas Baptist Association, *Minutes*, 1919, pp. 15–16; San Marcos Baptist Association, *Minutes*,
1919, pp. 7–8.
     [77] BGCT, *Proceedings*, 1919, pp. 93–94.

2

J. Frank Norris
and the Troublesome Twenties

THE 1920s began auspiciously for Texas churches. Membership was growing; impressive religious buildings were under construction; recent ratification of the Eighteenth Amendment reflected the power and influence of the righteous; and Texas Baptists quickly oversubscribed their apportionment of the Seventy-Five Million Campaign, an ambitious drive initiated in 1919 by the Southern Baptist Convention to raise at least $75 million in five years to fund its various agencies. But outward appearances were misleading. A turbulent storm was brewing, one that would adversely affect the progress of social Christianity. Fundamentalist J. Frank Norris of Fort Worth would soon become embroiled in a bitter struggle with other prominent Texas churchmen for control of the General Convention. The bombastic Norris accused his opponents of being modernists, thereby igniting a sharp debate over theological liberalism and evolution and intensifying doubts about the soundness of applying the Good News to society. To Norris, the "heresies" of liberalism, evolution, and social Christianity, which he easily fused together, had to be resisted with equal vigor. His accusations put advocates of social Christianity on the defensive. They began to find it difficult to address social concerns without arousing suspicion of theological infidelity. Joseph M. Dawson, for instance, a constant object of Norris's wrath, took pains to assure fellow Baptists of his faithfulness to the conservative traditions of the faith. Despite the tumult, Dawson never wavered from his commitment to social Christianity, and the annual reports of the Civic Righteousness and Social Service committees disclose that other churchmen, although a distinct minority, also were informed on and disturbed by social ills. So, if interest in social Christianity glimmered in the 1920s, it was not extinguished.

The modernist-fundamentalist controversy[1] that overtook Texas Baptists after World War I neither began nor ended in the 1920s and neither began nor ended with J. Frank Norris. But as church historian Sydney E. Ahlstrom noted, "that decade did witness the climactic confrontation of American evangelical Protestantism and modern thought,"[2] and that confrontation was especially strident in Texas because of the presence of Norris. In America the conflict began with the introduction of Charles Darwin's theories and the application of higher criticism to sacred scriptures. In the southern states, where conservative Protestantism held sway, modern scientific theories and new theologi-

[1]Two standard works on this subject are Stewart G. Cole, *The History of Fundamentalism* (New York: Richard R. Smith, 1931), and Norman F. Furniss, *The Fundamentalist Controversy, 1918–1931* (New Haven: Yale University Press, 1954), the latter of which until recently was regarded as the authoritative study on the topic. More current works, however, have called attention to the shortcomings of the Furniss book and sharpened our understanding of the modernist-fundamentalist conflict. Such studies, in order of publication, are Louis Gasper, *The Fundamentalist Movement* (Hague: Mouton, 1963), concentrating primarily on the American Council of Christian Churches and the National Association of Evangelicals; Richard Hofstadter, *Anti-intellectualism in American Life* (New York: Alfred A. Knopf, 1964), pp. 117–36, which offers illuminating insights on the "fundamentalist mind"; Willard B. Gatewood, Jr., ed., *Controversy in the Twenties: Fundamentalism, Modernism, and Evolution* (Nashville: Vanderbilt University Press, 1969), containing a perceptive introduction and a helpful bibliography; Ernest R. Sandeen, *The Roots of Fundamentalism: British and American Millenarianism* (Chicago: University of Chicago Press, 1970), which challenges the popular notion that fundamentalism was a southern rural phenomenon; Erling Jorstad, *The Politics of Doomsday: Fundamentalists of the Far Right* (Nashville: Abingdon Press, 1970), dealing with four contemporary fundamentalists and politics of the far right; George W. Dollar, *A History of Fundamentalism in America* (Greenville, S.C.: Bob Jones University Press, 1973), an account written from an extremely conservative viewpoint; C. Allyn Russell, *Voices of American Fundamentalism: Seven Biographical Studies* (Philadelphia: Westminster Press, 1976), an exceptionally good study that emphasizes the diversity and complexity of fundamentalism through the careers of seven prominent fundamentalists; James Barr, *Fundamentalism* (Philadelphia: Westminster Press, 1977), an insightful analysis; William R. Hutchison, *The Modernist Impulse in American Protestantism* (Cambridge: Harvard University Press, 1976), which, although primarily a treatment of Protestant liberalism over the past 120 years, sheds light on the nature of fundamentalism (see especially pp. 257–87); and George M. Marsden, *Fundamentalism and American Culture: The Shaping of Twentieth-Century Evangelicalism, 1870–1925* (New York: Oxford University Press, 1980), an excellent study depicting fundamentalism as a genuine religious movement with deeply rooted and intelligible beliefs rather than an amusing and temporary social aberration.

[2]Ahlstrom, *A Religious History of the American People* (New Haven: Yale University Press, 1972), p. 914.

cal interpretations made little headway. Methodists, Baptists, and Presbyterians effectively closed ranks against "unsound" teachings, and Alexander Winchell of Vanderbilt, Crawford H. Toy and William H. Whitsitt of Southern Baptist Theological Seminary, and James Woodrow of Columbia Theological Seminary felt the wrath of their respective denominations.[3] By contrast, churchmen in the North after the Civil War heatedly debated biological evolution and biblical authority. Several heresy trials involving seminary professors jarred the various denominations, but by the end of the nineteenth century the liberals, whether Baptist, Methodist, or Presbyterian, had generally prevailed. Science and religion had been reconciled to the satisfaction of those northern churchmen who were at peace with Darwin.[4] Indeed, in 1885 Henry Ward Beecher, the New York divine and leader among the religious liberals of his age, prematurely concluded that the age of strife between science and religion had "passed and closed."[5]

Although liberal ministers such as Beecher had reconciled themselves to the new science, numbers of other churchmen had not.[6] Increasingly troubled by the effects of Darwinism and higher criticism, religionists of a more conservative temperament regrouped and counterattacked. Often associated with such institutions as the Moody Bible Institute of Chicago, founded in 1886, and the Los Angeles Bible Institute, organized in 1907, these churchmen initiated a relentless attack on modernism early in this century. Established in 1902, the Bible League of North America bespoke the mood of such Christians. The league's purpose was "to meet and counteract the *Current Destructive teachings* concerning the truthfulness, integrity,

[3] Kenneth K. Bailey, *Southern White Protestantism in the Twentieth Century* (1964; reprint, Gloucester, Mass.: Peter Smith, 1968), pp. 9–24.

[4] Winthrop S. Hudson, *Religion in America: An Historical Account of American Religious Life* (New York: Charles Scribner's Sons, 1965), pp. 266–84; Furniss, *Fundamentalist Controversy*, pp. 10, 22.

[5] R. S. Wilson, ed., *Darwinism and the American Intellectual* (Homewood, Ill.: Dorsey Press, 1967), pp. 39–47. See also William G. McLoughlin, *The Meaning of Henry Ward Beecher: An Essay on the Shifting Values of Mid-Victorian America, 1840–1870* (New York: Alfred A. Knopf, 1970), pp. 49–54.

[6] Furniss, *Fundamentalist Controversy*, pp. 10–15.

and inspiration of the Bible as the Word of God."[7] This objective became a lifetime obsession with the indefatigable William Bell Riley, pastor of the First Baptist Church, Minneapolis, and, at least in the opinion of his friends, "the second Martin Luther of Protestantism." In behalf of the cause Riley wrote more than sixty books and countless articles, and he traveled extensively.[8]

An important development in the fundamentalist offensive was publication between 1910 and 1915 of *The Fundamentals*, a set of twelve pamphlets each about 125 pages in length. Published at the expense of Hyman and Milton Stewart, Presbyterian laymen and wealthy California oil men, and originally edited under the leadership of Amzi C. Dixon, a Baptist preacher who held pastorates in Baltimore, Brooklyn, and Boston, these booklets were distributed free of cost to ministers, seminary professors, theology students, Sunday school directors, and YMCA leaders throughout the country. Prominent conservative religionists, including Edgar Young Mullins, president of Southern Baptist Theological Seminary, and Charles B. Williams and J. J. Reeve, professors at Southwestern Baptist Theological Seminary, contributed to the effort. These pamphlets not only excoriated modernism but also enunciated what came to be the key tenets of fundamentalism: the infallibility of the Bible and the virgin birth, substitutionary atonement, bodily resurrection, and the second coming of Christ.[9] Finally, in 1919 fundamentalists meeting in Philadelphia succeeded in creating an organizational apparatus through which the assault on modernism could be channeled—the World's Christian Fundamentals Association (WCFA). Under the leadership of William Bell Riley and such like-minded believers as John Roach Straton, pastor of the Calvary Baptist Church, New York City; Jasper C. Massee, who occupied Baptist pulpits in both the North and South; and

[7] Quoted in ibid., p. 12.

[8] Russell, *Voices*, pp. 79–106; Furniss, *Fundamentalist Controversy*, pp. 11, 31–32, 49–52.

[9] Furniss, *Fundamentalist Controversy*, pp. 12–13; Barr, *Fundamentalism*, p. 2; Russell, *Voices*, p. 18; Sandeen, *Roots*, pp. 188–207. The term fundamentalist was not coined until 1920; see Russell, *Voices*, p. 221.

J. Frank Norris, this new organization embarked upon a militantly aggressive crusade to retrieve Christendom from the grasp of modernism.[10]

The religious discord of the 1920s was not an abrupt development. The debate had been in progress for three generations, and through it all Baptists in the South had remained relatively untouched. Conservative orthodoxy still reigned in their seminaries, colleges, and local congregations. So why did the denomination in the 1920s, particularly the General Convention of Texas, become so absorbed by the modernist controversy? Had the tainted doctrines of liberal theology suddenly gained a foothold in the southern Zion? In short, neither Southern Baptists in general nor Texas Baptists in particular had any cause for alarm. A new study by James J. Thompson, Jr., *Tried as by Fire*, stated the case plainly. "Despite the presence of a few genuine modernists," wrote Thompson, "the Southern Baptist denomination constituted a bastion of orthodoxy, defying the winds of theological change buffeting America in the 1920s."[11]

Still, many Southern Baptists, influenced by publication of *The Fundamentals* and the heated rhetoric of the modernist-fundamentalist feud, increasingly felt menaced. The denomination perceived a threat both from without and within, although none existed. According to Thompson, two events kindled a beleaguered-fortress mentality: the 1913 publication of Thomas T. Martin's *Redemption and the New Birth*, which questioned the theological fidelity of several professors at the University of Chicago, and the 1914 accusation of James B. Gambrell and Eugene C. Routh, then editors of the *Baptist*

[10]Gatewood, *Controversy in the Twenties*, pp. 18–19; Furniss, *Fundamentalist Controversy*, pp. 50–51; Sandeen, *Roots*, pp. 243–47; and Russell, *Voices*, p. 28. Although some scholars believe publication of *The Fundamentals* and creation of the WCFA mark the beginning of fundamentalism as a movement, one that climaxed in the 1920s, Sandeen, *Roots*, pp. 189, 208–32, argues to the contrary, that the unity of fundamentalism was already dissolving by about 1910. From that point on, divisive factionalism plagued the fundamentalists. Gatewood, *Controversy in the Twenties*, pp. 10–12, supports Sandeen.

[11]Thompson, *Tried as by Fire: Southern Baptists and the Religious Controversies of the 1920s* (Macon, Ga.: Mercer University Press, 1982), p. 79.

Standard, that Southern Baptist Theological Seminary sheltered a professor who denied the virgin birth. The Baptist Zion was endangered from without and imperiled from within. So in the 1920s, Thompson concluded, Southern Baptists, goaded by fundamentalists, transformed "modernism into an internal threat and turn[ed] upon their denomination for harboring heretics."[12] The response was especially strong in Texas, where J. Frank Norris, the South's leading fundamentalist, lashed out in all directions against fellow Baptists.[13]

There is irony in the bitterness between Norris and other Texas Baptists, for earlier in the century the flamboyant pastor appeared to be a rising denominational star. He graduated from Baylor University (1903) and Southern Theological Seminary (1905); he revitalized the flagging McKinney Avenue Baptist Church of Dallas (1905–1907); he purchased the *Baptist Standard* and made it a formidable voice for Texas Baptists (1907–1909); and his prestigious First Baptist flock in Fort Worth included such notables as B. H. Carroll and Lee Rutland Scarborough. But by the mid-1920s Norris had been expelled from the Baptist General Convention and "Norrisism" soon became a synonym among Baptists for demagoguery, innuendo, and schism. In a brief article entitled "The Fruits of Norrisism," Scarborough, who had succeeded B. H. Carroll as president of Southwestern Baptist Theological Seminary, now denounced his former pastor as being to "true religion what socialism and bol-

[12] Ibid., pp. 67–71.

[13] Scholarly accounts dealing with Norris are E. Ray Tatum, *Conquest or Failure? Biography of J. Frank Norris* (Dallas: Baptist Historical Foundation, 1966); Allyn Russell, "J. Frank Norris: Violent Fundamentalist," *Southwestern Historical Quarterly* 75, no. 3 (Jan., 1972): 271–73, which is included in the author's *Voices*, pp. 20-46; Royce Lee Measures, "The Relationship of J. Frank Norris to the Northern Fundamentalist Movement" (Th.M. thesis, Southwestern Baptist Theological Seminary, 1970), and "Men and Movements Influenced by J. Frank Norris" (Th.D. diss., Southwestern Seminary, 1976); C. Gwin Morris, "He Changed Things: The Life and Thought of J. Frank Norris" (Ph.D. diss., Texas Tech University, 1973), as well as "J. Frank Norris and the Baptist General Convention of Texas," *The Journal of Texas Baptist History* 1 (1981): 1–34; Roy E. Falls, *A Biography of J. Frank Norris, 1877–1952* (Euless, Tex.: published by the author, 1975); and Thompson, *Tried as by Fire*, pp. 137–66. A very useful source is *The Journal of Texas Baptist History* 1 (1981), the entire issue of which is devoted to Norris.

shevism are to politics and industry; wholly destructive in spirit and methods."[14] The explanation for this state of affairs lies partly in Norris's background and personal ambition.

Controversy and violence epitomized Norris. Born in Dadeville, Alabama, in 1877, he moved with his parents to a farm near Hubbard, Texas, in 1888. These early years in Texas were impoverished and painful. Norris's father, a sharecropper who evidently preferred drink to farming, beat his youthful son unmercifully on one occasion, breaking the child's nose and cutting his body. Despite such abuse, Norris later rushed to his father's aid when the latter was assaulted by horse thieves. In the process, the fifteen-year-old boy was shot three times. Because gangrene, followed by inflammatory rheumatism, set in, Norris's recovery took three years, two of which were spent in a wheelchair. His mother not only nursed him back to health, but also assured him that he was destined for greatness.[15] Having been converted at the age of thirteen, Norris chose the ministry as his vehicle to fame.

Pursuant to this objective, Norris enrolled in Baylor University in 1898, where he met Joseph M. Dawson. According to Dawson, "a coolness" between himself and Norris quickly "sprang up."[16] The two men eventually became bitter enemies, and the conflict between them symbolized, to some extent, the rift between Norris and Texas Baptists. The combative Norris, soon disillusioned with the Baptist establishment,[17] associated

[14] Scarborough, "The Fruits of Norrisism," (Fort Worth: privately printed for the author, n.d.), reprinted in *The Journal of Texas Baptist History* 1 (1981): 89.

[15] Norris obviously was devoted to his mother, and her influence upon him was considerable. See Louis Entzminger, "My First Meeting of Dr. Norris," in J. Frank Norris, *Inside History of First Baptist Church, Fort Worth, and Temple Baptist Church, Detroit: Life Story of Dr. J. Frank Norris* (published privately, 1938), p. 76; and Tatum, *Conquest or Failure?*, which stresses the influence of Norris's mother. Similarly, Norris's obsession with prohibition was in part the result of the devastating effects of alcohol on both his father and younger brother. See Tatum, *Conquest or Failure?* pp. 21–22; Falls, *Biography of Norris*, pp. 18–19. See also Russell, "Norris: Violent Fundamentalist," pp. 272–73; and Louis Entzminger, *The J. Frank Norris I Have Known for Thirty-Four Years* (privately published, n.d.), pp. 33–36.

[16] Oral Memoirs of Joseph M. Dawson, Waco, 1973, Baylor University Program of Oral History, p. 257.

[17] Norris, *Inside History*, p. 24.

Dawson with theological liberalism, Darwinism, atheism, and communism. Dawson was, said Norris, "the finished fruit of modernism."[18] The refined Dawson, highly respected in the denomination, accused Norris while at Baylor of indulging in cruel and malicious pranks and suspected him "of mishandling or embezzling a collection" Baylor students "had raised to aid a sick preacher." If anything, the passage of time hardened Dawson's judgment. In 1972 he recounted virtually every wrong attributed to Norris and in every instance suggested that the Fort Worth pastor was guilty as charged. He included rumors that Norris had pushed his father-in-law off the rear end of the Texas Special Railroad near San Marcos in order to use the insurance money to buy the *Baptist Standard* in 1907, charges that he had set fire to his own church and home in 1912, and accusations that he had murdered an unarmed Fort Worth businessman in 1926. Dawson concluded that Norris "was a coercive bigot" who bore "a striking resemblance in . . . personal characteristics" to Adolph Hitler.[19] If Norris initiated the conflict with fellow Baptists, as it seems he did, the Baptist establishment was fully capable, as Dawson's recollections show, of trading slander for slander.

Signs of tension between Norris and other Texas Baptists appeared early. In 1905, upon receiving the Th. M. degree from Southern Theological Seminary, Norris became pastor of the struggling McKinney Avenue Baptist Church of Dallas. This position brought the ambitious young minister into contact and competition with Dr. George W. Truett, the distinguished pastor of the First Baptist Church, Dallas. Norris aggressively promoted his own congregation, and the results were impressive. The first Sunday at McKinney Norris preached to only thirteen people. When he resigned in 1907, approximately a thousand

[18] J. Frank Norris, "Address on Dawsonism, Fosdickism, Darwinism and Agnosticism," *Fundamentalist*, Mar. 4, 1938, p. 4, and Norris, "Dawson Joins the Communist Ranks," *Inside History*, n.p.

[19] Oral Memoirs, Dawson, pp. 114–19, 254–60, 268, 278–83, 286–89. For a more moderate view of Norris by another prominent Texas Baptist, see Oral Memoirs of E. S. James, Waco, 1973, Baylor University Program of Oral History, pp. 56–57. See also Tatum, *Conquest or Failure?* pp. 221–40, and Falls, *Biography of Norris*, pp. 28–36.

members were meeting regularly in a new brick structure.[20] Dawson believed this accomplishment was tarnished, charging that Norris used "unscrupulous methods" to lure members away from Truett's fold. Among other things, the McKinney pastor supposedly hinted that his First Baptist colleague was an inter-denominationalist, a "sin" as abhorrent as modernism to many Baptists.[21] Upon leaving McKinney Avenue, Norris took the helm of the *Baptist Standard*. Immediately, he began using the paper to attack racetrack gambling in Texas. When other Baptist leaders subsequently failed to show sufficient enthusiasm for the new publisher's crusade, preferring less aggressive methods, Norris became impatient. Caustically, he needled his colleagues for timidity. This perhaps was the beginning of serious mistrust between Norris and other Baptist spokesmen. In 1908, for instance, Dawson resigned as editor of the *Standard* because of a dispute with owner Norris over editorial freedom. In any event, unable to secure adequate support from denominational leaders for his journalistic ventures, Norris in 1909 sold the Baptist paper, whose circulation had increased substantially under his management.[22]

As yet, Norris still enjoyed the confidence and support of the revered B. H. Carroll. While owner of the *Standard*, Norris had supported Carroll's decision to move Southwestern Seminary from Waco to Fort Worth, a relocation opposed by some prominent Baptists.[23] Shortly thereafter Carroll recommended Norris as pastor of the First Baptist Church, Fort Worth,[24] a position he held from 1910 until his death in 1952. With the same determination that had characterized his ministry at McKinney Avenue, Norris set about to forge the largest congregation in the world. A consummate showman with an eye for the dramatic, he attracted throngs. In manner and style, he easily could have

[20] Morris, "Norris and Baptist General Convention," p. 5.

[21] Oral Memoirs, Dawson, pp. 114–15, 258–59; Thompson, *Tried as by Fire*, pp. 22–25.

[22] Tatum, *Conquest or Failure?* pp. 89–94; Falls, *Biography of Norris*, pp. 28–29; Oral Memoirs, Dawson, pp. 117–18, 261–62; and Norris, *Inside History*, pp. 30–32.

[23] Tatum, *Conquest or Failure?* pp. 94–95; Norris, *Inside History*, pp. 34–37.

[24] Oral Memoirs, Dawson, pp. 114, 259, 263–64.

served as a model for novelist Sinclair Lewis's fictional evangelist, Elmer Gantry.[25] Roaming the platform, he shouted, ges-
tured, wept, and, on one occasion, paraded monkeys and apes in
front of the pulpit so that his followers could view the relatives of
Charles Darwin. Norris, as well as his loyal and longtime associate Louis Entzminger, acknowledged this penchant for the sensational, the results of which were remarkable. In 1909 the First
Church of Fort Worth had 1,200 members; in 1928 it had 12,000,
with an average Sunday morning attendance of 5,200.[26]

But all was not well. In 1911 approximately a thousand
members of Norris's Fort Worth flock withdrew their membership, including B. H. Carroll, who, in the opinion of Dawson,
"could not stomach the stuff Pastor Norris was preaching."[27] Although it has some validity, Dawson's claim does not fully explain
either Carroll's withdrawal or the general congregational rift.
Several factors accounted for the schism. By 1911 many prominent church members were offended by Norris's incessant, public attacks on Fort Worth's elected officials for alleged corruption;
others found his emotional and energetic pulpit style unappeal-
ing; and yet others felt uncomfortable with the newer church
members, many of whom were poor and crude.[28] In 1912, at a
time when the verbal slugfest between Norris and city hall was
gaining momentum, the pastor's church and home burned to the
ground. Norris was hastily indicted and tried for perjury and
arson. A month-long trial ended in acquittal. In 1927 Norris was
again on trial, having been charged this time with murder in the
1926 slaying of a Fort Worth businessman. On the first ballot an
Austin jury promptly acquitted the minister. The loyalty of most
of his flock was undiminished.[29]

[25]Several years after the publication of *Elmer Gantry*, Lewis did hear Norris
preach in Fort Worth. See Norris, *Inside History*, p. 5.

[26]See Russell, "Norris: Violent Fundamentalism," pp. 281–82; Norris, *Inside History*, pp. 51–56, 68; Tatum, *Conquest or Failure?* pp. 116, 161–68; and Oral Memoirs,
Dawson, pp. 264–65.

[27]Oral Memoirs, Dawson, p. 114.

[28]Tatum, *Conquest or Failure?* pp. 116–20; Falls, *Biography of Norris*, pp. 33–34;
Norris, *Inside History*, pp. 42–43, 47–52; and *Encyclopedia of Southern Baptists*,
(Nashville: Broadman Press, 1958), II, 983.

[29]Russell, "Norris: Violent Fundamentalist," pp. 278–90; Morris, "Norris and

His relations with the Baptist General Convention, meanwhile, had been steadily deteriorating. With growing frequency, Norris leveled cutting barbs at his ministerial colleagues. Sarcastically, he variously called Truett "the Infallible Baptist Pope," "His Allhighness," "The Great All-I-Am," and "The Holy Father"; Scarborough was "The Dictator"; Wallace Bassett, pastor of the Cliff Temple Baptist Church, Dallas, was dubbed "The Old Baboon"; Franz M. McConnell, editor of the *Baptist Standard* from 1928 to 1944, was dismissed as "The Old Woman Who Does the Best She Can"; and C. V. Edwards of College Avenue Baptist Church in Fort Worth was a "long, lean, lank yellow egg-sucking dog." Collectively, Norris labeled his opponents "denominational bishops," "ecclesiastical dictators," "the Texas Baptist machine," and "the Sanhedrin."[30] And with contempt, he now described Southwestern Seminary as "the *cemetery* over there" and mockingly denounced "their Hebrew, their Shebrew and the home brew."[31]

Resentful of Norris's attacks upon programs, agencies, and personalities, denominational loyalists retaliated, proving quite adept at exchanging barbs with their Fort Worth detractor. Scarborough, whose rhetoric could be as tart as Norris's, accused the pastor of being antimissionary and anti-institutional, inasmuch as his church spent "most of its money on itself—sometimes in court trials for perjury, arson and murder, and in sending out free literature seeking to destroy the causes other people try to build."[32] In 1923 Frank Groner, executive secretary of the General Convention, similarly characterized Norris as a "self-promoter and ardent lover of the limelight," an "unctious exponent and loquacious purveyor of interdenominationalism."[33] And in 1927 Joseph Dawson lashed back, retorting that assaults "by this paranoical performer were actuated by deep personal

---

Baptist General Convention," pp. 7–8; Tatum, *Conquest or Failure?* pp. 221–40; Falls, *Biography of Norris*, pp. 34–36; and Norris, *Inside History*, pp. 63–69, 83–101.

[30] Russell, "Norris: Violent Fundamentalist," p. 293; Morris, "Norris and Baptist General Convention," p. 8; Norris, *Inside History*, pp. 17, 32, 164, 166, 173–75.

[31] Oral Memoirs of R. A. Springer, Waco, 1971, Baylor University Program of Oral History, p. 53.

[32] Scarborough, "Fruits of Norrisism," p. 89.

[33] *Baptist Standard*, May 23, 1923, p. 8; June 7, 1923, p. 9.

pique and hatred originating in this aggrieved individual's student days." To Dawson, Norris was an opportunist who would use any means to advance himself.[34]

Riposting coincided with institutional action. Establishment Baptists moved quickly to exclude Norris from denominational forums. In 1914 he was removed from the Baptist Pastors' Conference of Fort Worth; in August, 1922, he was expelled by the Tarrant County Baptist Association; and in the fall, 1922, he was censured by the Baptist General Convention in Waco. At Galveston the following year the General Convention refused to seat him or any member of his congregation, and in 1924 Texas Baptists permanently barred the antagonistic pastor and his flock from denominational affairs.[35] By this stage, the anger of denominational loyalists toward Norris was equaled by the Fort Worth pastor's professed disenchantment with the Texas establishment. Upon assuming the pastorate at McKinney Avenue in 1905, remarked Norris, no Catholic priest had ever been more devoted to the papacy than he to "denominational headquarters at Dallas. What disillusionment was awaiting me!"[36]

The source of such reciprocal animosity was a struggle for power and influence within the Baptist General Convention, a struggle rooted primarily in Norris's psyche. Because of a "monumental ego and fiercely independent spirit," Norris "found it virtually impossible to cooperate with anything or anyone in a rigid and highly structured environment." Convinced of his own rightness, he expected acquiescence from others. According to one authority, Norris "saw himself as a patriarch, a messianic figure, a divinely ordained prophet."[37] Yet, paradoxically, one senses that Norris's overpowering need to succeed, his ambition to minister the largest Baptist church in the world, concealed a certain insecurity. His obsession with numbers, which some-

[34] Ibid., Dec. 1, 1927, p. 2.

[35] Russell, "Norris: Violent Fundamentalist," p. 293; Oral Memoirs, Dawson, p. 268; Morris, "Norris and Baptist General Convention," p. 9; Wayne Flynt, "One in the Spirit, Many in the Flesh: Southern Evangelicals," *Varieties of Southern Evangelicalism*, ed. David E. Harrell, Jr. (Macon, Ga.: Mercer University Press, 1981), p. 29.

[36] Norris, *Inside History*, pp. 24, 32.

[37] Morris, "Norris and Baptist General Convention," p. 3.

times caused him to exaggerate attendance and conversion figures, emanated apparently from a need simultaneously to boost
his ego and to prove himself to denominational leaders whom he
attacked.[38] Norris aspired to leadership and recognition within
the Baptist General Convention of Texas but, when rebuffed,
exalted himself by attacking the convention, its institutions and
programs, and successful establishment figures. The combative
cleric increasingly exhibited the qualities historians Richard
Hofstadter and Norman F. Furniss associated with militant
fundamentalism—egotism, harshness of thought, and violent
rhetoric.[39] Edward Newlon Jones, a faculty member at Baylor in
the 1920s and later president at Texas Tech University, put it
succinctly: "Norris was the type who would try to ruin what he
couldn't run."[40]

By 1920 Norris, representing a narrow fundamentalist viewpoint and an insistence upon absolute congregational autonomy,
and President Scarborough were on a collision course. The contest, which ultimately jarred the General Convention to its
foundation and redounded sharply to the disadvantage of social Christianity, turned on two primary issues—the Seventy-
Five Million Campaign, in which such prominent Texans as
Truett, Scarborough, and Dawson played leading roles, and
modernism.[41]

As the general director of the Seventy-Five Million Campaign, Scarborough assigned Norris's prosperous congregation a
quota, as he had done for Southern Baptist churches across the
South. Norris soon objected, calling the $100,000 quota an as-
sessment and charging that Baptists did not finance programs by

[38] Russell, "Norris: Violent Fundamentalist," pp. 283, 301.

[39] Hofstadter, *Anti-intellectualism*, pp. 118–19; Furniss, *Fundamentalist Controversy*, pp. 36–43.

[40] Oral Memoirs of E. N. Jones, Waco, 1973, Baylor University Program of Oral
History, p. 133. Louis Entzminger, Norris's devoted associate, attributed the hostility
largely to the jealousy of other Baptists at Norris's success. See Entzminger, "My First
Meeting" in Norris, *Inside History*, pp. 54–55; and Entzminger, *Norris I Have Known*,
pp. 59–60.

[41] Morris, "Norris and Baptist General Convention," p. 11; Falls, *Biography of
Norris*, pp. 48–49; Robert A. Baker, *The Southern Baptist Convention and Its People,
1907–1972* (Nashville: Broadman Press, 1974), pp. 393–94.

such means. To Norris, this was an encroachment upon congregational autonomy, a hallmark of the Baptist faith.[42] Dawson, the campaign's publicity director for Texas, sided with Scarborough and argued that Norris's stated objection was a facade. According to Dawson, Norris simply wanted "to escape any participation. . . . He didn't want to try to raise any money for the Seventy-Five Million Campaign."[43] A recent study gives weight to Dawson's charge. The Seventy-Five Million Campaign came in the midst of an effort by Norris to raise funds for a new sanctuary for his own congregation, and a large contribution to the denominational drive would have diverted sorely needed revenue from the local endeavor. Predictably, Norris's subsequent failure to support the regional project led to considerable ill will with Scarborough and other denominational loyalists. The sides exchanged bitter charges. Increasingly, the debate focused on personalities rather than issues.[44]

As the verbal bombast gained intensity, Norris raised the specter of Darwinism. There is little doubt that the Fort Worth minister genuinely objected to theological liberalism and evolutionary theories, but his discovery of such "heresies" was certainly timely. Opportunistically, he seized upon modernism to discredit his adversaries. The resulting debate, fraught with emotion, suited Norris. Drawing no distinction between evolution, liberalism, modernism, and the social gospel, he easily coalesced each "sin" with the others and thereby tapped the anxiety of conservative Texas religionists who were disturbed by numerous intellectual currents of the 1920s. And although Norris was usually the assailant, he intensified the sympathy of his devoted congregation by skillfully depicting himself as "the tired, persecuted, lonely prophet of God, whose legs would hardly carry him, whose head was about to burst, and whose nerves were ready to give way."[45] So in waging the Lord's battles

[42] Norris, *Inside History*, pp. 17, 160–62.

[43] Oral Memoirs, Dawson, pp. 265–66, 275.

[44] Morris, "Norris and Baptist General Convention," pp. 43–49; and Tatum, *Conquest or Failure?* pp. 185–200.

[45] Russell, "Norris: Violent Fundamentalist," p. 285.

against evolution, Norris enhanced his stature among his followers and gratified his ego.

Norris, of course, was not unique among Texas Baptists in opposing evolution. Most denominational leaders were as suspicious as he of anything that smacked of Darwinism. But whereas other Texans assumed the enemy was yet beyond the gate, Norris claimed the ramparts had already been breached and that Baylor University itself was tainted. In October, 1921, Norris accused Professor Grove Samuel Dow, head of the Baylor Sociology Department, of teaching evolution in his textbook, *Introduction to the Principles of Sociology*. The attack mushroomed. In sermons, radio addresses, and articles in his weekly paper, the *Searchlight*, Norris was soon challenging the views of President Samuel P. Brooks of Baylor, other members of the Baylor faculty, Truett, Scarborough, Dawson, who was serving on the Baylor Board of Trustees, and B. H. Carroll, who, though now deceased, was still revered. Norris insinuated that these prominent denominational figures "were not exactly sound Baptists."[46]

Clearly put on the defensive, Texas Baptists speedily moved to guard the integrity of their leaders and institutions. Eugene Coke Routh, editor of the *Baptist Standard*, assured readers that the General Convention "would not tolerate for one day any teacher who advocates Darwinian evolution in any Baptist school. . . . Our schools must be kept distinctly Christian."[47]

[46] Oral Memoirs, Dawson, pp. 114–15; J. Frank Norris, "Professor Dowe [*sic*] and Baylor University," *Searchlight*, Nov. 11, 1921, p. 1; Norris, *Inside History*, pp. 159–60; Tatum, *Conquest or Failure?* pp. 181–84. As documented by Pat Ledbetter, "Texas Fundamentalism: Secular Phases of a Religious Conflict, 1920–1929," *Red River Valley Historical Review* 6 (Fall, 1981): 38–52, the controversy over evolution affected secular as well as church politics in the 1920s. Although Texas never passed an anti-evolution law, Austin legislators debated the issue several times, many secular newspaper editors expressed opposition to the theory, and public school textbooks containing offensive evolutionary references were censored. According to Ledbetter, most Texans in the 1920s, whether in or out of the church, were unsympathetic to the theory of evolution. So when Norris raised the topic, he found a receptive audience among non-Baptists as well as Baptists. And in February, 1923, in the midst of his conflict with the General Convention, the Fort Worth pastor appeared before the Texas legislature to "skin the chimpanzee theory."

[47] *Baptist Standard*, Nov. 24, 1921, pp. 5, 8.

The Baptist editor had actually read the disputed textbook and carried out a personal investigation several months before Norris leveled his charges. Finding "three or four paragraphs . . . objectionable," Routh had exchanged letters with President Brooks and Professor Dow and the matter had been amicably resolved. As the editor explained, Dow had not only pledged to revise the controversial sections of his book but also had given assurances that he believed the biblical account of creation. "I have come to the conclusion," Dow wrote, "that science when properly understood is in harmony with the Bible account of creation." President Brooks, moreover, vouched for Dow's "loyalty to every doctrine held by Baptists, including . . . the acceptance of creation."[48]

Meanwhile, the Baptist General Convention addressed itself to Norris's charges at its Dallas meeting in November, 1921. Josiah B. Tidwell, head of the Baylor Bible Department, Scarborough, Truett, and others submitted a resolution that the messengers subsequently adopted without dissent. Texas Baptists, read the declaration, "unalterably" opposed "the teachings of Darwinian evolution or any other theory that discredits the Genesis account of creation." Reflecting how easily many churchmen associated evolution with social service, the messengers, in the same breath, also registered unyielding opposition to "rationalism, destructive criticism, and the substitution of social service and culture in the place of regeneration and personal evangelism." School presidents and boards of trustees were then instructed "to see to it that none of these false teachings" was "allowed in our schools." This would require, concluded the resolution, "that the most vigilant, painstaking and continual care be exercised in the selection of both teachers and textbooks."[49] President Brooks of Baylor not only endorsed the declaration but also recommended the establishment of a committee to investigate teaching at all Texas Baptist schools.[50]

By September, 1922, this investigative committee had

[48]Ibid., Nov. 3, 1921, p. 8.
[49]Ibid., Dec. 8, 1921, p. 1.
[50]Baptist General Convention of Texas, *Proceedings*, 1921, p. 35 (cited hereafter as BGCT, *Proceedings*).

cleared Baptist institutions of all charges. "It seems reasonably certain that no effort is being made in Baylor University or any of our schools to teach the theoretical science or any other subject in such a way as to undermine the faith of the student in God or in the credibility or authority of His Word," asserted the committee. "On the contrary, we have found strong evidence that the teachers were diligent in strengthening and stabilizing the faith of the pupils." The committee reported nearly unanimously; the one exception was a person who did not want to give the impression that he endorsed "theistic evolution, as . . . apparently held by at least two of the science teachers" at Baylor. Dr. Lula Pace, head of the Biology Department, and Dr. O. C. Bradbury, also of the Biology Department, both espoused theistic evolution.[51] President Brooks defended these faculty members and neither was dismissed. Professor Dow, whose textbook had initially sparked the controversy, was not interviewed by the committee because he had already resigned, unwilling "to spend his life in the tortures of such alleged errors."[52]

The committee did interview Dawson, who was vulnerable. That the Waco pastor interpreted scripture figuratively and espoused theistic evolution was undeniable. In December, 1921, with controversy brewing, he delivered a timely sermon on evolution. Discounting the literal six-day account of creation, he announced that "the days mentioned in the second chapter of the Book of Genesis could not be solar days of twenty-four hours each because the Scriptures declare the sun had not yet been created."[53] With President Brooks and most of the Baylor professors who were under investigation sitting in his congregation, it was almost as if Dawson was baiting Norris. The sermon certainly attracted attention. James B. Cranfill, then a trustee at Southwestern Seminary, took exception in a friendly rebuttal.[54]

[51] *Baptist Standard*, Sept. 14, 1922, pp. 6–7, 11–12; Thompson, *Tried as by Fire*, pp. 116–17.

[52] Oral Memoirs, Dawson, p. 148. See also Norris, *Inside History*, p. 10; Thompson, *Tried as by Fire*, pp. 116–17.

[53] Oral Memoirs, Dawson, pp. 142–44, 147, 266.

[54] *Baptist Standard*, Jan. 12, 1922, p. 6; Jan. 26, 1922, p. 7. See also Oral Memoirs, Dawson, p. 148.

To an unyielding literalist such as Norris,[55] however, such an approach to Genesis was unpardonable heresy. The Fort Worth minister reacted accordingly. As Dawson recalled, Norris "equated my interpretation with agnosticism and infidelity" and "never more relented from accusing me of being a menace to society."[56] Dawson, then, was a logical person to quiz. Candidly, the Wacoan subsequently informed the investigators that he was not particularly concerned about God's method of creation. "I believe God created man," he declared, "and you can freely call me a theistic evolutionist if you like." To Dawson's surprise, the committee was satisfied.[57]

In November, 1922, when the Baptist General Convention at Waco accepted the report of its investigative committee, thereby exonerating President Brooks and the faculty, Dawson considered it a victory for Baylor. According to the report, any complaint henceforth against a teacher, instead of being settled by an open and divisive debate on the convention floor, would be referred to the president or the board of trustees. This enabled Baylor and Texas Baptists to escape the trauma of a public trial of one of its faculty members.[58]

Norris, of course, was not silenced by the actions of the General Convention. He ridiculed the findings of the investigative committee, dismissed its members as toadies of the convention, and charged that evidence had been suppressed. As Frank Groner observed, the fact that the General Convention had exonerated Baylor "does not in the least faze this assailant of our Baptist enterprises, who imagines himself to be a paragon of orthodoxy."[59] But despite incessant attacks, Norris was unable to create a liberal-conservative schism among Texas Baptists, as was taking place in the North,[60] because most of the state's de-

[55] See Norris, *Inside History*, pp. 118–19, 152–53.
[56] Oral Memoirs, Dawson, p. 266. See also Norris, "Address on Dawsonism," p. 4; Falls, *Biography of Norris*, pp. 42–43.
[57] Oral Memoirs, Dawson, p. 148. See also Thompson, *Tried as by Fire*, pp. 118–19.
[58] Oral Memoirs, Dawson, p. 148.
[59] *Baptist Standard*, Apr. 19, 1923, pp. 5, 16–17. See also J. Frank Norris, "Notes from Jacksonville," *Searchlight*, June 2, 1922, p. 1, and "Two Main Issues Admitted but Not Settled," *Searchlight*, Oct. 27, 1922, p. 1; and Norris, *Inside History*, pp. 200–201.
[60] Furniss, *Fundamentalist Controversy*, pp. 103–18.

nominational leaders were as conservative as he on matters of theology and evolution. Scarborough, for instance, was ever concerned about doctrinal purity. In 1921 he assailed *The Old Testament in the Life of Today* by Dr. John A. Rice, a professor at Southern Methodist University in Dallas. The Baptist leader accused the Methodist scholar of denying the inspiration of the Old Testament, advocating Darwinism, and exalting social service above personal evangelism. It was "a dangerous book to Southern orthodoxy," Scarborough averred, and its influence was "already getting hold on the Methodist ministry of the South."[61]

No doubt to protect fellow Baptists against similar inroads, Scarborough wholeheartedly subscribed to the idea of "a Baptist confession of faith." A denomination had every right, he asserted, to demand orthodoxy of those who taught in its institutions.[62] So in 1925 the seminary president enthusiastically supported the creed adopted by the Southern Baptist Convention in Memphis, believing it established a "protective wall and hedge against the invasion of heresies such as rationalism, modernism, and other destructive doctrines."[63] For a denomination that had historically disparaged creeds, emphasizing instead religious liberty and freedom of conscience, this was a significant development. Scarborough, however, discouraged the convention from attempting to force seminary professors and employees of Baptist boards to sign the document. Such an intrusion would be not only unwise but also unnecessary. Scarborough explained that he planned to "recommend to the Board of Trustees of Southwestern Seminary that they adopt the Articles of Faith recommended by the Convention," and that he himself would "require, as formerly, each teacher in the Seminary to sign these Articles of Faith."[64] The traditional Baptist emphasis upon local

[61] *Baptist Standard*, Sept. 29, 1921, pp. 30–31.

[62] Ibid., Sept. 22, 1921, pp. 6–7; Sept. 29, 1921, p. 31.

[63] Ibid., Apr. 30, 1925, p. 9. See also Baker, *Southern Baptist Convention*, pp. 398–400.

[64] *Baptist Standard*, Apr. 30, 1925, p. 9. Despite his public posture, Scarborough evidently did not insist that faculty members at Southwestern sign such a declaration. Thomas B. Maston, for instance, a young member of the seminary faculty at that time, was never asked to sign anything. Thomas B. Maston to author, May 21, 1981.

autonomy no doubt coalesced at this point with a concern for presidential prerogatives.

In addition to identifying Baptists with such "great doctrines" as the inspiration of the Bible, the virgin birth, and the deity and bodily resurrection of Jesus, Scarborough praised the 1925 declaration for its stand against evolution. The teaching of evolution was "doing great damage to the cause of Christ," the seminarian declared, and that was "the reason" he favored the creed approved by the Memphis convention. As Scarborough put it, he would "sign almost any pronouncement against evolution. I am against it first, last and all time."[65]

With men such as Scarborough in positions of leadership, Norris's charges of heresy ultimately fell flat. Texas Baptists felt strongly about evolution, but they felt just as certainly that leaders such as Scarborough; Pat Neff, president of the Baylor trustees; and Josiah B. Tidwell, the staunchly conservative head of the Baylor Bible Department, would not tolerate unsound teachings in Baptist institutions.[66]

By the end of 1922 the Texas Baptist establishment was beginning to close ranks on Norris. In so doing it made it evident that doctrinal issues were not the crux of the furor. To be sure, many Texas Baptists did not share Norris's dispensational premillennialism, and they successfully resisted attempts to make such views a test of Christian orthodoxy.[67] Otherwise, Texas

---

[65] *Baptist Standard*, May 28, 1925, p. 7.

[66] See ibid., Jan. 5, 1922, p. 8; Jan. 12, 1922, p. 6; Jan. 26, 1922, p. 8; July 23, 1925, p. 7. See Apr. 19, 1923, pp. 5, 16–17; Oct. 9, 1924, p. 1, Oct. 16, 1924, p. 8, and Nov. 24, 1927, p. 5, for accounts of the Norris controversy. See also Oral Memoirs, Dawson, p. 116; Oral Memoirs, Jones, pp. 122–31; and Entzminger, *Norris I Have Known*, pp. 183–87.

[67] Thompson, *Tried as by Fire*, pp. 148–51. Premillennialism is the belief that steadily deteriorating world conditions (wars and rumors of wars) will precede the second coming, at which time Jesus will establish a thousand-year reign. Hence, Jesus will come before the millennium. Dispensational premillennialism was a theory popularized by C. I. Scofield of Dallas in 1909 and enthusiastically embraced by Norris. Scofield divided history into seven periods, or dispensations, each beginning with a divine covenant and ending with God's judgment. Scofield believed mankind was living in the sixth dispensation, which would soon end with the second coming and the beginning of the millennium. By contrast, postmillennial eschatology, popular among liberal social gospel ministers, held that steadily improving world conditions would culminate in the second coming. In this view, Jesus will come after a millennium of human progress.

churchmen had no problem with Norris's fundamentalism. They shared many of his theological views. But Texas Baptists could not tolerate Norris's belligerence, his abusive attacks upon denominational institutions.[68] So Norris was accused primarily of being a disruptive troublemaker. As Scarborough wrote in November, 1922, "Norrisism openly declares it is against all denominational drives, and this means opposition to the organized work of Southern Baptists." Bespeaking the sentiment of other Texans, the seminarian declared that he would not support anyone who attempted "to discount Southern Baptists, destroy their Sunday School Board and its work, their mission organizations, their schools, and their hospitals," and who sought "to win by misrepresentation and innuendo the leadership of this great people." Frank Groner even invoked the spirits of B. H. Carroll and James B. Gambrell, claiming that these recently deceased saints had predicted that Norris was "a mischief maker . . . destined to bring untold trouble to our cause."[69]

In September, 1924, when Norris at the Tarrant County Baptist Associational meeting rekindled the attack on Baylor, repeating the tired charges against Dow, Brooks, and evolution, a committee composed of Scarborough, John Milburn Price, William W. Barnes, all of Southwestern Seminary, and others bluntly rebuffed him. Since "the state convention has passed on this matter and settled it unanimously two or three times on thorough investigation," reported the committee, the issues raised by Norris had already been resolved.[70] A few weeks later Texas Baptists expelled the controversial pastor from the Baptist General Convention, officially ending his ties to the denomination.

Nevertheless, in 1927 the Baptist General Convention and Norris again exchanged salvos. The Fort Worth pastor once more challenged the orthodoxy of President Brooks and the Baylor

[68] Gatewood, *Controversy in the Twenties*, p. 6, for an explanation of different gradations of fundamentalism. See also Hofstadter, *Anti-intellectualism*, p. 118. To this day, some prominent conservative Texas Baptists still do not want to be described as fundamentalists because of the association that term has with J. Frank Norris. Thomas B. Maston, interview with author, Fort Worth, Mar. 16, 1979, pp. 7–8.

[69] *Baptist Standard*, Nov. 2, 1922, pp. 13, 27–28; Apr. 19, 1923, pp. 5, 16–17.

[70] Ibid., Sept. 24, 1924, p. 8.

faculty, prompting the General Convention at its annual meeting in November to review at length its stormy relations with Norris. Terming this latest charge "bitter, persistent and malicious," the convention voiced unequivocal "disapproval" of "this base-less . . . and conscienceless warfare against" its leaders and institutions and pledged itself "to defend these leaders and causes against misrepresentation, false accusation and sensational persecution until this propaganda . . . has been swept out of the hearts of our people."[71] Although Norris would continue to be an irritant, he was no longer a threat to the unity of the Baptist General Convention. Texas Baptists had washed their hands of their most tenacious and resourceful antagonist.

The controversy had been detrimental to social Christianity, however, because the General Convention's foremost exponent of applied religion, Joseph Dawson, had been such a frequent and vulnerable target. Now, in retrospect, a rift between Norris and Dawson seems unavoidable. In addition to being a theistic evolutionist, Dawson acknowledged in a sermon his intellectual indebtedness to Harry Emerson Fosdick, the noted liberal minister of Park Avenue Baptist Church in New York. Moreover, Dawson's associations were ecumenical; he joined with Methodists, Presbyterians, Episcopalians, Jews, and Catholics to form "an interfaith discussional society for confronting social problems." He wrote an article on changing views of hell, which prompted "a terrific [radio] attack" from Norris, and he published a controversial study, *Christ and Social Change*, in 1937.[72] To a narrow dogmatist like Norris, Dawson was clearly a modernist.[73] Moreover, one suspects that Dawson was much that Norris desired to be—an accepted member of a small circle of such influential Texas Baptists as B. H. Carroll, Samuel P. Brooks, George W. Truett, and Lee Rutland Scarborough; a highly regarded denominational leader who held important positions on numerous state and regional boards; and a scholar whose writings reached a national audience. By impugning such a de-

[71] Ibid., Nov. 24, 1927, pp. 5–6.
[72] Oral Memoirs, Dawson, pp. 115–16, 147, 266, 172–73.
[73] See *Fundamentalist*, Mar. 4, 1938, p. 4; Falls, *Biography of Norris*, pp. 42–43.

voted, loyal, and successful denominational figure, Norris could call attention to himself and at the same time belittle the denomination Dawson represented and the men with whom he was a confidant.

Whatever the exact reason, Norris's continuing attack upon Dawson placed churchmen like him in an awkward position. While striving to apply the gospel to society, they might too vigorously advocate social involvement; however worthy the objective, such advocacy could easily arouse suspicion of one's theological soundness. Consequently, socially alert Texas Baptists often coupled social pronouncements with declarations of scriptural fidelity. This was certainly true of Dawson. The Wacoan, who was convinced his concern for "the social applications of Christianity" was responsible for much of Norris's rancor, frequently felt it necessary to emphasize his devotion to personal evangelism. Indeed, in fending off his Fort Worth adversary, Dawson shrewdly linked himself to B. H. Carroll, whose orthodoxy was beyond dispute with most Texans. As the Waco pastor liked to emphasize, the "fundamental Bible doctrines" of the revered founder of Southwestern Seminary still prevailed at the First Baptist Church of Waco, where Carroll had pastored from 1870 to 1899.[74]

In addition to intensifying the discomfiture of socially concerned Baptists, Norris also contributed to the popular notion that social religion was synonymous with theological liberalism. Much like Victor I. Masters, the widely read editor of the *Western Recorder*,[75] who "construed the whole thing [social gospel] to mean running soup kitchens and collecting worn out garments for the poor as a sort of substitute for a divine regeneration,"[76] Norris continually fused evolution, liberal theology, and social Christianity, insisting ipso facto that one led to the other. Hence, it was during the 1920s that Texas Baptists grew increasingly suspicious of any kind of social activism, automatically as-

[74] Oral Memoirs, Dawson, pp. 114, 267. See also *Baptist Standard*, Nov. 15, 1928, p. 2; July 4, 1929, p. 2; and Apr. 10, 1930, p. 4.

[75] See Thompson, *Tried as by Fire*, pp. 9–11, 37, 53.

[76] Oral Memoirs, Dawson, pp. 137–38.

sociating it with Darwinism and theological heterodoxy. Actually, there was no difference between Norris and Scarborough at this point. In 1921 the seminary leader drew a straight line from Darwinian evolution to social Christianity. A modernist, he proclaimed, was "an evolutionist" who believed "man evolved from lower animals instead of being created by the power of God"; a rationalist who embraced "the dictates of reason and the findings of science instead of the authority of God"; a "destructive critic" whose denial of the "integrity, inspiration and binding authority" of the Bible culminated in a rejection of "the supernatural and miraculous . . . and the virgin birth and essential deity of Christ"; and a believer "in the power of social service, a reform rather than regeneration and personal evangelism." Although Scarborough later acknowledged that Southern Baptists as yet had "had very little trouble . . . with Modernism," he nonetheless felt the denomination needed "to be on . . . guard against the subtle and insidious efforts of Rationalism to entrench itself within our ranks." Otherwise, Southern Baptists *could* go the way of Northern Baptists.[77]

Evident in Scarborough's alert was a belief that Northern Baptists, as well as other denominational bodies above the Ohio, had already succumbed to "modern evils." Despite the vigorous efforts of fundamentalists such as William Bell Riley, John Roach Straton, and J. Gresham Machen, liberal churchmen in the North had steadily gained the upper hand.[78] This, too, was detrimental to social Christianity in Texas, for Texas Baptists could easily see that many of the same northern liberals who occupied prominent denominational positions, such as Shailer Mathews, dean of the Divinity School of the University of Chicago, and Harry Emerson Fosdick, were also leading advocates of the social gospel. This not only strengthened the tie many Texas Baptists saw between social Christianity and other presumed evils but also fueled latent sectional hostility.[79] Social Christianity

[77] *Baptist Standard*, Sept. 22, 1921, pp. 6–7; Jan. 17, 1924, p. 6.
[78] See Furniss, *Fundamentalist Controversy*, pp. 110–18, 127–41, 149–76.
[79] *Baptist Standard*, Oct. 16, 1924, p. 7; Oral Memoirs, Dawson, p. 137; Oral Memoirs of T. B. Maston, Waco, 1973, Baylor University Program of Oral History,

subsequently suffered because Texas churchmen, in responding to these presumed heresies, fervently proclaimed their innocence on all counts. They were no more guilty of harboring evolutionists and theological liberals than of promulgating a false social gospel.

In November, 1921, for instance, the General Convention, reacting to J. Frank Norris's original charges, unequivocally served notice that it opposed not only evolution and liberal teachings but also "the substitution of social service . . . [for] personal evangelism." Much of the rank and file concurred. A few weeks later a contributor to the *Baptist Standard* called the social gospel "a religious sham" that sought to replace the gospel of Jesus with social involvement. Satisfied that the primary purpose of Christianity was to save individuals rather than reform society, the writer condemned the social gospel as "an adulterated mixture of socialism, humanitarianism, Unitarianism and infidelity." Even Wallace Bassett, who had previously been sympathetic to social religion, shifted to a more traditional emphasis upon personal evangelism. In a sermon to the Southern Baptist Convention in Louisville, Kentucky, May, 1927, the Dallas pastor told fellow Baptists that "our greatest service is not to feed the hungry, or clothe the needy, . . . [but] to make God known." Elaborating, Bassett contended that "the only gospel" that could endure was "the one that works from the inside out and not from the outside in." [80]

This theme was reiterated time and again throughout the 1920s and into the 1930s, as the Baptist General Convention unequivocally reasserted the primacy of personal evangelism and pointedly disparaged social Christianity. The 1920 report of the Social Service Committee was typical. It declared that social service was "temporal and material," whereas "the work of the church" was "eternal and spiritual." As if to accentuate the sec-

pp. 23–25; Maston, interview with author, p. 4; George B. Tindall, *The Emergence of the New South, 1913–1945* (Baton Rouge: Louisiana State University Press, 1967), pp. 208–18.

[80] *Baptist Standard*, Dec. 8, 1921, p. 1; Feb. 23, 1922, p. 12; May 12, 1927, pp. 10–11, 17.

ondary role of social Christianity, it concluded that social service sought merely "to improve the housing problem in the slums" and dealt "in soap as the means of cleanliness," whereas the church pointed "to mansions in the skies" and labored "for cleansing through the blood of Christ." Two years later at the convention in Waco the committee repeated itself, insisting that Baptists rendered the highest social service where they were the most evangelistic. To prove the point, the committee cited the establishment of orphanages, hospitals, and local charities in communities where Baptists promoted personal evangelism. Furthermore, such eleemosynary endeavors were advanced "without calling it a social program at all." The 1922 Baptist General Convention then proceeded to consolidate the Civic Righteousness and Social Service committees, thus creating the Committee on Civic and Social Service.[81]

Thereafter, the General Convention, disturbed by evidence of decay in homes, churches, and schools, flailed away at such "sins" as dancing; divorce; smoking, especially among women; sabbath desecration; racetrack gambling; lotteries; and, as always, alcohol. Even if Al Smith, the 1928 Democratic nominee, had been a Protestant, his views on prohibition would have made him unacceptable to most Texas Baptists. They objected to advertising which encouraged people to drink and as early as 1927 adopted a resolution opposing any presidential candidate who renounced prohibition.[82] They objected to rodeos on Sunday, specifically the Huntsville Prison Rodeo which took place each Sunday in October, and were concerned about the spread of crime, especially among juveniles. And though fearful of the corrupting and destructive influence of movies, Baptists also

---

[81] BGCT, *Proceedings*, 1920, p. 80; 1922, p. 148; 1923, p. 171.

[82] Ibid., 1927, pp. 97–99. A good analysis of the 1928 campaign in Texas, one that concludes that it was not Catholicism per se that made the New Yorker unacceptable to Texans, is in Norman D. Brown, *Hood, Bonnet, and Little Brown Jug: Texas Politics, 1921–1928* (College Station: Texas A&M University Press, 1984), pp. 374–422. See also Tatum, *Conquest or Failure?* pp. 247–50, for a brief account of J. Frank Norris's vigorous efforts in behalf of Herbert Hoover. See J. Frank Norris, "Information Needed in Campaign," *Fundamentalist*, Oct. 26, 1928, p. 1, and "And the Mule under Him Went Away," *Fundamentalist*, Nov. 9, 1928, p. 1; and *Baptist Standard*, Sept. 29, 1927, p. 7; Feb. 2, 1928, p. 2.

recognized the educational and constructive potential of this popular medium.[83]

Usually, Texas Baptists responded to these "maladies" unimaginatively. They offered simplistic cures and issued calls for law and order. Characteristically, they tended to blame the individual for social ills and to suggest that personal involvement was the solution. Pat Neff put it aptly in the 1925 report of the Committee on Civic Righteousness. "The bad citizenship of good people," he said, was responsible "for the things that go wrong in our government life." This same committee the following year, after asserting that crime permeated "our social, political, and commercial life," could only suggest that "the need of this hour" was "to stimulate in the minds of men, women and children respect for and obedience to God, His laws and the laws of the land." And the home was the place to begin. As late as 1942 this committee was still attributing crime, sabbath desecration, gambling, and other ills to the civic unrighteousness of nominal Christians and still suggesting that the answer was sincere Christianity.[84]

Still, despite obvious resistance, there continued throughout the 1920s to be some emphasis upon the social applicability of the gospel. At Southwestern Seminary in Fort Worth, despite President Scarborough's own preference for evangelism, courses on social Christianity were offered regularly. When Thomas B. Maston, who would eventually become the General Convention's foremost exponent of social Christianity, joined the seminary faculty in 1922, Scarborough gave the young instructor every encouragement.[85] Meanwhile, John Milburn Price, who di-

[83] See BGCT, *Proceedings*, 1922, pp. 142–45; 1926, p. 164; 1929, pp. 167–71; 1930, p. 139; 1931, pp. 157–60; 1932, pp. 152–54; 1933, pp. 154, 157; 1934, p. 159; 1936, pp. 145–47; 1937, pp. 145–58; and 1940, pp. 160–61.

[84] Ibid., 1925, pp. 176–77; 1926, pp. 164–65. This pattern was much the same at the regional level. See Yance, *Religion Southern Style: Southern Baptists and Society in Historical Perspective*, Perspectives in Religious Studies, Special Studies Series, no. 4 (Danville, Va.: Association of Baptist Professors of Religion, 1978), pp. 16–18.

[85] Letter from Maston to author, May 21, 1981. Although Scarborough was very supportive, his emphasis on personal evangelism was so intense that Maston sometimes felt ill at ease. Maston, interview with author, p. 29.

rected the School of Religious Education, taught "The Social Teachings of the Bible," out of which evolved *Christianity and Social Problems*. Price urged fellow Baptists not to neglect social reform. "We should work both on the individual and his environment," he wrote, "if the best results are to follow."[86]

The same point was made by the seminary's most respected theologian, Walter Thomas Conner. Joining the Southwestern faculty in 1910, Conner taught systematic theology at the Baptist institution for thirty-nine years. He studied at Baylor (B.A., 1906, and M.A., 1908); Rochester Theological Seminary in New York, where he encountered Walter Rauschenbusch; Southern Baptist Seminary, Louisville (Th.D., 1916, and Ph.D., 1931); and the University of Chicago. In 1927, shortly after the General Convention summarily dismissed Norris's latest charges, Conner observed that there had been "a good deal of meaningless discussion" regarding the purpose of religion—whether it was to save the individual or to save society. To the theologian, there was "no such thing as an individual apart from social relationships." To save the individual was "to save him in his social relations." But conversely, added Conner, "the only way to save society is to save individuals composing society, and save them in all their social relations."[87]

Joseph Dawson, however, continued to be the denomination's most important and articulate spokesman for social Christianity. In April, 1928, he called attention to the urban and industrial trends of the South, declaring that the churches could not ignore the plight of "the multiplied thousands" of men and women "in these new industrial centers." Illiteracy, more prevalent among whites and blacks alike in the South than elsewhere, was particularly disturbing to the Wacoan. Indeed, as so many of the victims of "this disgraceful condition" were Baptists, the churches were obligated to grapple with the issue. When Dawson in November, 1928, repeated his remarks about illiteracy, he took a swipe at J. Frank Norris. "The pestilential warfare against

---

[86] Price, *Christianity and Social Problems* (Nashville: Sunday School Board, 1928), pp. 41–43.

[87] *Baptist Standard*, Dec. 15, 1927, p. 2. See also Walter T. Conner, *Gospel Doctrines* (Nashville: Sunday School Board, 1925).

our schools by those who charged that they were teaching evolution," Dawson asserted, had hindered Baptists in dealing with inadequate schooling in the South.[88]

Although rare, there were some collective expressions of support for social Christianity. In 1924 the Committee on Civic and Social Righteousness, although blandly suggesting that business morality had improved as a result of luncheon clubs and commercial credit associations, nevertheless emphasized the need for upgrading Texas penal institutions. Accusing the public of being indifferent to the physical needs of prisoners, the committee urged the Texas legislature to establish a "blue ribbon" panel to study penal reforms and examine criminal laws. Such statements, of course, depended largely upon the composition of the Civic and Social Righteousness committee. And since it was not unusual for committee membership to change entirely at frequent intervals, there was little continuity in social pronouncements from one convention to the next. So a progressive statement on social issues one year was often followed by inconsequential reports. After the 1924 report, for instance, the annual statements of the Civic and Social Righteousness committee were devoid of meaningful social content for the next several years.[89]

If Baptist men as a body were reluctant to apply the scriptures to society, it was not so of the women. Ladies of the General Convention proved to be much bolder than their male counterparts, especially by the end of the decade. In 1928 the Committee on Civic Righteousness for the Woman's Missionary Union, an auxiliary of the Baptist General Convention, although giving an expected emphasis to home, family, and law and order, also endorsed child welfare efforts, called for improvement in industrial conditions, and supported international peace. The following year the women were not only more specific but also more insistent that action replace rhetoric. Industry, they declared, should be closely scrutinized in order to safeguard women and children from long and dangerous hours of toil and to

[88] *Baptist Standard*, Apr. 19, 1928, p. 3; Nov. 15, 1928, p. 2; July 4, 1929, p. 2.
[89] BGCT, *Proceedings*, 1924, pp. 157–58; 1925, pp. 176–77; 1926, pp. 164–65; 1927, p. 97; 1928, pp. 116–17; 1929, pp. 167–71.

protect the public from disease-causing practices detrimental to community health. Racial justice, they added, should be pursued through the creation of local interracial committees. The women further suggested that it would be helpful for Texas Baptists to study the policies and methods of social service in other organizations.[90]

Such progressive statements were not uncommon for southern churchwomen in the 1920s. A recent study documents the social concerns of those Methodist ladies, admittedly a minority, who, as a result of their home missionary endeavors, became "convinced that Christian missions should meet the physical and social as well as spiritual needs of people."[91] So the pronouncements of Texas Baptist women were not an isolated occurrence. Ladies of the Methodist Episcopal Church, South, voiced similar concerns, and in 1929 they challenged the "industrial communities" to compensate laborers adequately enough "to share in the abundant life."[92]

But whether uttered by men or women, even such implied criticism of business and industry was rare in the 1920s, for the basic economic values of business were shared by Texas Baptists. Sounding much like Russell Conwell, the Philadelphia Baptist who had advised previous generations to get rich, Walter Conner, for instance, attributed the "acquisition instinct" to God and saw nothing wrong with the attainment of wealth, so long as it was used in "the service of humanity." And Joseph Dawson? He had already intimated that Jesus opposed neither private property nor capital accumulation.[93] Moreover, the popularity of *The*

[90] Ibid., 1928, pp. 61–62; 1929, pp. 46–47.

[91] McDowell, *Social Gospel in the South*, p. 4.

[92] Quoted in ibid., pp. 47–48; see also pp. 60–143. See also Patricia S. Martin, "'Keeping Silence': Texas Baptist Women's Role in Public Worship, 1880–1920," *Journal of Texas Baptist History* 3 (1983): 15–30; L. Katherine Cook, "Texas Baptist Women and Missions, 1830–1900," *Journal of Texas Baptist History*, 3 (1983): 31–46; Lillian Smith, *Killers of the Dream* (New York: Norton, 1978), pp. 138–55; Jacquelyn Dowd Hall, *Revolt against Chivalry: Jessie Daniel Ames and the Women's Campaign Against Lynching* (New York: Columbia University Press, 1979), pp. 159–91; Leon McBeth, *Women in Baptist Life* (Nashville: Broadman Press, 1979); and Thelma Stevens, "A Place of Their Own," in *On Jordan's Stormy Banks, Religion in the South: A Southern Exposure Profile*, ed. Samuel S. Hill, Jr. (Macon, Ga.: Mercer University Press, 1983), pp. 33–36.

[93] *Baptist Standard*, Dec. 15, 1927, p. 2; Oct. 1, 1914, p. 3.

Man Nobody Knows (1925), in which Bruce Barton portrayed
Jesus as an enterprising entrepreneur, and the utilization by the
churches of managerial techniques to boost enrollments and
contributions,[94] further suggests that Texas churchmen essentially were at ease with cultural values of the 1920s. But with the
onset of depression and war the mood changed in the 1930s.

[94] Lynn Ray Musslewhite, "Texas in the 1920s: A History of Social Change," (Ph.D.
diss., Texas Tech University, 1975), pp. 315, 336–37; Robert A. Baker, *The Blossoming
Desert: A Concise History of Texas Baptists* (Waco: Word Books, 1970), pp. 202–204.

3

The Impact of Depression and War, 1930–1945

JUST as the churches had shared in the prosperity of the 1920s, they experienced the hard times associated with the Great Depression and World War II. Across the nation congregations slashed budgets, curtailed programs, released ministers, and struggled to stay alive. Such privation evoked varied responses from the faithful. As church historian Sydney E. Ahlstrom observed, "religious views gravitated to the extremes." While many churchmen looked inward for explanations, suggesting that world crises reflected God's displeasure with individual sinners, others scrutinized the environment, finding in flawed economic and political institutions the sources of human distress. So these years witnessed disparate religious tendencies. Simultaneously, there was an intense revival among Holiness and Pentecostal groups, "perhaps because the Depression so enlarged their constituencies among the disinherited," and a revitalization of the social gospel. "Nearly all the churches," Ahlstrom wrote, especially Northern Methodists, exhibited "an increased willingness to speak out on social issues in a distinctly critical manner."[1] In Texas, the Baptist General Convention mirrored these trends.

Actually, Texas Baptists had encountered financial straits long before the crash of 1929. Carried along by the optimism immediately following World War I, as well as denominational

---

[1] Ahlstrom, *A Religious History of the American People* (New Haven: Yale University Press, 1972), pp. 919–22. See also Robert Moats Miller, *American Protestantism and Social Issues, 1919–1939* (Chapel Hill: University of North Carolina Press, 1958), pp. 65–71; Robert T. Handy, *A History of the Churches in the United States and Canada* (New York: Oxford University Press, 1976), pp. 387–91, and "The American Religious Depression, 1925–1935," *Church History* 24 (Mar., 1960): 3–16; and Kenneth K. Bailey, *Southern White Protestantism in the Twentieth Century* (1964; reprint, Gloucester, Mass.: Peter Smith, 1968), p. 115.

pressure to meet the challenge of the Seventy-Five Million Campaign, many congregations overextended themselves. So by the early 1920s pledges to the campaign fell behind, despite the fervent appeals of Lee Rutland Scarborough to "DENOMINA-TIONAL HONOR" and "ALL THE INTERESTS WHICH WE HOLD DEAR,"[2] and loans negotiated in better times to fund ambitious building projects could not be paid. Baptist churches throughout the state faced economic ruin. And the condition of the General Convention was no better. In 1926 the indebtedness of its institutions was more than $6 million. This prompted state denominational leaders to launch a statewide fund-raising drive called the Conquest Campaign reminiscent of the Seventy-Five Million Campaign, but the effort was blunted by depressed economic conditions. From 1926 to 1929 the General Convention consistently operated in the red. In 1928 and 1929, respectively, its liabilities exceeded its assets by approximately $830,000 and $732,000. Hence, the stock market crash of October, 1929, and the succeeding years of the Great Depression only intensified an already painful economic situation.[3]

Despite hard times, Texas churches experienced significant numerical growth during the depression and war years. From 1930 to 1945 church membership expanded from 521,462 to 920,952, and the number of churches increased from 2,973 to 3,262.[4] For Texas Baptists, the tangible effects of the depression were measured primarily in financial terms. Contributions for missions and other programs, along with church property values, declined sharply. Between 1930 and 1933 total gifts to the General Convention fell by approximately 30 percent.[5] Such a decline dramatically affected the academic institutions owned

[2]James J. Thompson, Jr., *Tried as by Fire: Southern Baptists and the Religious Controversies of the 1920s* (Macon, Ga.: Mercer University Press, 1982), p. 196.

[3]*Encyclopedia of Southern Baptists* (Nashville: Broadman Press, 1958), II, 1381–82; Joseph M. Dawson, *A Century with Texas Baptists* (Nashville: Broadman Press, 1947), pp. 87–95; Robert A. Baker, *The Blossoming Desert: A Concise History of Texas Baptists* (Waco: Word Books, 1970), pp. 206–21; Carr M. Suter, Jr., *O Zion, Haste: The Story of the Dallas Baptist Association* (Dallas: Dallas Baptist Association, 1978), pp. 95–96.

[4]Baker, *Blossoming Desert*, p. 219. See also Robert C. Cotner et al., *Texas Cities and the Great Depression* (Austin: Texas Memorial Museum, 1973), pp. 62–63.

[5]*Encyclopedia of Southern Baptists* II, 1389; Baker, *Blossoming Desert*, p. 218.

by the state convention. Rusk Academy, as well as other academies, and Burleson College at Greenville, which had been in
operation since 1895, were closed in the early 1930s.[6] At Baylor,
where the economic crisis seemed all the more acute as a result
of the death of President Samuel P. Brooks in May, 1931, the
faculty was paid in scrip, which local merchants sometimes redeemed at no more than 70 percent of face value. Moreover,
upon the death of Brooks, the Baylor trustees in June, 1932,
selected Pat Neff, who was then chairman of the Baylor board, as
president. It was felt that the school needed at the time someone
of Neff's business and administrative talents. Far more authori-
tarian than his predecessor, the former Texas governor, without
consulting the faculty, set about combining departments to
reduce administrative costs and slashing budgets. Joseph Dawson believed these measures saved the Baptist school from
bankruptcy.[7]

Similar conditions plagued Southwestern Seminary in Fort
Worth, ownership of which had been assumed by the Southern
Baptist Convention in 1925. Although its faculty was never paid
in scrip, salary money from Nashville arrived irregularly and un-
predictably. And when it did reach Fort Worth, there was never
enough to pay faculty members their full earnings. Whatever
amount was sent from Nashville was parceled out, often in small
sums of no more than $20 or $30. Thomas B. Maston recalled
that one year he received only $1,036.[8] Such financial difficulty,
coupled with declining student enrollment, forced the seminary
to cut faculty positions. Faculty members who were retained
usually "moonlighted," while students did maintenance work for
the seminary in return for room and board.[9]

Local congregations, large and small, rural and urban, were
likewise affected. Budgets were cut, salaries reduced, workers

[6] Oral Memoirs of R. A. Springer, Waco, 1971, Baylor University Program of Oral
History, pp. 101–102; Baker, *Blossoming Desert*, p. 220.
[7] Memoirs of E. N. Jones, Waco, 1973, Baylor University Program of Oral History,
pp. 74–76; Oral Memoirs of Joseph M. Dawson, Waco, 1973, Baylor University Program
of Oral History, p. 40; Dawson, *Century with Texas Baptists*, pp. 90–91.
[8] Oral Memoirs of T. B. Maston, Waco, Baylor University Program of Oral History,
p. 63.
[9] Ibid., pp. 64, 68–70.

dismissed, and mission programs scaled down. The First Baptist Church, Amarillo; the South Main Baptist Church, Houston; and the First Baptist Church, San Marcos, all of which had begun substantial building programs in the 1920s, now faced severe hardship.[10] The plight of the First Baptist Church, San Antonio, was common. Its annual receipts plunged from more than $200,000 in the late 1920s to $54,256 in 1932.[11] And in smaller communities such as Cisco and Belton, where Acker C. Miller pastored, "the salaries had to be cut terribly and the budget by at least a third."[12] William Richardson White, executive secretary of the Baptist General Convention from 1929 to 1931, drew a bleak picture in Sepember, 1931. Unable to pay salaries, numerous churches were without pastors; other congregations could not meet current expenses; and many clergymen were among the unemployed. Burdened with debt, said White, many churches would surely go bankrupt "were it not for the mercy and good judgment of their creditors."[13]

External conditions influence thought; to what extent did this crisis affect the theological assumptions and social attitudes of Texas Baptists? As was true of religious bodies nationally,[14] the buoyant mood of the 1920s in Texas was broken and the exuberant self-confidence was shaken, but the theological effects on the Baptists in the state were negligible. Unlike those pundits, both secular and religious, whose optimism gave way to despair in the face of depression and war,[15] Texas Baptists underwent no soul-searching. The neo-orthodoxy movement, which stressed the tenacity of sin and the transcendence of God and discarded the

[10] Oral Memoirs of W. R. White, Waco, 1971, Baylor University Program of Oral History, pp. 100–101; Cotner et al., *Texas Cities and the Great Depression*, p. 42.

[11] Cotner et al., *Texas Cities and the Great Depression*, pp. 62–63.

[12] Oral Memoirs, Miller, p. 44.

[13] *Baptist Standard*, Sept. 10, 1931, p. 1.

[14] Ahlstrom, *Religious History*, p. 919; Handy, *History of Churches*, p. 393; and Thompson, *Tried as by Fire*, pp. 195–208.

[15] William Warren Sweet, *The Story of Religion in America* (New York: Harper and Brothers, 1950), pp. 450–51. See also George L. Mosse, *The Culture of Western Europe: The Nineteenth and Twentieth Centuries* (New York: Rand McNally, 1961), pp. 331–40; Edwin Scott Gaustad, *A Religious History of America* (New York: Harper and Row, 1974), p. 334; Ahlstrom, *Religious History*, pp. 932–39; and Handy, "American Religious Depression," pp. 10–11.

overly sanguine outlook of the social gospel, struck a responsive chord among many Americans of the 1930s and 1940s.[16] And Texas Baptist leaders such as Professor Thomas B. Maston at Southwestern Seminary were certainly familiar with the ideas of neo-orthodoxy, but the movement generated little excitement within the denomination. As theological conservatives, Texas Baptists had always stressed the darker aspects of human nature and had always been skeptical of human reason and progress. So the pessimistic outlook of such neo-orthodox thinkers as Karl Barth, Emil Brunner, and Reinhold Niebuhr, whose influence was extensive in the 1940s and 1950s, was nothing new to Texas Baptists.

But the tumult of depression and war did affect social attitudes and pronouncements, although not in dramatic or uniform ways. Puzzled by such unsettling times, many communicants simply fell back upon archaic nostrums. The Baptist General Convention blamed greed for the trouble and, as in years past, condemned modern dancing, objected to smoking, rebuked the movie industry, and urged enforcement of prohibition.[17] Southern Baptists, of course, were not alone in this obsession with liquor. "How often," observed one scholar, "did the reader of the church press in the depression start an editorial or article entitled 'The Need of the Hour,' 'A Time of Crisis,' 'The President Must Lead,' 'Moral Issues in the Election,' 'The Stakes in the Election,' 'It Is Time for the President to Act,' only to discover that, far from dealing with the economic crisis, it was concerned with prohibition!"[18]

Even after almost a decade of want and poverty the editor of the *Baptist Standard*, Franz M. McConnell, concluded that

[16] Ahlstrom, *Religious History*, pp. 937–48; Handy, *History of Churches*, p. 393; Cushing Strout, *The New Heavens and New Earth: Political Religion in America* (New York: Harper and Row, 1974), pp. 265–84.

[17] Baptist General Convention of Texas, *Proceedings*, 1933, p. 158; 1931, pp. 157–60; 1932, pp. 152–54; 1936, pp. 136–38; 1938, pp. 151–55; 1939, pp. 148–50; 1940, pp. 160–61; 1941, pp. 180–82; 1942, pp. 208–11; and 1945, pp. 184–85 (cited hereafter as BGCT, *Proceedings*).

[18] Miller, *American Protestantism*, p. 120. See also Ahlstrom, *Religious History*, p. 925.

"the greatest menace to this nation and to civilization in the world" was "the destruction of the Christian Sabbath." The Baptist journalist believed that if individuals would help individuals, the world crisis would be solved.[19] In 1942 a minister from Kosse, Texas, William H. Sealy, recommended "a revival of preaching the doctrine of punishment in hell" as a cure for current ills, a remedy J. Frank Norris had already pursued in an "Old Fashioned Heaven-Sent Fire-Baptized Holy Ghost Sin-Convicting Mourners-Bench Shouting Revival" in Amarillo.[20] And in 1944 David M. Gardner, who succeeded McConnell as editor of the Texas Baptist weekly, recommended evangelism as a means of exorcising the demons of poverty and war.[21] For Americans who were struggling to feed, clothe, and shelter their families, there was little "good news" in this.

As for social Christianity, many Texas Baptists continued to view it with scorn. Editor McConnell, whose tenure at the *Standard*, 1928–1944, coincided with years of international distress and unparalleled national want, was typical. Supposedly to grapple with a wide range of public concerns, the Baptist weekly in 1933 introduced a feature page entitled "Christianity and Civic Righteousness." One subject dominated the feature. Like that of so many other Baptists, McConnell's social awareness generally ended with prohibition. In the columns of the "Christianity and Civic Righteousness" page, he and other contributors urged enforcement of prohibition laws, fought the repeal of the Eighteenth Amendment, and detailed the concomitant evils of legalized drink. McConnell gives validity to Sydney Ahlstrom's claim that repeal of the Eighteenth Amendment "was the greatest

[19] *Baptist Standard*, Feb. 17, 1938, p. 3.

[20] Ibid., May 21, 1942, p. 16; Thompson, *Tried as by Fire*, p. 209. Although Norris was always fervently evangelistic and unsparingly critical of the social gospel, his Fort Worth congregation nevertheless matched, perhaps surpassed, the efforts of socially alert Texas Baptists in feeding, clothing, sheltering, and offering medical attention to the destitute during the Great Depression. And, initially, Norris applauded the New Deal. See Roy E. Falls, *A Biography of J. Frank Norris, 1877–1952* (Euless, Texas.: privately printed, 1975), pp. 89–94.

[21] *Baptist Standard*, Mar. 9, 1944, p. 2. See also May 13, 1943, p. 3, and Oct. 14, 1943, p. 1.

blow to their pride and self-confidence that Protestants as a collective body had ever experienced."[22]

McConnell, furthermore, rarely missed an opportunity to disparage both social Christianity and the efforts of other churchmen to apply the scriptures more broadly. In 1934 he dismissed "the so-called 'Social Gospel' . . . [as] no gospel at all," adding that there was "no other gospel" for the individual than that of Jesus Christ. Somewhat later he attributed the decline of Northern Baptists to the social gospel, explaining that they, taken in by social gospel ministers, had reduced religion to "a matter between man and man and not a matter between man and his God." Devoid of sound theological content, religion among Northern Baptists had lost its appeal.[23]

Ironically, in 1935 the *Baptist Standard* used the "Christianity and Civic Righteousness" page to oppose the creation of a Social Research Bureau by the Southern Baptist Convention. Dr. Edwin M. Poteat, Jr., a highly respected North Carolina Baptist whose commitment to a social application of the gospel was unswerving, wanted Southern Baptists to establish such an agency to investigate social and moral issues and to suggest ways that the convention could pursue worthy social programs.[24] Joseph M. Dawson of Waco supported this effort, but James B. Cranfill of Dallas dissented, sarcastically labeling the proposed agency the "Poteat Pimple Bureau" and the "South-wide Smelling Committee." The *Standard* sided with Cranfill and urged Texas Baptists to vote decisively against Poteat at the upcoming Southern Baptist Convention in 1936. Baptist money was more urgently needed, the Texas journal reasoned, "to send the gospel to the nations of the earth and evangelize our own great country."[25] Poteat lost, as did churchmen who shared his social vision.

[22]Ibid., Feb. 2, 1933, p. 6; Mar. 16, 1933, p. 6; Oct. 26, 1933, p. 6; Nov. 16, 1933, p. 6; Apr. 12, 1934, p. 6; Mar. 28, 1935, p. 6; and Aug. 22, 1935, p. 2; Ahlstrom, *Religious History*, p. 925.

[23]*Baptist Standard*, Jan. 4, 1934, p. 3; Jan. 30, 1936, p. 3.

[24]See Bailey, *Southern White Protestantism*, pp. 124–25; John Lee Eighmy, *Churches in Cultural Captivity: A History of the Social Attitudes of Southern Baptists* (Knoxville: University of Tennessee Press, 1972), pp. 132–40.

[25]Joseph M. Dawson, *A Thousand Months to Remember: An Autobiography* (Waco: Baylor University Press, 1964), p. 167; Eighmy, *Churches in Cultural Captivity*,

For Baptists of the persuasion of McConnell and Cranfill, the Great Depression failed to spark much concern for social issues. Aside from prohibition and evangelism, these churchmen had little encouragement for Americans who were struggling with the problems spawned by a faltering economy. Sounding like latter-day Ben Franklins, they viewed the economy in terms of the Protestant ethic and explained want in terms of individual laziness. Aphoristically, a contributor to the *Baptist Standard* said it plainly in 1933. The country, he asserted, had "too many spendthrifts and not enough thrifty spenders." He added that the current impoverishment of many Americans was "self-inflicted," the result of too much "prodigal and riotous living."[26]

The depression prompted more thoughtful reexamination, however, from other Texas churchmen. With so many unemployed Americans vainly searching for work, it was difficult to attribute the national calamity to personal deficiency. Numbers of Texas Baptists, consequently, increasingly challenged the motives of business, viewed more sympathetically the plight of industrial labor, and glimpsed the importance of institutions in shaping human behavior. Although the General Convention never recommended socialism, as did the National Council of Methodist Youth in 1934, nor consistently promoted the objectives of social Christianity, as did Northern Methodists,[27] it nonetheless issued statements on social concerns reminiscent of its earlier posture in 1917–1918. And the social thought of individual churchmen closely approximated that of their northern brethren. Sydney Ahlstrom's observation is not altogether applicable to Texas. "In the South," he maintained, "the tradition of ecclesiastical silence on social issues (aside from Prohibition) was so strong that conservatives rarely had cause for complaint."[28] It was not so among Texas Baptists.

---

p. 136; *Baptist Standard,* Nov. 28, 1935, p. 6. See also May 2, 1935, p. 19, and Feb. 6, 1936, p. 4; Norman A. Yance, *Religion Southern Style, Southern Baptists and Society in Historical Perspective* ("Perspectives in Religious Studies," Special Studies Series, no. 4; Danville, Va.: Association of Baptist Professors of Religion, 1978), pp. 34–35.

[26] *Baptist Standard,* Mar. 9, 1933, p. 6.

[27] Ahlstrom, *Religious History,* p. 922; Miller, *American Protestantism,* pp. 65–71.

[28] Ahlstrom, *Religious History,* p. 924.

When the Southern Baptist Convention in 1938 praised the American economic system as the "best in the world,"[29] it did not speak for substantial numbers of communicants in the Lone Star State. Prominent Texas Baptists joined a chorus of national religious critics who rebuked business in general and denounced capitalism, laissez faire, and especially the profit motive. As one scholar noted, "the 'religion of business' lost votaries in droves" during the 1930s.[30] Like other Americans of the depression era, many Texas Baptists accepted the unflattering thesis that business, obsessed with profits, had engineered the United States into World War I. Drawing upon the sensational Nye Committee hearings, Frank Groner, then president of the East Texas Baptist College at Marshall, told fellow Baptists in 1934 that the Du-Ponts benefited from international tensions and made profits from war. The Baptist leader concluded from this that armament factories "should no longer be owned and operated by men who . . . exact profit out of an industry deliberately designed for the destruction of human life." The following year Wallace Bassett of Dallas similarly reported to the General Convention that "we know now that the last war was brought about largely through false propaganda and that it never should have been fought at all." To prevent a recurrence, said Bassett, "we believe that profit should be taken out for the profiteers, [and] that the makers of war should be compelled to do the fighting."[31]

The depression also gave impetus to social Christianity. Acker C. Miller, pastor of a small, struggling congregation in Belton, near Waco, recalled that the general privation of the period made him more aware of the material needs of people, and his "preaching and teaching" subsequently "had a great deal of emphasis" upon such matters.[32] And, importantly, Texas Baptists as a body similarly gave attention to the problems of people who were hungry, ill-housed, and jobless. The 1930 report of

[29] *Annual* of the Southern Baptist Convention (Nashville, 1938), p. 104.

[30] Ahlstrom, *Religious History*, p. 920. See also Bailey, *Southern White Protestantism*, pp. 115–23.

[31] BGCT, *Proceedings*, 1934, pp. 158–59; 1935, pp. 144–45.

[32] Oral Memoirs of Acker C. Miller, Waco, 1973, Baylor University Program of Oral History, pp. 45–46.

the Civic Righteousness Committee to the General Convention was unique for Texas Baptists in tone and scope. After summarizing the shift from an "extreme individualistic conception of Christianity" to the social gospel emphasis upon saving "both individuals and society . . . by means of a changed environment," the committee concluded that the two views were not antagonistic. Rather, they were "the two parts of the whole. The hope of the individual" was "in right relation to God, while the hope of society" was "in the right relation of man to man."[33]

With candor and perception, the Civic Righteousness Committee added that churchmen rarely objected so long as religion restricted itself to saving individuals and flailing personal sin. But "stern resistance" was "often encountered" when attention was turned to such industrial injustices and antisocial conditions as low wages, long hours, improper housing and working conditions, and employment of children. Nevertheless, it behooved organized Christianity to address itself to "the ever present conflict between capital and labor." Specifically, declared the committee, "the profit motive as the sole, or chief objective in business cannot be justified. Human rights must precede property rights, human welfare must come before profits and dividends." The committee concluded that industry existed for man, not man for industry. The need for racial justice was touched upon, though only briefly. Although succeeding reports lacked such breadth, they often, albeit in general terms, placed human rights ahead of property rights.[34]

Meanwhile, even the intensely evangelistic editor of the *Baptist Standard*, Franz M. McConnell, who had never been hospitable to social Christianity, frequently endorsed legislation designed to achieve social justice. He considered the Social Security Act of 1935, for instance, to be "one of the best laws ever enacted in this country." And in January, 1938, claiming that a company recently had laid off 30,000 workers in one day, he exclaimed that "there is no excuse" for Congress's allowing "such a social danger to exist. They should have so framed the laws of

[33] BGCT, *Proceedings*, 1930, p. 136.
[34] Ibid., pp. 137–39; 1933, pp. 154–58; and 1935, pp. 144–45.

this country that the turning out of 30,000 people in one day by one concern would have been impossible." "Surely," thought McConnell, legislation could be enacted that would "provide food and clothing and shelter for laborers when they are in crisis." In a strong plea for justice the journalist concluded: "This is just. One baby is worth more than a factory. Human beings are worth more than property."[35]

Two weeks later, seeking to reassure those readers who had interpreted his remarks as hostile to business, McConnell struck a more balanced pose. "It ought not to be possible in this country for an organized strike to do vast damage and harm to business"; he said, "and it ought not to be possible for a vast number of families to be thrown out of employment and be compelled to face starvation . . . without anything to buy the necessaries of life." This was more consistent with the view the Baptist editor had expressed in his book *The Rights and Obligations of Labor According to the Bible* (1937), in which he had blandly advised both sides to abide by the golden rule.[36] Nevertheless, despite a highly individualistic conception of religion, McConnell was beginning to see that the achievement of social justice in certain situations required more than moral suasion.

This same lesson was also learned by Walter Conner and Joseph Dawson, whose social thought matured during the depression era. By the late 1930s Conner no longer suggested that social ills could be resolved by individual conversion. The relationship between society and individuals was more complex than that, as Conner told Mercer University students in Macon, Georgia, in 1939. "I agree with those who say that the gospel of Christ is the remedy for all the ills of our modern world," he said, "but I do not believe that those ills will all be remedied merely by the conversion of individual men to the Christian life." As the Southwestern theologian explained, "evil institutions and ill adjustments in life" that had developed over hundreds of years could not "all be adjusted over night by the con-

---

[35] See *Baptist Standard*, Aug. 4, 1938, p. 3; Oct. 26, 1939, p. 4; Sept. 12, 1935, p. 3; Jan. 27, 1938, p. 3.

[36] Ibid., Feb. 10, 1938, p. 3; Apr. 22, 1937, p. 15.

version of individual men." Furthermore, it was "not always easy to" sort out what was "good and valuable" from what was "bad and dangerous" in aged institutions and customs. Although Conner still believed it necessary "to get individual men and women converted," he now considered that to be "just the beginning of the task."[37]

Conner's influence at Southwestern Seminary was far-reaching, but Dawson continued to be the most important spokesman for social Christianity among Texas Baptists. Through sermons, addresses, and writings, the articulate pastor continually called attention to the broader social dimensions of faith. By the 1930s, moreover, Dawson's own social thought had undergone significant shifts. Although still fervently conservative in his understanding of human nature and still very much a Southern Baptist in his commitment to personal evangelism, Dawson now closely paralleled the northern social gospel ministers of the early twentieth century and many Northern Methodists of his own generation. Historian Robert M. Miller said of this era that many Protestant churches, influenced by the neo-orthodoxy of Reinhold Niebuhr, "went to the Right in theology and to the Left in politics."[38] In Dawson's case, this was only half true. Without ever straying from the theological right, the Baptist leader definitely ventured somewhat further to the left in social pronouncements. Like Walter Rauschenbusch or George Herron or leaders of the Methodist Episcopal Church, who tended to be the sharpest critics of capitalism within American Protestantism,[39] the Waco pastor now readily rebuked the nation's economic system, particularly its headlong pursuit of profits. In a 1934 address at Gatesville, Texas, to the District Sunday School and Baptist Training Union Convention, Dawson declared that capitalism had "become unbearable through its profit motive, its insatiable lust for profits." This did not mean that the Baptist spokesman was attracted to the communist alternative. Indeed, he dismissed communism as "the selfish effort of a class,

[37] Ibid., Oct. 5, 1939, p. 3.
[38] Miller, *American Protestantism*, p. 64.
[39] Ibid., pp. 65–71.

on a materialistic and atheistic basis, to control all wealth." This, too, Dawson considered "a most sinister thing."[40]

The following year Dawson forcefully argued that "social regeneration" was as fundamental to the message of Jesus as "personal regeneration." Addressing the Dallas General Pastors' Association, he declared that it was "never intended" that Martin Luther's doctrine of individual salvation by faith "should be construed to the neglect of social improvement." Rather, Luther "really preached the creation of redeemed individuals in a redeemed society." Without being specific, Dawson maintained that "the present world welter" compelled one to recognize "that a whole gospel" encompassed "the redemption of the individual and the redemption of society." Elaborating on this point somewhat later, Dawson discounted the notion, popular among Southern Baptists, that all social problems would be resolved if evangelistic campaigns were successful. Were that so, asked Dawson, why has there been "such little desirable social change" in regions where evangelism has been so intense? Dawson believed the reason, especially among southern churches, was the failure to understand that salvation, although a private and personal experience, entailed a commitment to social regeneration. And within the social realm, concluded the Waco pastor, Christian social concern should go beyond liquor and gambling to "gross economic injustice and human exploitation."[41]

The extent to which Dawson's social thought had shifted was most fully revealed in a series of lectures presented at a summer assembly of the Baptist Ministers' Conference in South Carolina. Subsequently published in 1937 as *Christ and Social Change*, these essays were remarkably close to the tone and content of Walter Rauschenbusch's work and the 1932 resolution of the General Conference of the Methodist Episcopal Church. Although Dawson joined neither the Rochester cleric nor Northern Methodists in advocating a socialized economy, he was nonetheless unrestrained in his denunciation of the existing system of capitalism. "Our present pagan economic system," he declared,

[40] *Baptist Standard*, Apr. 5, 1934, p. 1.
[41] Ibid., Apr. 18, 1935, pp. 2, 10; Sept. 29, 1938, p. 9.

based on an insatiable pursuit of profits, prostituted the humane Christian values of cooperation, sharing, and service to humanity. Echoing his Methodist brethren in the North, who labeled the prevailing industrial system "unchristian, unethical and antisocial, because it is largely based on the profit motive, which is a direct appeal to selfishness,"[42] Dawson unequivocally condemned the profit motive, since it rendered "men predatory, with unmistakable selfishness, greed and inconsiderateness." Like southern slavery, Dawson believed the present economic system was harmful to everyone. It too often made the economically privileged, who lived self-indulgently off the toil of others, selfish, arrogant, and unsympathetic to the poor; on the other hand, it left the economically unfortunate—who were exploited and degraded—envious, sullen, and potentially violent enemies of the existing order.[43]

Significantly, this increasingly critical perception of the economic system led Dawson to reexamine the interrelationship between individuals and institutions. And unlike his 1914 sermons, in which he had urged practical stewardship in the form of better wages, the cleric now conceded the inadequacy of such a course. "The system [itself] as operated is immoral and inhumane," he wrote, "no matter how many individual employers as such are guiltless, and no matter how much of good was in the system itself in the past." So, irrespective of the worthiness of certain individual capitalists, the system, driven by a materialistic ethic, exercised a harmful influence over society as a whole. Furthermore, the harmful effects of institutions could not be overcome solely by the saving of individuals. It was fallacious, Dawson argued, to believe that because individuals controlled institutions, the church had only to create "a new heart in as many of those individuals as possible." As the Waco Baptist put it, changing through salvation the personal attitudes of a few

[42] Quoted in Miller, American Protestantism, p. 66.

[43] Joseph M. Dawson, Christ and Social Change (Boston: Judson Press, 1937), pp. 80–86. Broadman Press, the publishing arm of the Southern Baptist Convention, refused to print these lectures. So Dawson submitted them to the Judson Press, a Northern Baptist agency, which immediately accepted them. See Dawson, Thousand Months to Remember, p. 168.

capitalists in no way altered "the life-shaping, depersonalized systems under which they regularly work."[44] The system, then, along with the individual, had to be restructured.

Whether he knew it or not, Dawson analyzed the relationship between individuals and society exactly as Walter Rauschenbusch had in 1917. The noted Rochester minister had already pointed out that regeneration was a social matter, inasmuch as individuals, regardless of how much they changed, were shaped and bound by common social sins. "The apparently free and unrelated acts of individuals are also the acts of the social group," Rauschenbusch had observed, and "when the social group is evil, evil is over all." And it was folly to expect speedy cures, for common evil often carried the weight of centuries. "The evils of one generation are caused by the wrongs of the generations that preceded," noted Rauschenbusch, "and will in turn condition the sufferings and temptations of those who come after."[45] Such observations account for Rauschenbusch's popularity among socially alert Texas Baptists. His optimism was tempered by a realization of the tenacity of sin, both personal and social.

Dawson, however, could not embrace Rauschenbusch's vision of the ideal economic order. Whereas the Rochester seminarian believed that the achievement of full social justice, industrial democracy, equal treatment, and cooperation required a socialized economy,[46] the Waco pastor, while striving for the same objectives, never ventured that far to the political left. Indeed, quite unlike many Protestants in the North whose antagonism to capitalism led to a forthright espousal of socialism,[47] Dawson was vague concerning specific structural changes in the economy. He would only suggest that in an age of large corporations in which a few persons exerted inordinate influence, there was a need for some form of social control to ensure equitable treatment for the masses. Blandly, he declared that "economics

[44] Dawson, *Christ and Social Change*, pp. 86, 116–23.

[45] Walter Rauschenbusch, *A Theology for the Social Gospel* (New York: Macmillan, 1917), pp. 69–72, 78–81.

[46] C. Howard Hopkins, *The Rise of the Social Gospel in American Protestantism, 1865–1915* (1940; reprint, New Haven: Yale University Press, 1967), pp. 224–27.

[47] Handy, *History of Churches*, p. 391; Ahlstrom, *Religious History*, p. 922; Miller, *American Protestantism*, pp. 70–71.

must be redirected so that business will be turned toward the common good."[48] Historian Robert M. Miller was correct: "Southern soil—whether watered by Baptist immersion or non-Baptist sprinkling—did not nourish collectivist notions."[49]

If Dawson was imprecise regarding the form of the desired economic system, he was quite clear about the role to be played by the church. The Texan rejected the approach of theologian and social activist Reinhold Niebuhr, who in *Moral Man and Immoral Society* (1932) had advised the use of political force to accomplish worthy social objectives.[50] Despite "the mood of our generation . . . for using force," said Dawson, the church ought not to become involved in power politics, for this violated the basic Christian concept of love. The Waco pastor recommended more conventional alternatives. Through its pronouncements, both written and spoken, and through "some kind of program of social education," the church could focus public attention on specific social abuses and inform its membership on such issues as race, international relations, liquor control, and the causes of crime. Additionally, the church could become directly involved in social action through its own service agencies, which minister to the lonely, the aged, orphans, the underprivileged, the sick, and the mentally ill. And this could be done, Dawson believed, "without thrusting the churches as such into politics, or committing them to the programs of economic parties."[51]

Clearly, Dawson's social thought had progressed considerably since his memorable 1914 sermons on social Christianity. But as the Wacoan often reassured fellow Southern Baptists, he remained steadfast to his conservative theological upbringing.[52] Moreover, when compared to his contemporaries, brothers Reinhold and H. Richard Niebuhr, Dawson was also conservative politically. While he and the Niebuhrs shared a common goal for social justice, they differed widely over means. To theologian Richard Niebuhr, who faulted the early twentieth-century

[48] Dawson, *Christ and Social Change*, pp. 41–44, 78–79, 89, 92.

[49] Miller, *American Protestantism*, p. 74.

[50] Reinhold Niebuhr, *Moral Man and Immoral Society: A Study in Ethics and Politics* (New York: Charles Scribner's Sons, 1960), pp. 200–230.

[51] Dawson, *Christ and Social Change*, pp. 124–27, 133–40, 142–43, 146–47, 199.

[52] *Baptist Standard*, Sept. 29, 1938, p. 2; Feb. 26, 1942, p. 1.

social gospel movement for the same reason, it was unrealistic to expect the church to substantially change society through the kind of educational endeavors suggested by Dawson. To Niebuhr, this was a policy of indirection in which the churches attempted to get some other agency to redress intolerable conditions. That is, the churches lobbied legislatures to enact desirable laws, encouraged schools to teach responsible social attitudes, and pressured political parties to adopt specific programs.[53] Theologian and activist Reinhold Niebuhr accused the early social gospel ministers of being sentimentalists for supposing that such instructive methods would bring about a more benevolent social order.[54]

Dawson stressed educational means and stopped short of the political activism of Reinhold Niebuhr, but his position on social involvement was neither sentimentalist nor altogether indirect. Indeed, at a time when many churches, overwhelmed by the troubles of the period, were abandoning their responsibility for welfare and relief to the New Deal,[55] Dawson gently reminded fellow churchmen that it had always been the prerogative of the church to feed the hungry, care for the sick, and minister to the underprivileged. And Baptists, he asserted, could do this directly through their own service institutions.[56] As for expectations, Dawson's conservative theological teachings made him a realist. Like social gospel proponent Rauschenbusch, the Wacoan understood the human propensity to evil, but he nevertheless remained hopeful about the future.

Such a theological outlook stood Dawson and other Texas Baptists in good stead during the troubled years of world crisis that lay ahead. As the sounds of war in the distance grew louder, Texas Baptists, like religionists elsewhere, were hesitant. The blatant militarism of the churches during World War I had produced a strong pacifist movement in the 1920s,[57] a pacifism

[53] H. Richard Niebuhr, "The Attack upon the Social Gospel," *Religion in Life* 5 (Spring, 1936): 176–80.

[54] Niebuhr, *Moral Man and Immoral Society*, pp. 72–76.

[55] Gaustad, *Religious History of America*, p. 336.

[56] Dawson, *Christ and Social Change*, pp. 142–45.

[57] Ahlstrom, *Religious History*, p. 930; Sweet, *Story of Religion*, p. 428.

fueled in part by the popular belief that greedy munitions dealers had manipulated the nation into entering the European conflict on the false premise of making the world safe for democracy.
Texas Baptists were not immune to such sentiment. At the 1934
General Convention in San Antonio Professor Frank E. Burk-
halter of Baylor University presented a long paper against warfare. The delegates subsequently adopted resolutions sharply
rebuking armaments manufacturers.[58] The following year the
convention applauded the Kellogg-Briand Pact, which had been
concluded in 1928, and urged national leaders to use pacific
means to resolve global disputes. "We know that the world is
worse off now," the delegates concluded, "than it was before
[World War I] was fought."[59]

Just weeks before Pearl Harbor Thomas B. Maston gave
thoughtful attention to the problem of war. The Southwestern
ethics professor advised Baptist ministers "to keep cool," lest
they again get caught up in the war hysteria and "the spirit of
intolerance" currently "so rampant in the world." Believing the
ministry during the previous world war had made a "tragic mistake" in using the pulpit "to whip up patriotism . . . and to encourage young men to enlist in the army," Maston now counseled the clergy to neither dwell upon nor glorify war. And to
identify the kingdom of God with the outcome of the conflict
was equally misguided, for God's kingdom was spiritual and thus
not dependent upon "this or any other war." Maston knew most
Christians probably would support the war effort if the United
States became involved, but he insisted that "such participation
should not be defended as being Christian." To the seminarian,
war negated "every basic principle found in the teachings of
Jesus."[60]

Maston's suspicion regarding the churches was correct. Ap-
palled by the aggressiveness of Japan and Germany, as well as
the latter's anti-Semitism, most American congregations ultimately did support the nation's war effort. And in Texas, despite

---

[58] Dawson, *Century with Texas Baptists*, p. 95; BGCT, *Proceedings*, 1934, p. 158.
[59] BGCT, *Proceedings*, 1935, p. 145.
[60] *Baptist Standard*, Oct. 31, 1940, p. 2.

Maston's plea for calm, many churchmen were quickly overcome
by the martial spirit after the Pearl Harbor attack. In January,
1942, for instance, W. W. Melton, executive secretary of the
General Convention, proclaimed that Pearl Harbor had made it
impossible for him to remain uninvolved. Emotionally, the denominational spokesman declared: "My silence would shame
me. My ravaged home would mock me. The blood of my slain
sons would cry out from the ground to condemn me." Melton
was not alone.[61] Even so, the stridence of evangelist Billy Sunday, who had described World War I as "Hell against Heaven"
and had contemptuously dismissed "all this talk about not fighting the German people" as "a lot of bunk,"[62] was not to be repeated. As Sydney Ahlstrom put it, chastened by the Great Depression and sobered by the pessimism of neo-orthodoxy, "the
churches did not repeat the unrestrained capitulation to the war
spirit which had left them disgraced after 1918."[63]

The involvement of this nation in World War II definitely
affected Texas Baptists, although in diverse ways. Just weeks
after Pearl Harbor, for instance, Joseph Dawson hinted that recent events confirmed the conservative Christian view of history
and had sparked a trend "among all churches . . . toward the
historic, conservative interpretation of Christianity."[64] A few
months later Shelton G. Posey, pastor of the First Baptist
Church, Austin, suggested to the General Convention that the
world conflagration demonstrated the failure of the social gospel, in that the war had come despite the recent emphasis of the
churches "upon the social and economic welfare of both the individual and nation."[65]

[61] Ibid., Jan. 22, 1942, p. 1; see BGCT, Proceedings, 1942, pp. 207–11; Baptist
Standard, Mar. 25, 1943, p. 5.

[62] Quoted in Sweet, Story of Religion, p. 402. Joseph Dawson called attention to
the fact that Texas Baptist churches became caught up in the martial spirit of World War I
and "constantly waved the flag"; he himself was a "four-minute man" for the Committee
on Public Information (the Creel Committee) and thus gave speeches in behalf of the
war in theaters. See Dawson, Century with Texas Baptists, p. 96.

[63] Ahlstrom, Religious History, pp. 930–31, 949–50. See also Handy, History of
Churches, p. 395; and Sweet, Story of Religion, pp. 400–403, 428–29.

[64] Baptist Standard, Feb. 26, 1942, p. 1.

[65] BGCT, Proceedings, 1942, pp. 207–11; Baptist Standard, Mar. 25, 1943, p. 5.

For the most part, however, the war prompted Texas Baptists to give renewed emphasis to historic and traditional objectives. Criticism of the business community, which had often been severe during the depression, now ceased. Convention concern focused on gambling, sabbath desecration, and prohibition.[66] The Civic Righteousness Committee reflected the mood of the convention. In 1945, after victory had been achieved in Europe and Asia, it recommended stiff measures to deal with domestic crime, censorship of the movies, more stringent divorce laws, and another national crusade for prohibition.[67] Nor were evangelism and missions ignored. With military victory accomplished, David M. Gardner, editor of the *Baptist Standard*, asserted that it was time to send "an army of Crusaders to pagan lands with Bibles instead of bombs, with the message of life instead of missiles of death." As a contributor to the Baptist journal declared, "in this atomic era . . . Christ must be made known to the people of the world."[68] And the evangelistic intent of Texas Baptists was backed up by contributions from the faithful. By the late 1930s the denomination's improving economic situation was reflected in donations for missions. From a low of $310,072 in 1933, Texas Baptists steadily increased their mission gifts to $710,272 in 1939, $1,292,395 in 1942, and $2,944,370 in 1945.[69] This was obviously a propitious moment for the youth evangelism movement, which fanned out from the Baylor University campus in the late 1940s.[70]

And what of social Christianity? Despite the educational efforts of leaders such as Joseph Dawson, editor Gardner, who insisted that social accomplishments were concomitants of fervent evangelism, was probably closer to the hearts of most Texas Baptists in the 1940s. Personal evangelism, the editor believed, was the taproot from which emerged hospitals, orphanages, schools, and other social endeavors. Hence, the remedy for all

[66] BGCT, *Proceedings*, 1942, pp. 208–11; 1943, pp. 157–60; 1944, pp. 171–73.
[67] Ibid., 1945, pp. 184–85.
[68] *Baptist Standard*, Aug. 23, 1945, p. 3; Nov. 1, 1945, p. 12.
[69] Baker, *Blossoming Desert*, p. 218.
[70] Oral Memoirs, White, p. 158. See also *Baptist Standard*, Aug. 9, 1945, p. 12.

social ills was evangelism, and the need of the hour was for devoted evangelists.[71] As for Dawson, he increasingly devoted attention in the 1940s and thereafter to matters of church and state.[72] Furthermore, in 1945 the sixty-seven-year-old minister resigned his long pastorate at the First Baptist Church, Waco, to become the first full-time executive director of the Baptist Joint Committee on Public Affairs in Washington, D.C.

Although Dawson would remain an important figure among Texas Baptists, the mantle of leadership for social Christianity devolved by the mid-1940s upon a younger generation headed by Thomas B. Maston at Southwestern Seminary in Fort Worth. Though Maston labored to apply Christian ideals to all areas of life, racial justice absorbed his energy in the late 1940s and 1950s. World War II, specifically Nazi racism, and the emerging rivalry of the United States and Russia in the Third World heightened the awareness of racial discrimination, and in Texas, Maston strove tirelessly to help Baptists overcome attitudes demeaning to blacks. The seminarian was not alone. Texas Baptists, individually and collectively, had been grappling with this perplexing issue since 1900.

[71] *Baptist Standard*, Mar. 9, 1944, p. 2; Oct. 19, 1944, p. 1.

[72] Ibid., Dec. 7, 1944, p. 1. See also Oral Memoirs, Dawson, pp. 158–59, 207–25; Dawson, *Thousand Months to Remember*, pp. 185–205.

4

Racial Attitudes,
1900–1950

DURING the late nineteenth and early twentieth centuries the southern states steadily refined and extended the Jim Crow system, with little opposition from the federal government. The Spanish-American War of 1898 led to a coalescence of national and southern racial practices. Federal policymakers were no more willing to grant political and social equality to Puerto Ricans and Filipinos than southern whites were to blacks. As a result of its own discriminatory policies in distant places, the federal government lost its moral leverage in the South. And the Supreme Court's decisions in *Plessy* v. *Ferguson* (1896), which gave constitutional legitimacy to the "separate-but-equal" doctrine, and *Williams* v. *Mississippi* (1898), which approved the 1890 Mississippi plan for determining voter eligibility, signaled the collapse of virtually all outside resistance to southern racial patterns. Indeed, as historian C. Vann Woodward observed, by the turn of the twentieth century the southern way in matters of race had become "the American Way."[1]

---

[1] Although Texas Baptists often commented on other minority groups, such as Germans, Mexicans, and Orientals, this chapter concentrates solely on black-white relationships. C. Vann Woodward, *Origins of the New South, 1877–1913* (1951; reprint, Baton Rouge: Louisiana State University Press, 1964), p. 325; H. Shelton Smith, *In His Image, But . . . : Racism in Southern Religion, 1780–1910* (Durham, N.C.: Duke University Press, 1972), pp. 261–64. Other fine studies detailing the spread of segregation are Paul Lewinson, *Race, Class, and Party: A History of Negro Suffrage and White Politics in the South* (New York: Universal Library, 1965), pp. 61–131; George B. Tindall, *The Emergence of the New South* (Baton Rouge: Louisiana State University Press, 1967), pp. 143–83; C. Vann Woodward, *The Strange Career of Jim Crow* (New York: Oxford University Press, 1966), pp. 67–110; Albert D. Kirwan, *Revolt of the Rednecks: Mississippi Politics, 1876–1925* (New York: Harper Torchbooks, 1965); Rayford W. Logan, *The Betrayal of the Negro: From Rutherford B. Hayes to Woodrow Wilson* (New York: Collier Books, 1965), originally published in 1954 as *The Negro in American Life and Thought: The Nadir, 1877–1901*; Gunnar Myrdal, *An American Dilemma: The Negro Problem and Modern Democracy* (New York: Harper and Brothers, 1944), pp. 452–504; and Harvard

Although Texans never held a constitutional convention to deal with "the Negro problem" as did their neighbors in several southern states,[2] they nevertheless took steps to ensure the subordination of blacks. The years preceding World War I were particularly momentous. In 1902 Texans adopted a poll tax amendment, and individual cities across the state took steps to restrict racial commingling. Fort Worth forbade sexual intercourse between whites and blacks within the city limits; Texarkana prohibited white males, except for doctors, bill collectors, and deliverymen, from entering the homes of black women; and Houston followed suit, barring interracial cohabitation in 1922. Meanwhile, state lawmakers, motivated by this same fear of racial intimacy, grappled with laws concerning transportation, housing, prisons, mental institutions, and amusements. The legislatures of 1907 and 1909 were especially busy, formalizing local customs and codifying segregation statutes dating from the late nineteenth century. Solons in 1907 allowed amusement places to either provide separate facilities for blacks or refuse them service altogether and instructed officials involved in all forms of public transportation to institute segregated seating policies. Similarly, the 1909 legislature ordered railroads to provide separate waiting rooms at depots and commanded penal authorities to house blacks separately from whites.

Racial separation became more extensive as the century progressed. In 1923 it became unlawful for blacks to vote in the Democratic primary, and in 1927, despite invalidation by the courts of a similar ten-year-old Dallas ordinance, the state permitted cities to withhold building permits from individuals or firms seeking to construct houses for blacks in white neighborhoods. And in 1935 the state further codified transportation laws, declaring that all systems of public transportation had to maintain separate accommodations for blacks and whites. Eight years later state legislators decreed that blacks traveling on buses that had made no provision for separate seating arrangements were to take seats in the rear of the vehicle. Curiously,

Sitkoff, *The Struggle for Black Equality, 1954–1980* (New York: Hill and Wang, 1981), pp. 1–7.

[2]Woodward, *Origins of the New South*, p. 321.

the state failed to extend Jim Crow to water fountains, rest-
rooms, and swimming pools, but local customs made up for the
lack of legislation. As late as 1956 a poll of Texas Democrats
disclosed continuing support for the antimiscegenation
legislation.[3]

Although Texas Baptists rarely commented on specific Jim
Crow laws, they clearly approved the pattern of segregation buttressed by such legislation. Most denominational leaders were
paternalistic racists in the tradition of Atticus G. Haygood, a
distinguished Methodist minister, editor, and educator from
Georgia; Jabez L. M. Curry, a prominent Baptist minister and
educator from Alabama; Charles Betts Galloway, a native Mississippian and influential Methodist leader; and Henry W. Grady of
Georgia, the region's leading apostle of the New South.[4] Hence,
editors of the *Baptist Standard*, state executives, and pastors
looked upon blacks as childlike beings dependent upon superior
whites for protection and tutelage. The influential and respected
James B. Gambrell, journalist, educator, and denominational
spokesman, consistently voiced such sentiment from the 1880s
until his death in 1921. Thereafter, the tradition of paternalism
was carried on by other prominent churchmen. Significantly,
however, a few denominational leaders challenged the prevailing
racial stereotypes. Throughout this period Joseph M. Dawson
championed the cause of blacks; Thomas B. Maston increasingly
after 1930 focused attention upon racial issues. Although the
more progressive views of these men gradually won some support within the General Convention, paternalistic attitudes generally prevailed, particularly in the early part of the century.

Like whites elsewhere in the nation,[5] Baptists in Texas prior

[3]Bruce A. Glasrud, "Jim Crow's Emergence in Texas," *American Studies* 15
(Spring, 1974): 53–56; David G. McComb, *Houston: A History* (Austin: University of
Texas Press, 1981), pp. 108–14; Norman D. Brown, *Hood, Bonnet, and Little Brown
Jug: Texas Politics, 1921–1928* (College Station: Texas A&M University Press, 1984),
pp. 150–51, 362–64.

[4]See Smith, *In His Image, But . . .* , pp. 227–89; George M. Frederickson, *The
Black Image in the White Mind: The Debate on Afro-American Character and Destiny,
1817–1914* (New York: Harper and Row, 1971), pp. 204–16; and Paul M. Gaston, *The
New South Creed: A Study in Southern Mythmaking* (Baton Rouge: Louisiana State University Press, 1970), pp. 125–26, 136–40, 148–50.

[5]Excellent studies documenting national racial attitudes and shedding light on the

to World War I were imbued with the spirit of Anglo-Saxon superiority. As the Committee on Negro Population told the Baptist
General Convention in 1906, blacks had the strength of "brute
force and numbers," but "the Saxon [had] all the qualities that
make kings." And the report echoed other current racial stereotypes. The "high animal propensities" and natural super-
stitiousness of blacks, for instance, stemmed from their proximity to "the jungle," from which they were "only a few
generations" removed.[6] Given such attitudes, the posture of
churchmen on specific matters was predictable—since enfranchisement after the Civil War was considered to have been a
tragic mistake, schemes to eliminate black voters were applauded; anything smacking of social equality was denounced;
demeaning racial stereotypes were easily accepted; and the activities of whisky dealers and Catholic priests among blacks were
feared and resented.[7] Concern over this last item was long-
standing. In 1889 President Rufus C. Burleson of Baylor University informed the General Convention that Texas Baptists had to
"save our colored brethren from the triple monster evils of ignorance, whisky and Catholic delusions." Disclosing deeper ap-
prehensions, the Baylor official added that those "wily Jesuits"
were "deceitfully flattering the colored man with amalgamation
and social equality."[8]

   It was abundantly clear that Texas Baptists believed the gospel of Jesus was the solution to the nettlesome racial problem.
But it was equally apparent they did not expect Christianization
to advance the cause of racial equality. This led many church-

idea of Anglo-Saxon supremacy are John Higham, *Strangers in the Land: Patterns of
American Nativism, 1860–1925* (New York: Atheneum, 1963), pp. 132–57; Thomas F.
Gossett, *Race: The History of an Idea in America* (Dallas: Southern Methodist University Press, 1963), pp. 253–408; I. A. Newby, ed., *The Development of Segregationist Thought* (Homewood, Ill.: Dorsey Press, 1968); and Fredrickson, *Black Image*,
pp. 97–129.
      [6]Baptist General Convention of Texas, *Proceedings*, 1906, pp. 88–89 (cited here-
after as BGCT, *Proceedings*).
      [7]Ibid., 1887, pp. 20–21; 1889, p. 50; 1906, pp. 88–89; 1909, p. 89; 1914, p. 133.
See also *Baptist Standard*, May 5, 1904, p. 2; Apr. 21, 1910, p. 10–11; and July 28,
1910, p. 7.
      [8]BGCT, *Proceedings*, 1889, p. 50; see also 1887, pp. 20–21.

men into ambiguity. They simultaneously applauded and feared signs of progress among blacks.[9] Such contradictory sentiment was obvious in the report of the Committee on Negro Population to the General Convention in 1906. While commending blacks for economic and educational improvement, the committee also argued that such advancement invariably created demands for political and social equality. The committee concluded that in dealing with the vexatious problem of race, Texas Baptists should strive for a solution in which blacks freely acquiesced to white authority, for "never before was the Saxon more determined to dominate." The committee then reviewed and dismissed several possible solutions. Amalgamation was unacceptable as long as there was "a drop of Saxon blood in the South," and colonization was impractical. Even a more equal national distribution was undesirable, for blacks did not want to leave the South and southern whites needed their labor. And education, even of an industrial sort, was potentially dangerous. As the committee explained, schooling, however desirable, was "like putting rifles in the hand of the unfriendly Indian." Finally, the only solution was evangelism, and even here the committee hedged. Southern Baptists should concentrate their efforts on black leaders, thereby avoiding the mistake made by Northern Baptists of working among the masses.[10] If successful, this would make allies of the black clergy in keeping blacks in "their place." Among Texas Baptists of the early twentieth century there was little doubt that society should be directed by whites of ability, means, and intelligence.

Although most Texas Baptists considered blacks inferior, denominational spokesmen never sanctioned the extreme negrophobia so common in the late nineteenth and early twentieth centuries.[11] At no time did convention leaders revile the

---

[9] As shown by Smith, *In His Image, But . . .* , pp. 266–77, southerners throughout the region were troubled by the idea of progress among blacks.

[10] BGCT, *Proceedings*, 1906, pp. 88–89. See also *Baptist Standard*, May 5, 1904, p. 2.

[11] See Woodward, *Origins of the New South*, p. 352; Fredrickson, *Black Image*, pp. 276–82.

black population after the fashion of such politicians as James K. Vardaman of Mississippi or "Pitchfork" Ben Tillman of South Carolina, who depicted the black man as "a fiend, a wild beast, seeking whom he may devour."[12] Indeed, by the 1890s the Baptist press in Texas condemned without reservation lynching and other forms of mob violence. No crime, however heinous, excused lynching, declared James B. Cranfill, editor of the *Texas Baptist Standard*, and any person engaging in such action should be considered a murderer.[13] Editorial policy on this issue never wavered. Similarly, denominational leaders promptly repudiated the scurrilous antiblack literature of the early twentieth century. In 1902 the General Convention specifically repudiated *The Negro a Beast* (1900) by Charles Carroll, calling upon "our ministers, teachers and membership everywhere to expose and denounce the insulting and outrageous book now circulating in the South, which professes loudly to prove from the Bible that the Negro is not human, but a beast without a soul."[14] The following year Cranfill rebuked Thomas Dixon, Jr., for his book *The Leopard's Spots* (1902). To the Baptist journalist, the tone of Dixon's novel, suggesting that the black was "a brute," further inflamed the already tense racial situation in the South.[15] And on many occasions Baptist leaders criticized politicians who exploited racial fears for political advantage.[16]

Essentially, Texas Baptists were paternalists who believed the presumed superiority of whites carried with it responsibilities. Allegedly inferior and childlike blacks, instead of being humiliated, were to be under the watchful tutelage of the "superior" Saxons. A churchman from Teague, Texas, said it tersely in 1910. Although "degenerate and immoral," blacks were "a trust committed to us [whites]" by God.[17] The General Convention

---

[12]Quoted in Frederickson, *Black Image*, p. 276.

[13] *Texas Baptist Standard*, Nov. 2, 1893, p. 4; Sept. 20, 1894, p. 4; Aug. 4, 1898, p. 1; and Nov. 4, 1899, pp. 4–5. See also *Texas Baptist and Herald*, Feb. 16, 1893, and Jan. 26, 1899.

[14]BGCT, *Proceedings*, 1902, p. 55.

[15] *Baptist Standard*, Feb. 5, 1903, pp. 1, 5.

[16]Ibid., June 13, 1907, p. 1; June 30, 1910, p. 1; Oct. 31, 1912, pp. 10–11; Aug. 22, 1918, p. 14.

[17]Ibid., Apr. 14, 1910, p. 7. See Myrdal, *American Dilemma*, pp. 592–95.

concurred, acknowledging its obligation to "this docile and trac-
table race" in 1914.[18]

James Bruton Gambrell, an influential leader for two generations, epitomized Texas Baptist paternalism. He was born in
South Carolina in 1841. Four years later the family moved to
northeast Mississippi, where Gambrell attended school and
grew to maturity. His family owned slaves, and during the Civil
War Gambrell scouted for Gen. Robert E. Lee, fought at Get-
tysburg, and eventually rose to the rank of captain. Following
the war he entered the University of Mississippi. After a stint as
pastor of the Oxford Baptist Church, he became editor in 1877 of
the *Baptist Record*, the denominational weekly in Mississippi.
Gambrell retained this position until 1893, when he was elected
president of Mercer University in Macon, Georgia. After three
years at the helm of this Baptist school he ventured to Texas in
1896, where he remained until his death in June, 1921.

The former Mississippian quickly established himself as a
leader among Texas Baptists. He was state superintendent of
missions from 1896 to 1910, when he resigned to become editor
of the *Baptist Standard*. In 1912, while continuing as editor of
the Baptist journal, Gambrell joined the faculty at Southwestern
Seminary. But in 1914 he relinquished both positions to become
executive secretary of the Board of Missions and Education of
the General Convention, a post he held for six years. Meantime,
in 1917 Gambrell was elected president of the Southern Baptist
Convention, serving four one-year terms.[19] Highly regarded,
Gambrell's voice carried considerable weight.

On matters of race, Gambrell repeatedly expressed concern
for the well-being of blacks, but it was the paternalistic solici-
tude of an alleged superior for a presumed inferior. Actually,
Gambrell's racial outlook was shaped before he left Mississippi,
and it never changed. When he told Texans in 1907 that "enfranchisement of the Negroes . . . was more than a blunder; it was a
crime against a weak, untrained race, and a high crime against
civilization,"[20] the Baptist leader was merely reiterating a theme

[18] BGCT, *Proceedings*, 1914, p. 133.
[19] *Encyclopedia of Southern Baptists* I, 523–24.
[20] *Baptist Standard*, June 13, 1907, p. 1.

voiced a generation earlier in his home state. As editor of the *Baptist Record* in Mississippi, Gambrell had not only supported disfranchisement of blacks but had also utilized the Baptist press to mobilize public opinion for the cause. As early as 1881 he had argued that black suffrage "was a stupendous blunder in whatever light it is viewed." It "was a broad mistake to think that 4,000,000 ignorant Africans," accustomed to obeying rather than ruling, "could control 8,000,000 Anglo-Saxons, with all their intelligence, property and traditions." If black rule had succeeded, added he, "civilization must have perished." "Intelligence and property will control here," he concluded, "as everywhere else."[21]

In 1889, on the eve of Mississippi's constitutional convention,[22] Gambrell wrote a series of articles and editorials advocating black disfranchisement. Although illiteracy and incompetence were sufficient grounds for denying blacks the ballot, Gambrell was more alarmed lest fraudulent tactics used by whites to control or obtain black votes would erode white morality. "Ballot box stuffing," he declared, "is teaching our young men to be mean, sneaking, and the perjury which goes with it, is undermining all truth and honor in them."[23] This was a common argument across the South. As C. Vann Woodward noted, "repugnance for corrupt elections was put forward everywhere as the primary reason for disfranchisement."[24] The preservation of southern character, then, as well as the assurance of white supremacy, required the elimination of black votes. When the Mississippi constitutional convention subsequently adopted an "understanding clause" in 1890 requiring potential voters to read and understand any portion of the state constitution, Gambrell was dissatisfied. He had hoped for a more forthright educational qualification, even if it meant disfranchising some un-

---

[21] *Baptist Record* (Meridian and Jackson), Mar. 31, 1881.

[22] For accounts of the 1890 constitutional convention in Mississippi, see Woodward, *Origins of the New South*, pp. 328–44; Kirwan, *Revolt of the Rednecks*, pp. 59–68; and Vernon Lane Wharton, *The Negro in Mississippi, 1865–1890* (New York: Harper Torchbooks, 1965), pp. 206–15.

[23] *Southern Baptist Record*, July 25, 1889; Aug. 8, 1889; Jan. 16, 1890; May 1, 1890.

[24] *Origins of the New South*, p. 326.

lettered whites. "This irresponsible, ignorant, tramp vote [black voters] ought to be cut off and it would be cut off without a moments' [sic] hesitation," he asserted, "if it were not that some white men would be cut off too." [25]

During the quarter century Gambrell lived in Texas, his racial views never changed. Time and again he disparaged black enfranchisement during Reconstruction and defended the removal of blacks from the polls in the 1890s. Additionally, he often argued that slavery, although indefensible, had been the means by which blacks had been taught economic skills and Christianized by "the foremost race on earth." And he agreed readily with fellow churchmen that evangelical religion would resolve racial ills. "To a remarkable degree," he maintained, blacks "have the child-heart. They believe it [Bible] just like it is written, and never stop to quibble." Consequently, Gambrell believed untutored blacks were "a thousand leagues ahead of a great many university professors." [26] Gambrell again reiterated his racial philosophy just a few months before his death. Now, however, he suggested that some intelligent blacks should be allowed to vote and hold office. Whites would have nothing to fear in this, he explained, since blacks constituted a minority of the total population. [27]

Actually, Gambrell, an admirer of Booker T. Washington, was convinced the best avenue of advancement for blacks was not politics, but homemaking, education, religion, and industry. Washington's acclaimed Atlanta address of 1895, in which he urged blacks to work hard and to avoid political confrontation, had struck a responsive chord among Southern Baptists. [28] Gambrell was no exception. In 1915, just days after the renowned

---

[25] *Southern Baptist Record*, Sept. 25, 1890. Ironically, only two years earlier, the Mississippi Baptist Convention had commented favorably on black voters, stating that "they are learning to read and are using more conscience in the exercise of the ballot." Mississippi Baptist State Convention, *Proceedings*, 1887, p. 23.

[26] *Baptist Standard*, Mar. 10, 1910, p. 1; Mar. 24, 1910, p. 1; and June 30, 1910, pp. 1–2.

[27] Ibid., Mar. 3, 1921, p. 6.

[28] John W. Storey, "The Rhetoric of Paternalism: Southern Baptists and Negro Education in the Latter Nineteenth Century," *Southern Humanities Review* 12, no. 2 (Spring, 1978): 106–107.

Tuskegee educator died, Gambrell presented a resolution to the Baptist General Convention praising Washington as an example to both races.[29] The resolution was readily accepted, for other prominent churchmen shared Gambrell's sentiment. In 1911, for instance, James B. Cranfill, who had heard the black educator address a mixed audience in Dallas, proclaimed Washington to be "the greatest negro in the world" and as good an orator as William Jennings Bryan, B. H. Carroll, or George W. Truett. Washington's advice to blacks to be industrious and property-owning citizens, coupled with a sharp denunciation of "thrift-lessness, idleness and crime" among his race, had especially impressed the Baptist journalist.[30] Baptists such as Gambrell and Cranfill admired Washington because they saw in him a reflection of their own racial philosophy. One scholar's observation regarding southern white paternalists is also applicable to many Texas Baptists: they "were so close to Washington in their basic racial philosophy and drew so much inspiration from him that it would not be far from the mark to call them white Washingtonians."[31]

Praise to the contrary notwithstanding, however, Texas Baptists were no more willing to accept a person of Washington's stature as a social equal than they were a lowly, unlettered field hand. The reaction to the Roosevelt-Washington dinner at the White House in October, 1901, illustrates the point.[32] No doubt verbalizing the sentiment of other Baptists, Cranfill exclaimed that President Roosevelt had "committed a great breach, both of social ethics and good sense," and the consequences would be "disastrous."[33] To a great extent, Texas Baptist esteem for Booker T. Washington must be weighed against the feelings of hostility churchmen felt for more militant blacks, such as William E. B. DuBois. The Tuskegee educator was honored because he repre-

[29] BGCT, *Proceedings*, 1915, p. 21.
[30] *Baptist Standard*, Oct. 19, 1911, p. 13. See also Feb. 5, 1903, p. 5.
[31] Fredrickson, *Black Image*, p. 293.
[32] See Dewey W. Grantham, "Dinner at the White House: Theodore Roosevelt, Booker T. Washington, and the South," *Tennessee Historical Quarterly*, 17 (June, 1958): 112–30; Louis R. Harlan, *Booker T. Washington: The Making of a Black Leader* (New York: Oxford University Press, 1972), pp. 304–24.
[33] *Baptist Standard*, Feb. 5, 1903, p. 5.

sented a solution, so perceived at least by whites, that coincided with Baptist expectations regarding the proper station of blacks in American society. Actually, Baptist homage for the black leader emanated from a misconception. Whereas Washington considered industrial training the ultimate doorway to full economic and political equality for his race, Baptists believed the Alabama educator was simply preparing blacks to fulfill a subordinate status more efficiently.[34]

Again, Gambrell sheds light on the dominant attitudes of Texas Baptists. He expected blacks, however worthy their accomplishments, to remain subservient. Although acknowledging that black soldiers performed commendably during World War I,[35] for instance, the Baptist leader did not expect this show of patriotism and valor to alter social practices at home. This was evident in his explanations for the violent race riots of 1919. Beginning in early July in Longview, Texas, and climaxing in October near Elaine, Arkansas, the nation was rocked by some twenty-five riots during this "red summer" of violence. Casualties were substantial. In the Chicago riot alone at least thirty-eight people were killed—fifteen whites and twenty-three blacks.[36] Gambrell showed no appreciation for the varied causes of such strife. Simplistically, he traced the trouble to the affections shown black soldiers by European women during the war. Consequently, he argued, black doughboys returning home assumed that their social station in American society had changed, but they were "fearfully mistaken." "The white race is dominant in America," asserted Gambrell, and "it always will be."[37] Other Baptists concurred.[38] Nevertheless, in spite of such superficial

[34] Storey, "Rhetoric of Paternalism," p. 107. See also John Hope Franklin, *From Slavery to Freedom: A History of Negro Americans* (New York: Alfred A. Knopf, 1967), pp. 392–93; Harlan, *Booker T. Washington*, pp. 204–28; and Myrdal, *American Dilemma*, pp. 739–44.

[35] *Baptist Standard*, Aug. 22, 1918, p. 14.

[36] See Franklin, *From Slavery to Freedom*, pp. 480–84; Tindall, *Emergence of the New South*, pp. 151–56; William M. Tuttle, Jr., *Race Riot: Chicago in the Red Summer of 1919* (New York: Atheneum, 1980); and Arthur J. Waskow, *From Race Riot to Sit-In, 1919 and the 1960's: A Study in Connections Between Conflict and Violence* (Garden City, N.Y.: Doubleday, 1966).

[37] *Baptist Standard*, Sept. 4, 1919, p. 1.

[38] Ibid., Aug. 7, 1919, p. 8.

analysis, Texas Baptist leaders, as they had done since the late nineteenth century, unequivocally condemned the mob violence of the postwar era.[39]

As Gambrell reflected on the racial turmoil of this period, the paternalism of his thought was readily apparent. Indeed, his career gives support to the thesis of Lawrence J. Friedman, *The White Savage* (1970). According to Friedman, the clamorous debate following the Civil War over integration actually masked "a deeper Southern abhorrence of 'uppity niggers.'" More than anything else, said Friedman, postbellum southerners wanted docility from blacks, and this was sought through "differential segregation." This policy allowed blacks who knew "their place" to associate with superior whites while rigidly ostracizing "uppity" blacks who aspired to equality.[40] Similarly, from 1919 to 1921 Gambrell repeatedly acknowledged the responsibility of the "stronger" toward the "weaker" race but at the same time restrictively defined the degree and nature of interracial contact. Within this paternalistic context, his remarks sounded unusually progressive. This was "not only the white man's country," he wrote in 1919, "but the country of all the people." Hence, "all the avenues of progress must be open to all the peoples of the many races on our shores," for this was "fundamental justice." And although convinced that separate churches were preferable, Gambrell nonetheless announced that he "would not belong to a church that . . . [denied] a place to worship [to anyone] because of race prejudice."[41] Furthermore, the Baptist churchman favored expanded educational and job opportunities for blacks, demanded full protection of the law for all citizens, and asserted that if blacks paid the same fare as whites for public transportation they were entitled to "comfortable accommodations."[42]

The key was "comfortable accommodations." This did not

[39] Ibid., Sept. 4, 1919, p. 1; June 8, 1922, pp. 8–9; and June 15, 1922, p. 2.

[40] Lawrence J. Friedman, *The White Savage: Racial Fantasies in the Postbellum South* (Englewood Cliffs, N.J.: Prentice-Hall, 1970), pp. 26–27, 32–33, 53–54, 73–74, 119–21.

[41] *Baptist Standard*, Apr. 17, 1919, p. 8.

[42] Ibid., Feb. 24, 1921, pp. 6–7.

mean equal accommodations, and it certainly did not mean the same accommodations provided for whites. Gambrell's sense of propriety did not allow for racial equality, and his declarations of concern did not extend to "uppity blacks" who grasped for too much. Racial traits were innate, Gambrell believed, and "the South, for the sake of both races, must . . . safeguard racial integrity."[43] And this required restraints, legislatively enforced if necessary, against social commingling. Characteristically, Gambrell applied the injunction against social commingling in the broadest possible sense. He defended segregated railroad coaches, for instance, on the same grounds that many churchmen would defend segregated schools in the 1950s. Integrated passenger cars, like integrated schools, would result in social equality,[44] which in turn would lead to racial mongrelization.[45]

So Gambrell, like many other whites from all walks of life, preferred "good Negroes" to "bad Negroes." The former were simple, loyal, duly grateful for the favors of whites, and docile; the latter strove for social equality, belonged to the National Association for the Advancement of Colored People (NAACP), and were aggressive agitators.[46] Whites would tolerate a degree of familiarity with the former because they did not challenge white authority. But the latter were rebuked and shunned because they threatened established practices.

This pattern of thought was remarkably durable. The *Baptist Standard* featured stories about the "good Negro" as late as 1932.[47] And even after the painful and shattering years of the Great Depression and World War II, many Texas Baptists still explained the struggle for racial justice prosaically. In August, 1945, David M. Gardner, editor of the *Baptist Standard* during the troubled years from 1944 to 1954, attributed the South's difficulties to outside "racial rabble rousers," and he insisted southerners would find "a commonsense solution" to their racial ills if

[43] Ibid., Aug. 7, 1919, p. 1.
[44] Ibid., Feb. 24, 1921, pp. 6–7.
[45] Ibid., Aug. 7, 1919, p. 1.
[46] Foy D. Valentine, "A Historical Study of Southern Baptists and Race Relations, 1917–1947" (Th.D. diss., Southwestern Baptist Seminary, 1949), pp. 50–58.
[47] *Baptist Standard*, Oct. 26, 1932, p. 16.

"the pestiferous pettifoggers who" were "employed and paid fabulous sums to promote strife and trouble" would leave the region alone.[48] The reactionary nature of Gardner's racial thinking was further disclosed a few months later. In October, 1945, he endorsed racial justice, so long as it was accomplished "within the [various] racial groups." Elaborating, Gardner explained that "neither Christianity, common justice, nor common sense would justify an amalgamation of the races." Falling back upon an ancient theme, the journalist declared that "God created and established the color line in the races, and evidently meant for it to remain."[49] Although temperamentally and intellectually ill-suited for the racial developments unfolding by mid-century, Gardner was in tune with a broad segment of the Baptist faithful. An extensive survey of Southern Baptist Sunday school manuals and other denominational literature revealed extensive agreement with the editor's position, not only in Texas but across the South.[50]

Although perhaps representing dominant sentiment, Gardner did not speak for all Texas Baptists. For half a century a counterview, one that challenged prevailing racial stereotypes, had been evolving. For the most part, it was the denomination's leading exponents of social Christianity who most clearly saw the discrepancy between ideals and practices in matters of race. Indeed, with regard to race these Texas Baptists, though not yet as cognizant of the corporate nature of evil as the social gospel ministers of the North, surpassed their northern counterparts. Josiah Strong, for instance, was an avid disciple of the manifest destiny of Anglo-Saxons, and the racial thought of Washington Gladden, George Herron, and Walter Rauschenbusch was ambiguous.[51] By contrast, pre–World War I Texas Baptists such as Benjamin Franklin Riley and Joseph M. Dawson were more in the tradition of such noted southern liberals as George Washing-

[48] Ibid., Aug. 15, 1945, p. 3.

[49] Ibid., Oct. 4, 1945, p. 3. See also Oct. 7, 1948, p. 4.

[50] Davis C. Hill, "Southern Baptist Thought and Action in Race Relations, 1940–1950" (Th.D. diss., Southern Baptist Theological Seminary, 1952), pp. 96–115, 141–50, 288–90, 299–301.

[51] Gossett, Race, pp. 176–97; Smith, In His Image, But . . . , pp. 262–63; Fredrickson, Black Image, pp. 303–304.

ton Cable, *The Silent South* (1885), and Lewis Harvie Blair, *A Southern Prophecy* (1889).[52]

Riley was born in Monroe County, Alabama, in 1849. His intellectual horizons were broadened by extensive travels and educational training. He attended Erskine College (B.A., 1871), Southern Baptist Seminary, and Crozer Theological Seminary in Pennsylvania, 1874–76. He toured Europe and the United States and wrote numerous scholarly studies. After pastoring several small congregations in Alabama and Georgia, Riley became president of Howard College, a Baptist school in Birmingham, Alabama, in 1888. He resigned the post after five years to join the faculty at the University of Georgia, where he served as a professor of English from 1893 to 1900. At the turn of the century Riley accepted a call to the First Baptist Church, Houston, and promptly joined Texas Baptists in the ongoing crusade against liquor. Indeed, in 1907 he relinquished his Houston pulpit to become head of the Anti-Saloon League of Texas. And in 1909 he returned to Birmingham, Alabama, as organizer and leader of the Southern Negro Anti-Saloon Federation.

Although deeply involved in the prohibition movement, Riley's social concern, like that of his central Texas colleague, Joseph M. Dawson, extended to other public issues, including race.[53] His principal writings on this topic appeared after he returned to Alabama, but the *Baptist Standard*, no doubt because of his prominence while in Texas, provided ample coverage of his views. Riley's most important statements on race, besides numerous articles, were *The White Man's Burden* (1910), published at his own expense, and *The Life and Times of Booker T. Washington* (1916).

Riley was by no means completely free of stereotypes and biases. He uncritically accepted the simple analysis that slavery, although wrong, had taught blacks important lessons; he patronizingly recounted the virtues of the "black Mammy"; he depicted blacks as essentially docile; he voiced pride in dominant Anglo-Saxons; and he considered enfranchisement of blacks

[52] Gossett, *Race*, p. 431. See also Carl N. Degler, *The Other South: Southern Dissenters in the Nineteenth Century* (New York: Harper and Row, 1974), pp. 313–14.

[53] See BGCT, *Proceedings*, p. 91; Fredrickson, *Black Image*, p. 288.

immediately after the Civil War to have been a mistake.[54] Of course, other southern whites whose racial thought was otherwise progressive were not altogether free of bias either.[55] But Riley did recount the role of blacks in American history since the Revolution; he encouraged blacks to be proud of their racial heritage; he argued that southern regional progress was linked to advancement of the black community; and he pointedly dismissed the notion of black inferiority, calling attention to the swift advancement of blacks, both individually and as a group, since the Civil War. And whites who attempted to discredit evidence of progress, claiming that only those blacks with an admixture of white blood showed signs of improvement, evoked Riley's ridicule. If blacks were given "a fair chance in the race of life," he retorted, they possessed sufficient ambition and native talent to succeed. He admitted that blacks as a group still lagged behind whites as a group but said this was because of environment rather than innate racial differences.[56]

Stereotypes, particularly those depicting blacks as naturally lazy and shiftless, especially offended Riley, and it disappointed him that southern whites who knew better remained silent. Why, he asked, should those whites who reviled blacks as liars, thieves, and murderers go unchallenged by other whites who knew blacks to be thrifty, hard-working, and law-abiding? The former Houstonian answered his own question. "Many [whites] are lacking in manly and moral courage by failing to say that certain expressed sentiments are not true," thus allowing "the tide of unfair denunciation to sweep on . . . for fear of unpopularity."[57] To Riley, it was hypocrisy to send missionaries to Africa while demeaning blacks at home.[58]

Riley was aware of the achievements of militant blacks, and

[54] Benjamin Franklin Riley, *The White Man's Burden* (Birmingham, Ala.: Riley, 1910), pp. 40–49, 124–25; and *The Life and Times of Booker T. Washington* (New York: Fleming H. Revell Co., 1916), pp. 23, 73, 154, 217, 247. See also Fredrickson, *Black Image*, pp. 288–89.

[55] Friedman, *White Savage*, p. 101.

[56] Riley, *White Man's Burden*, pp. 9, 13, 74–84, 95; and *Life and Times of Booker T. Washington*, pp. 18–19, 21–23, 243–44.

[57] *Baptist Standard*, Sept. 5, 1912, pp. 4–5.

[58] Ibid., Jan. 14, 1915, pp. 3, 11.

cited William E. B. DuBois and Monroe Trotter as examples of racial progress. Like other southern moderates,[59] however, he preferred the gradualism of his friend Booker T. Washington. Riley had met Washington while the latter was on tour in Texas, and a symbiotic relationship soon developed. Washington's success gave confirmation to Riley's belief in gradual racial accommodation, and Riley's public support helped Washington counter the view of white southern extremists. Riley sought Washington's advice on *The White Man's Burden*, delivered two addresses at Tuskegee, and joined Washington at a New York City meeting in behalf of Tuskegee.[60] Unlike many fellow churchmen, Riley knew that the Tuskegee educator expected blacks to be more than a permanent mudsill. And unlike militant blacks,[61] Riley did not see Washington as an Uncle Tom. According to the Baptist scholar, critics who accused Washington of kowtowing to whites did not appreciate the intensity of racial animosity in the latter nineteenth and early twentieth centuries. The Tuskegee principal "was neither cowardly nor sycophantic"; rather, he was a pragmatist who saw the futility of "uselessly inveighing against the impossible." So Washington encouraged blacks to forgo momentarily the quest for political equality, striving instead for economic independence. To Riley, this was a "wise and level-headed" course, for had the black leader "been violent, or even offensive, he would have cut short his career, obliterated his influence, and undone that already achieved."[62] This assessment is shared by some recent observers.[63]

The impact of Riley's writings is difficult to gauge. His schol-

[59] Fredrickson, *Black Image*, pp. 292–93; Franklin, *From Slavery to Freedom*, p. 392–93.

[60] Louis R. Harlan, *Booker T. Washington: The Wizard of Tuskegee, 1901–1915* (New York: Oxford University Press, 1983), pp. 256–57, 259.

[61] For an account of the growing rift between Washington and other black leaders, see Elliott M. Rudwick, *W. E. B. DuBois: Propagandist of the Negro Protest* (New York: Atheneum, 1969), pp. 63–76, 94–118, 179–80, 300–303; Franklin, *From Slavery to Freedom*, pp. 393–95; and Harlan, *Booker T. Washington: Wizard*, pp. 259–78.

[62] Riley, *Life and Times of Booker T. Washington*, pp. 99, 144–48, 243–44.

[63] Irving Howe, "Remarkable Man, Ambiguous Legacy," *Harper's*, Mar. 1968, pp. 143–49; Samuel R. Spencer, Jr., *Booker T. Washington and the Negro's Place in American Life* (Boston: Little, Brown, 1955), pp. 187–201; Harlan, *Booker T. Washington: Wizard*, pp. 238–65.

arly works probably were not widely read. Nevertheless, at least a few Texas Baptists agreed with the former Houston pastor. William Thomas Tardy of Marshall praised his "courageous and scholarly treatment of this hugest [sic] American issue" and concurred that anyone attempting to apply Christian principles to race usually aroused the contempt and scorn of fellow churchmen.[64]

One Texas Baptist who bravely ran this risk was Joseph M. Dawson. During his long ministry in Waco he consistently strove to improve race relations, sometimes to the irritation of fellow Baptists. The origins of Dawson's racial concern are obscure. While he was growing up, his contact with blacks had been quite limited. Indeed, by his own admission, Dawson knew little about racial attitudes until assuming the pastorate of the First Baptist Church, Waco, in 1915. He was then in his late thirties.[65]

Shortly after arriving in Waco Dawson witnessed a grisly act of racial savagery. Jesse Washington, a seventeen-year-old black youth accused of murdering a middle-aged white woman near Waco, was burned to death and mutilated by a frenzied mob in front of city hall on May 15, 1916. Helpless to stop the incident, Dawson watched in horror. With "five thousand monsters" participating, he later asked plaintively, "who was I, a lone individual, to do anything about it?" When rumors circulated that Washington was innocent, Dawson was further dismayed that the "only comment . . . heard around town . . . was, 'Well, it's fine. At last, they got the right Nigger.'" Although he had made no effort to save Washington, Dawson's subsequent action was courageous. The week following that incident he presented a strong resolution to the Waco Pastor's Association condemning the act. The resolution passed, although it was not supported by all the ministers.[66] Indeed, the NAACP was disappointed by the failure of the local clergy to respond more vigorously to "The Waco Horror," as the incident was described in the organization's

[64] *Baptist Standard*, Oct. 31, 1912, pp. 10–11; see also Mar. 10, 1910, pp. 1–2; Sept. 5, 1912, p. 8; and Sept. 14, 1916, p. 3.

[65] Oral Memoirs of Joseph M. Dawson, Waco, 1973, Baylor University Program of Oral History, p. 64.

[66] Ibid., pp. 53–55; Dawson, *Thousand Months to Remember*, p. 165.

publication, *Crisis*. W. E. B. DuBois, editor of the journal, bitingly commented that "any talk of the triumph of Christianity . . . is idle twaddle so long as the Waco lynching is possible."[67] In addition to Dawson, the Baylor University faculty and the Reverends Frank P. Culver of Austin Avenue Methodist Church, Charles T. Caldwell of the First Presbyterian Church, and Frank S. Groner of Columbus Street Baptist Church condemned the brutal lynching.[68]

After this barbarous act Dawson consistently denounced racial violence from the pulpit. His outspokenness was daring, for some members of his Waco congregation belonged to the Ku Klux Klan and only recently had invited their new pastor to join them in the secret organization. Dawson declined, denouncing the hooded organization instead. Moreover, he subsequently supported the gubernatorial candidacy of Mrs. Miriam A. "Ma" Ferguson, despite his distaste for her husband, because "she opposed the Ku Klux Klan."[69] Given the power and influence of the Texas Klan in the early 1920s, as well as the fact that Waco was one of five Texas cities selected as a headquarters for the secret society,[70] Dawson's stand reflected some boldness. This is all the more significant in view of the failure of Texas Baptists as a body to take a similar stance. In 1922, an election year in which the Klan was especially active and in which violence again flared in Waco, Dawson forthrightly rebuked the mobs. His courage elicited praise from James B. Cranfill, the former editor of the *Baptist Standard*, who singled out the Wacoan as one of the few pastors manly enough to address such issues from the pulpit. Cranfill, too, held the Klan in contempt.[71]

Dawson promoted racial understanding in other ways. Al-

[67] Quoted in James M. SoRelle, "The 'Waco Horror': The Lynching of Jesse Washington," *Southwestern Historical Quarterly* 86, no. 4 (Apr., 1983): 534.

[68] Ibid., pp. 529, 532.

[69] Oral Memoirs, Dawson, pp. 36, 52, 55–57; Brown, *Hood, Bonnet, and Little Brown Jug*, pp. 265, 330.

[70] David M. Chalmers, *Hooded Americanism: The History of the Ku Klux Klan* (New York: Franklin Watts, 1975), pp. 39–48; and Brown, *Hood, Bonnet, and Little Brown Jug*, pp. 49–87.

[71] *Baptist Standard*, June 15, 1922, p. 12; Brown, *Hood, Bonnet, and Little Brown Jug*, p. 55.

though never allowed to become members, blacks were invited to attend Sunday worship services at First Baptist, which many frequently did. Dawson, moreover, encouraged black ministers to attend the weekly pastors' luncheons held in his church. This aroused the ire of the white ladies of First Baptist, who, fiercely resistant to anything resembling racial equality, refused to serve the blacks. And there were other occasions when Dawson made fellow churchmen uncomfortable. As a trustee for thirty years of Bishop College in Marshall, a black school founded by Northern Baptists, he was keenly interested in Negro education. In 1927 he wrote an article entitled "Baptist Illiteracy in the South" for a national magazine, *Plain Talk*, in which he argued that blacks were being kept illiterate as a result of shamefully low appropriations for black schools.[72] This evoked a sharp rebuke from many fellow Baptists, including Edgar Young Mullins, longtime president of Southern Baptist Seminary and a former president of the Southern Baptist Convention. A few years later Pat Neff, president of Baylor, despite a close friendship with the First Baptist pastor, vehemently objected upon hearing a rumor, later proven false, that Dawson was arranging a joint discussional between white and black youths. Baylor students, the former governor summarily announced, would not be allowed to participate.[73]

In May, 1946, shortly before ending his long pastoral career in Waco, Dawson again pricked the conscience of his denomination. He chided Southern Baptists in an address broadcast from Miami, Florida, during "The Baptist Hour." Despite the preponderance of Baptists, said the Wacoan, the South still endured the "greatest" illiteracy, the "most serious" economic exploitation of the helpless, and the "worst" prejudices.[74] Dawson's commitment to racial justice never failed. In 1957 the seventy-eight-year-old minister appeared before a hostile state senate committee in Austin to oppose pending legislation detrimental

---

[72]Joseph M. Dawson, "Baptist Illiteracy in the South," *Plain Talk*, Oct., 1927, pp. 440–45.

[73]Oral Memoirs, Dawson, pp. 39–40, 64–65, 160. See also *Baptist Standard*, Apr. 19, 1928, p. 3; Nov. 15, 1928, p. 2; and Joseph M. Dawson, "Religion Down South," *Christian Century*, June 25, 1930, p. 812.

[74]*Baptist Standard*, May 29, 1946, p. 2.

to blacks, and the following year in *Christianity Today* he expressed disappointment in Gov. Price Daniel, a fellow Baptist, for failing to take a more enlightened stand on race.[75]

By the mid-1930s important institutional developments regarding race began to unfold. Although external pressures stemming from the depression and World War II were important, they were not entirely responsible for the chain of events that culminated in 1950 in the Christian Life Commission of Texas, an agency dedicated to the cause of social Christianity. Within the General Convention itself the influential J. Howard Williams, a practical man who believed the church should address itself to the material as well as the spiritual needs of people,[76] was the mainspring. Licensed to preach in 1910, the Dallas native served as a chaplain during World War I. Afterward, he entered Southern Seminary in the spring, 1919, but transferred within a few months to Southwestern in Fort Worth. In 1921 he returned to Southern, this time completing residence requirements for a doctorate in 1923. After successful pastorates at Sulphur Springs and Corsicana, Williams became executive secretary of the General Convention in 1931.[77] He held this important denominational position for five years during the depression era, during which time his administrative skills and leadership talents were put to the test.

During the difficult years of the depression Williams saw more clearly than many fellow Baptists the disastrous effects the economic crisis had on blacks. "If the economic situation through which we have recently passed was a depression for the white people," he observed, "it has been a calamity for the Negroes." And, implicitly at least, the Baptist executive dismissed the popular assumption that personal behavioral traits accounted for the condition of the black community. Reminiscent of Benjamin F. Riley, Williams chided whites for indiscriminately condemn-

[75] James M. Dunn, "The Ethical Thought of Joseph Martin Dawson" (Th.D. diss., Southwestern Baptist Seminary, 1966), pp. 161–62.

[76] See *Baptist Standard*, June 6, 1946, p. 1.

[77] H. C. Brown, Jr., and Charles P. Johnson, eds., *J. Howard Williams: Prophet of God and Friend of Man* (San Antonio: Naylor, 1963), pp. 2–7, 46–48, 76–77.

ing all blacks as shiftless and worthless, thus deliberately ignoring those who were honest, conscientious, and law abiding.[78]

At this stage, however, Williams's own thought still reflected traces of racial stereotypes. He regarded blacks as basically happy, imitative, and "not likely" to rise, as a race, above whites. And there was an air of paternalism about his demeanor. He spoke in terms of what Texas Baptists should do *for* rather than *with* the black community. Nevertheless, in 1934 Williams took an important step toward moving the denomination forward in the area of race. He recommended that local white congregations create a Committee on Colored Work, which, "by tactful suggestion," could assist blacks with various church-related programs. Williams believed such committees, by enhancing communications between blacks and whites, were essential to improved race relations. Williams also suggested that the General Convention employ someone, white or black, to work with black ministers, conducting interracial conferences throughout the state. This would enable the General Convention to work for better race relations by cultivating goodwill among black Baptist leaders. A few months later, in March, 1935, Williams himself held two conferences for black preachers, one in Houston and one in Dallas. A key speaker at the Dallas meeting was the elderly Charles T. Alexander, an exceptional teacher with a long record of accomplishments among Southern Baptists.[79]

Williams, supported by numerous black Baptist leaders, subsequently prevailed upon Alexander, who was then sixty-six years old, to work as a missionary for the General Convention among blacks throughout Texas. This was an excellent choice. Alexander was known and respected by Baptists across the South. A man of wit, he wrote humorous poetry as well as scholarly articles. A native of Cumby in northeast Texas, Alexander was educated at Sam Houston State Teachers College, Baylor University, Southern Seminary, and Cumberland University in Tennessee, where he studied law. As a young preacher in Huntsville, such dissimilar figures as Gov. James Hogg and bandit John

[78] *Baptist Standard*, Nov. 8, 1934, p. 6.
[79] Ibid., July 4, 1935, p. 2.

Wesley Hardin responded to his call for repentance. Rising rapidly among Texas Baptists, Alexander was chairman of the Committee on Liquor Traffic for the General Convention in 1901.[80] Some years later B. H. Carroll invited the scholarly minister to deliver a series of lectures at Southwestern Seminary.[81] Following pastorates at Cisco, Cleburne, and Sulphur Springs, Alexander left Texas for Alexandria, Louisiana. Success again characterized his ministry. From Alexandria, he went to New Orleans as pastor of the First Baptist Church. During his long ministry in New Orleans, the transplanted Texan was elected president of the Louisiana Baptist Convention. In 1929 Alexander returned to Texas, settling in Dallas, where he joined Gaston Avenue Baptist Church.[82]

Long interested in racial matters, Alexander spoke often to black congregations and served as a trustee of Bishop College in Marshall until his death in 1950. Moreover, he had journeyed years earlier to Tuskegee Institute to meet Dr. George Washington Carver.[83] In 1936 when Alexander went to work for the General Convention, there were almost 400,000 black Baptists in Texas divided among three separate state conventions—the General Baptist Convention of Texas, the Missionary and Educational Baptist Convention, and the Texas Baptist Convention.[84] As perceived by Alexander, his task was to approach the racial problem from the "top instead of the bottom," thereby bringing "into closer bonds of helpful fellowship and cooperation the leadership of both races." But how could this be achieved without arousing the anxiety of white Baptists who were fearful of racial equality? There was no cause for alarm. Although white and black Baptists "would become more closely allied," they would "develop along parallel lines" and remain in "different circles."[85] To have proposed anything else at this time would

[80] BGCT, *Proceedings*, 1901, p. 76.

[81] *Baptist Standard*, Aug. 19, 1948, p. 5.

[82] Ibid., June 1, 1950, p. 1. See also *Dallas Morning News*, Part 3, May 19, 1950, p. 2.

[83] *Baptist Standard*, Apr. 8, 1945, p. 2.

[84] Ibid., June 8, 1944, p. 5.

[85] BGCT, *Proceedings*, 1936, p. 99; *Baptist Standard*, Aug. 27, 1936, p. 2.

have been very risky. In the late 1930s churches were rigidly segregated, not only in the South but throughout the nation. Of the nation's approximately 8 million black Protestants, one scholar has estimated that only about 8,000 actually worshiped with whites in 1940.[86]

Despite age and increasingly poor health, Alexander embraced his new task with the vigor of a much younger person. He never, however, pushed himself "into their fellowship." Rather, he made his availability known and waited for blacks "to open the door of their own accord."[87] They did so generously. Between 1936 and 1943, when failing health forced him to retire, Alexander tirelessly worked with leaders of the three black Baptist conventions of Texas; visited similar bodies in Missouri, Kentucky, Arkansas, Alabama, and Louisiana; attended national meetings of black religious bodies; pointed out the need for literature dealing with interracial matters; and conducted in 1942 alone twenty-five one-week interracial Bible conferences and institutes across the state.[88] At such a meeting in Waco Joseph Dawson cooperated with Alexander.[89] All the while Alexander was striving to establish interracial contacts of a lasting institutional nature. With a penchant for organization, he continually encouraged local congregations, black as well as white, to form standing committees on race relations. This would bring local leaders together. And at the state level he advocated the creation of a Texas Baptist Interracial Commission. This body would consist of representatives from the three black bodies and the Baptist General Convention.[90]

In November, 1942, in his last report to the Baptist General Convention, Alexander, with justifiable pride, informed the messengers that he had opened the doors to the black community. Meaningful relationships with black leaders had been forged. Now was the time, he believed, for Texas Baptists to move ahead

[86] Robert Moats Miller, *American Protestantism and Social Issues, 1919–1939* (Chapel Hill: University of North Carolina Press, 1958), p. 297.

[87] *Baptist Standard*, Aug. 27, 1936.

[88] BGCT, *Proceedings*, 1942, pp. 82–84.

[89] *Baptist Standard*, Mar. 17, 1938, p. 4.

[90] Ibid., Feb. 4, 1937, p. 4. See also BGCT, *Proceedings*, 1941, pp. 86–87.

aggressively in this important work. The Convention took Alexander's advice, appointing a Committee on Interracial Relations to study matters.[91]

Without minimizing the significance of Alexander's labors, one must acknowledge the impact of other developments. The subsequent course of the General Convention, like that of church bodies elsewhere in the South,[92] was influenced by international events, especially the violent racism of Nazi Germany. As early as November, 1940, J. Howard Williams, then outgoing president of the General Convention, glimpsed the signs of change. He praised the work of Alexander but then added prophetically: "The day is not far distant when the South is going to see acute race problems arise."[93] Three years later, with the nation in the midst of a global conflict, the recently established Committee on Interracial Relations clearly disclosed the influence of external events upon denominational pronouncements. "The world is at war now because of race prejudices and hatred," declared committee chairman E. S. Hutcherson. "Some races," he continued, "have the feeling that they are superior and are to dominate other races." Such an attitude was contrary to biblical teachings, Hutcherson argued. Moreover, judged by the biblical standard, "the treatment of the colored race" was "impossible to justify" in America.[94]

Prompted by the study of its Interracial Relations Committee, the General Convention created the Department of Interracial Cooperation in November, 1943. This new agency was to work with all ethnic groups in Texas, thereby consolidating under the direction of one person what Texas Baptists had been doing piecemeal through several men for a decade. A director and an advisory council of twelve associates would guide the agency's activities. Contrary to Alexander's recommendation, this new department did not include representatives from the three black conventions. In March, 1944, the General Conven-

---

[91] BGCT, *Proceedings*, 1942, pp. 82–84; 1943, pp. 67–68.
[92] Bailey, *Southern White Protestantism*, pp. 136–41.
[93] *Baptist Standard*, Dec. 12, 1940, p. 1.
[94] Ibid., June 10, 1943, p. 15.

tion named Acker C. Miller, who had been coordinating the convention's work among soldiers since January, 1941, to lead this endeavor. One of the twelve associates was Professor Thomas B. Maston.[95]

In the tradition of Charles T. Alexander, the Department of Interracial Cooperation immediately embarked on a two-pronged campaign—organizational and educational. By the end of 1945 the department had established local interracial committees in 47 of the 113 Baptist associations in Texas, secured from the General Convention $10,000 for Butler College in Tyler to foster black ministerial education, persuaded the Woman's Missionary Union, an auxiliary of the General Convention, to contribute $5,000 toward scholarships for promising black students, and was preparing a body of literature based upon the Bible to promote racial understanding.[96]

The agency's accomplishments were impressive. By 1950, when it was absorbed by the newly fashioned Christian Life Commission of Texas, the Department of Interracial Cooperation had been responsible for substantial contributions to black colleges and students; had offered extension courses on race in conjunction with Southwestern Seminary in such key urban areas as San Antonio, Austin, Beaumont, and Dallas; had conducted interracial conferences across the state; had supplemented the salaries of several black ministers in weak churches; and had employed a young Southwestern Seminary graduate student, Foy Valentine, a protégé of Professor Maston, to work among black college students. In 1948 Valentine had pioneered in an interracial youth revival in Brownwood.[97] Budget allocations suggest that convention leadership supported these endeavors. From 1943 to 1950 the budget for the Department of Interracial Cooperation increased from $15,000 to $75,000, and the number of workers whose salaries were supplemented by the agency grew from nineteen to ninety-three.[98]

[95] BGCT, *Proceedings*, 1944, p. 187. See also Oral Memoirs of Acker C. Miller, Waco, 1973, Baylor University Program of Oral History, pp. 79–80.

[96] BGCT, *Proceedings*, 1945, pp. 193–94.

[97] Ibid., 1945, pp. 174–75; 1947, p. 199; and 1948, p. 184.

[98] Ibid., 1950, pp. 170–71. Actually, the name of the Department of Interracial

Equally significant in these years was the shift in the racial thought of Acker C. Miller. In 1945, and again in 1946, Miller stressed that his new agency was committed to the concept of brotherhood in which there was "neither Greek nor Jew." "We must demonstrate to the world," he said, "that Christianity does unite all mankind into a genuine brotherhood."[99] But what was Miller's concept of brotherhood? And what practical effects would the application of such a concept have on society? As other pronouncements show, Miller's racial attitudes had not as yet caught up with his lofty rhetoric. The new director of inter-racial cooperation did not expect significant changes in southern society. "Under existing social customs and conditions," he wrote in 1944, "it is better to develop within our own races." Since "real Christian fellowship" did not require "mixed membership in our churches," explained Miller, race relations could be improved without "the submergence or gradual extinction of our racial integrity." In December, 1945, Miller again emphasized racial peculiarities and declared that "each race should strive to preserve its own identity that it may better fulfill its racial mission."[100] Although such primitive views seem at odds with the progressive objectives of the Department of Interracial Cooperation, they probably were characteristic of most Texas Baptists in the mid-1940s. Other prominent Baptist officials certainly shared them.[101]

But Miller changed. By 1949 he saw more clearly the complexity of the racial issue and vowed to seek a "practical application of the very gospel I accept and so loudly proclaim."[102] His report that year to the General Convention ended with a stinging denunciation of racism. "Instead of using our advantage to lift people from their low estate, we have permitted these racial differences to develop within us the revolting evil of racism," Miller declared. "This may be a new word for us," he continued,

---

Cooperation had been changed to the Ministry with Minorities in 1947. See Oral Memoirs, Miller, p. 63.

[99] BGCT, *Proceedings*, 1945, p. 195; 1946, p. 175.

[100] *Baptist Standard*, May 4, 1944, p. 5; Dec. 6, 1945, p. 12.

[101] Ibid., May 18, 1944, p. 5.

[102] Ibid., Dec. 15, 1949, p. 6.

"but it is a word that makes its bed with nazism, fascism, communism, and many other evils that are abroad in the world." He concluded that racism violated both democratic and Christian principles. Later, he challenged Texas Baptists to come to grips with racial discrimination in the areas of education, housing, and jobs.[103]

The reasons for such an altered outlook can only be surmised. International developments were a factor. Miller saw that the world had changed profoundly since 1945. Black nations, as reflected in the composition of the United Nations, figured more prominently in world affairs. Of the sixty members of the world body, forty or more had either black majorities or large black minorities. Consequently, like other missionary-minded Southern Baptists, Miller quickly realized that mistreatment of blacks at home adversely affected foreign missions. Americans, he observed, could no longer proclaim abroad what they failed to practice at home.[104] And at home, Miller was obviously aware of the signs of change. In 1948 President Harry Truman had taken steps to desegregate the armed services and to broaden the fair employment program. That same year the national Democratic party committed itself to the advancement of civil rights, sparking the Dixiecrat revolt led by Strom Thurmond of South Carolina. The following year several northern and western states followed the presidential example. By 1949 New Jersey, Indiana, Illinois, and Arizona had sought to curb segregation in public schools. The most dramatic headway against racial discrimination, however, was made by the Supreme Court. In 1944 *Smith* v. *Allwright* laid to rest the white primary and opened the door of the southern political process to significant numbers of blacks. Then, on June 5, 1950, the justices, in a series of momentous decisions, swept away the foundation of the South's separate-but-equal society. Dixie would never be the same after *Sweatt* v. *Painter*, *McLaurin* v. *Board of Regents*, and *Henderson* v. *United States*. Respectively, these rulings gained blacks admission to the University of Texas' School

[103] BGCT, *Proceedings*, 1949, pp. 144–49; 1950, p. 173.
[104] Ibid., 1940, pp. 172–74. See also Franklin, *From Slavery to Freedom*, p. 622.

of Law, equal access with whites to classrooms and other facilities in the University of Oklahoma's graduate and professional
schools, and the right to eat in integrated railway dining cars.[105]

As important as these events were, they were not wholly
responsible for the shift in Miller's racial views. Association with
Thomas Maston was also important. A major objective of the
Department of Interracial Cooperation had always been educational. Consequently, the agency held group discussions and
seminars at Baptist encampments, encouraged Baptist schools to
offer courses on race relations, placed books in church and college libraries, and prepared and circulated informative literature.[106] Professor Matson was ideally suited for such endeavors.
His first publication on race and the Bible was "Racial Revelations," a pamphlet that the Woman's Missionary Union of the
Southern Baptist Convention had printed in 1927.[107] This was
followed in 1933 by a series of Sunday school lessons for the
Southern Baptist Sunday School Board, one of which was entitled "The Christian Attitude toward Other Races." And by the
early 1940s Maston had developed several ethics courses at the
seminary dealing primarily with race relations in the South.[108]
Given such a background, it was logical that Maston, while serving on the advisory council of the Department of Interracial Cooperation, should again address the issue of race. In 1946 the
seminarian published *Of One*, a candid and controversial study.
Maston later explained that this publication grew out of a sense of
need. Race "was a major issue," he said, and *Of One* would help
fellow Baptists grapple with it from the standpoint of scripture.[109]

[105] Numan V. Bartley, *The Rise of Massive Resistance: Race and Politics in the
South During the 1950's* (Baton Rouge: Louisiana State University Press, 1969), pp. 5–6;
Darlene Clark Hine, "The Elusive Ballot: The Blacks' Struggle against The Texas Democratic White Primary, 1932–1945," *Southwestern Historical Quarterly* 81, no. 4 (Apr.,
1978): 371–92; and Sitkoff, *Struggle for Black Equality*, pp. 13–20.

[106] BGCT, *Proceedings*, 1944, p. 188.

[107] W. T. Moore, *His Heart Is Black* (Atlanta: Home Mission Board, Southern Baptist Convention, 1978), p. 61.

[108] Oral Memoirs of T. B. Maston, Waco, 1973, Baylor University Program of Oral
History, pp. 71–72; William M. Pinson, Jr., *An Approach to Christian Ethics: The Life,
Contribution, and Thought of T. B. Maston* (Nashville: Broadman Press, 1979), p. 62.

[109] Oral Memoirs, Maston, p. 138.

Of One was a forceful statement in behalf of racial equality based on the premise that God is no respecter of persons and on the attitude of Jesus toward the Samaritans. To many Baptists, such an argument invariably raised the specter of social equality and intermarriage. Maston did not evade these emotional subjects. Spiritual equality, he maintained, involved social equality. More to the point, the ethicist insisted that human relationships should rest upon individual, as opposed to racial, considerations. As for intermarriage, Maston dismissed it. Blacks wanted economic equality and job opportunities, not white women.[110] *Of One* not only established Maston as the leading spokesman for racial justice among Texas Baptists, it also influenced the tone and substance of the Interracial Cooperation Department's subsequent reports to the General Convention. And although neither man acknowledged it, Maston's presence on the advisory council surely contributed to the maturation of Miller's racial thinking.

Popular reaction to *Of One*, meanwhile, bespoke the divided mind of Texas Baptists by mid-century. A San Antonio woman who identified herself as "a Southern Baptist . . . and a loyal and patriotic American" asserted that *Of One* "is not Christian, or American!" "And if that," added she, "is what you teach in the Seminary, and elsewhere, you should not be allowed to teach, or instruct. I never want one of my children to become indoctrinated with such nonsense!"[111] But Arthur B. Rutledge, pastor of the First Baptist Church, Marshall, who had minored in ethics at Southwestern under Maston, warmly commended his former mentor for such timely and helpful advice. "Let me thank you for your excellent book," Rutledge wrote, "and assure you of my desires and prayer that the book may do much good in the realization of the Christian ideal in race relations." Such a study, added the pastor, was "certainly needed among us Southern Baptists."[112]

While the San Antonio woman perhaps mirrored the opin-

[110]Thomas B. Maston, *Of One* (Atlanta: Home Mission Board, Southern Baptist Convention, 1946), pp. 8–17, 60–71, 90–97.

[111]Letter to T. B. Maston, Mar. 21, 1952, Maston Collection.

[112]Rutledge to Maston, May 9, 1946, Maston Collection.

ion of most Texas Baptists, Rutledge reflected the sentiment of a growing number of church leaders who were striving to achieve racial justice through a practical application of Christian ideals. Maston's vision of social justice, however, went beyond race. Although his efforts in behalf of blacks never ceased, by the late 1940s the seminarian was searching for a way to apply Christian principles to all aspects of daily life. This led Maston and likeminded Texas Baptists to forge the Christian Life Commission of Texas in 1950.

5

Thomas Maston and the Origins
of the Christian Life Commission

In 1963 Thomas Buford Maston retired from Southwestern Seminary after forty-one years of distinguished service. Although an unassuming and essentially shy man, his influence on fellow Baptists across the nation was enormous.[1] Through former students alone his reach extended to all levels of denominational life. Several thousand undergraduates took at least a few of Maston's courses in applied Christianity; a substantial number minored under him in ethics; and forty-nine of his candidates completed doctoral requirements.[2] Bill Moyers, an aide to former President Lyndon B. Johnson and more recently a commentator for CBS News, studied under Maston and would have majored in ethics had he remained at the seminary.[3] As pastors, denominational executives, professors, and foreign missionaries, Maston's doctoral students became involved in every aspect of Baptist life. At various times, forty-seven have been pastors; twenty-one, denominational executives; fifteen, seminary professors; thirteen, missionaries; and three, seminary and college presidents. Two other seminary presidents minored in ethics under Maston. Outside the denomination, two of his majors served as military chaplains, and four others became government officials.[4]

[1] Much of the material in this chapter was previously published in John W. Storey, "Thomas Buford Maston and the Growth of Social Christianity among Texas Baptists," *East Texas Historical Journal* 19, no. 2 (1981): 27–42.

[2] Thomas B. Maston to author, Oct. 18, 1978; William M. Pinson, Jr., ed., *An Approach to Christian Ethics: The Life, Contribution, and Thought of T. B. Maston* (Nashville: Broadman Press, 1979), p. 91.

[3] Thomas B. Maston, interview with author, Fort Worth, Mar. 16, 1979, p. 21. All citations from this interview are taken from a typed transcript of taped conversations.

[4] Pinson, *Approach to Christian Ethics*, pp. 91–92, 94–96; Maston to author, Oct. 18, 1978.

In Texas the vehicle through which Maston's protégés exerted considerable influence was the Christian Life Commission. Devoted to expanding the social vision of fellow churchmen, this agency has been dominated by Maston graduates. With the exception of Acker C. Miller, the first director of the Christian Life Commission, and Phil Strickland, the current leader [1985], all directors of the commission have been Maston students: Foy Valentine, 1953–60; Jimmy Allen, 1960–68; and James Dunn, 1968–80. And upon resigning from the Texas agency, each of these men moved to other influential denominational positions. Valentine became executive secretary of the Christian Life Commission of the Southern Baptist Convention, a post he still held in 1985. Allen went to the First Baptist Church, San Antonio, where during a twelve-year ministry his racially integrated congregation implemented an impressive array of social programs.[5] In the meantime, he served as president of the Baptist General Convention of Texas, 1970–71, and of the Southern Baptist Convention, 1978–79. In 1980 Allen gave up his San Antonio pastorate to become president of the Radio and Television Commission of the Southern Baptist Convention in Fort Worth. And Dunn went to Washington, D.C., to head the Baptist Joint Committee on Public Affairs in 1981.

When asked why he had never carried placards or marched in protest parades, as other people who shared his concern for social justice had done, Maston replied, "There is a place for some folk who stay primarily right here in the classroom at the seminary." The activities of his students would seem to bear him out. As Maston observed, they "have gotten involved in ways that I could not and ways in which I would not feel comfortable."[6]

Who was T. B. Maston? Why should a Texas Baptist such as he, who spent his academic career in a conservative environment, be so concerned about social Christianity? Why was he able to rise above his culture on an issue such as race, especially when so many of his contemporaries, whether in or out of the

[5]Oral Memoirs of Jimmy Raymond Allen, Waco, 1973, Baylor University Program of Oral History, pp. 173–88.

[6]Maston, interview with author, pp. 8–9.

church, were unable to do so? What made him such a dynamic and unique force among fellow Baptists? Maston's family background and educational development shed some light.

The seminarian's interest in social issues was kindled by his family environment. "I know some folks move away and forget [their origins]," recalled Maston, "but I definitely think this had a definite influence in my life," especially in "the concern about people."[7] Maston was born in Jefferson County, Tennessee, in 1897. His parents were very poor. His father, who grew up in east Tennessee after the Civil War, toiled as a farm laborer, a section hand on a railroad, and a sharecropper. Pursuit of work led the Maston family to a small Ohio village, College Corner, in 1901. After a decade the family returned to Tennessee, settling on a farm near Fountain City, where Maston grew to maturity. Despite a rather humble and migratory existence, the Maston family was stable. The parents enjoyed a successful marriage and exerted a positive influence on their children. As Maston was especially close to his father, the elder man's influence on the son was considerable.[8]

Inasmuch as his family was poor, Maston always identified with underprivileged people. Because of his father's experience as a railroad section hand, for instance, he rather early developed a sympathy for unionism. His father, while not an activist committed to any particular social program, joined the railroad union for practical reasons. It helped the laborers. So Maston saw the benefits of unionization and thus could later identify with those southern miners, mill hands, lumberjacks, and agricultural laborers who struggled against formidable odds to organize in the early twentieth century. Family conditions, then, Maston later recalled, "have explained to some degree what I hope has been a genuine, sincere interest in the underprivileged, the poor, and the disinherited in general in our society."[9]

But why should Maston's concern for the underprivileged cut across racial lines? Why should the son of a poor white la-

[7] Ibid., p. 3.
[8] Oral Memoirs of T. B. Maston, Waco, 1973, Baylor University Program of Oral History, p. 10.
[9] Ibid., pp. 1–6.

borer from east Tennessee develop such an interest in racial justice? Historically, poor southern whites in general and laborers in particular have often resisted efforts by blacks to improve their status in society. Motivated by economic and social fears, these southern whites frequently released their frustrations in aggressive acts against blacks and often excluded them from local unions.[10] So why was Maston different? There is some temptation to account for this in terms of Maston's upbringing in eastern Tennessee, a mountain region noted in the antebellum era for its opposition to slavery. But this does not mean that Maston was reared in a prejudice-free environment. On the contrary, east Tennesseans, whether before or after the Civil War, were no more willing to accept blacks as equals than were most other white Americans. Their abolitionism, for instance, had usually been coupled with plans for deportation of blacks.[11] Again, Maston's home more so than its geographical location explains his racial progressiveness. "My folks seemingly had no racial prejudice, [and I] never heard it expressed at all," he observed.[12]

Maston, moreover, was affected by biblical stories dealing with racial equality. "I think the attitude that I early developed grew *primarily* out of my reading and study of the New Testament and the attitude of Jesus, particularly toward the Samaritans," he said, "because they were the most hated group by the Jews of that time."[13] But even Maston could not explain why those biblical stories made such an impression upon him, par-

[10] See C. Vann Woodward, *Origins of the New South, 1877–1913* (1951; reprint, Baton Rouge: Louisiana State University Press, 1964), pp. 228–29, 360–66; John Dollard, *Caste and Class in a Southern Town* (Garden City, N.Y.: Anchor Books, 1957), pp. 75–76, 93–94, 250–52; W. J. Cash, *The Mind of the South* (New York: Vintage Books, 1961), pp. 120–23, 305–306; and Thomas D. Clark and Albert D. Kirwan, *The South since Appomattox: A Century of Regional Change* (New York: Oxford University Press, 1967), pp. 312–14.

[11] Carl N. Degler, *The Other South: Southern Dissenters in the Nineteenth Century* (New York: Harper and Row, 1974), pp. 79–81; Lawrence J. Friedman, *The White Savage: Racial Fantasies in the Postbellum South* (Englewood Cliffs, N.J.: Prentice-Hall, 1970), pp. 27–28; Roger L. Hart, *Redeemers, Bourbons and Populists: Tennessee, 1870–1896* (Baton Rouge: Louisiana State University Press, 1975), pp. 124–25; and Lester C. Lamon, *Black Tennesseans, 1900–1930* (Knoxville: University of Tennessee Press, 1977), pp. 2–3.

[12] Maston, interview with author, p. 40.

[13] Ibid.

ticularly when so many other whites of similar background were unaffected by them. Indeed, despite scriptures alluding to racial justice, southern religion, for most whites at least, tended to reinforce cultural norms regarding the status of blacks in the South. As church historian Rufus B. Spain pointed out, "theories of race were as much a part of Southern Baptist thinking as the Virgin Birth or Second Coming."[14] This could be said of Baptist thought well into the twentieth century.

Perhaps the nature of Maston's early association with blacks was important. Because few blacks lived in the Tennessee and Ohio communities where he grew up, Maston actually had little contact with blacks during his formative years. There were only two black families in College Corner, where Maston entered public school. Although limited, this association was positive. He sat across the aisle in school from a black child and played with him at recess on the playground. This in itself was significant, for in the segregated school systems of the South such an experience would have been unlikely. Furthermore, unlike southern whites whose fears sometimes were accentuated by the preponderance of blacks in that region, the Maston family never felt threatened. Upon returning to Tennessee in 1911, for instance, the family had little contact at all with blacks.[15] This did not change until Maston entered Yale University in the 1930s. So, from childhood to maturity Maston's contact with blacks was positive, albeit limited. And despite humble origins, Maston, first at College Corner and later at Yale, had opportunities to associate with blacks on a basis quite different from that of southern whites who never ventured outside the region. Whatever the precise reasons, Maston, from early life on, genuinely cared for underprivileged people, black as well as white. "But why that attitude [of caring for blacks existed], I don't know," acknowledged Maston. "I really don't." Perhaps, he said, it was

[14]Rufus B. Spain, *At Ease in Zion: A Social History of Southern Baptists, 1865–1900* (Nashville: Vanderbilt University Press, 1967), p. 120. The same point is made by H. Shelton Smith, *In His Image, But . . . : Racism in Southern Religion, 1780–1910* (Durham, N.C.: Duke University Press, 1972); and Lillian Smith, *Killers of the Dream* (Garden City, N.Y.: Anchor Books, 1963), pp. 29–43, 69–74, 83–96.

[15]Maston, interview with author, p. 40.

"partly due to the fact that we were so poor that we had sympathy for these folks [blacks] who were [also] underprivileged."[16]

Although the exact origins of Maston's concern for racial justice cannot be pinpointed, his educational development no doubt broadened his understanding of social issues, including race. Maston's mother and father, who completed only the third and eighth grades, respectively, were eager for their son to attend college, although they were unable to afford the cost. A timely loan from a local Fountain City high school English teacher and campus jobs as a custodian of sorts and a waiter in the men's dorm enabled Maston to attend Carson-Newman College in Jefferson City, Tennessee, from 1916 to 1920. Maston's recollection of his undergraduate education was not particularly flattering. There were no memorable teachers or courses. As for the social gospel, "I remember hearing of [Walter] Rauschenbusch, but that was all," said Maston.[17]

But in 1920, beginning an institutional relationship that lasted forty-three years, Maston entered the fledgling Southwestern Baptist Seminary in Fort Worth, where he studied in some depth the social applications of Christianity. Despite the Norris imbroglio of the early 1920s, the seminary offered on a regular basis several courses on social Christianity. Dr. John M. Price offered "Social Teachings of the Bible," and James B. Gambrell taught "Christian Ethics." Maston took both courses during his first year in Fort Worth. And in 1921, when the School of Religious Education was formed under Price's leadership, applied Christianity became an established part of the curriculum.[18] Indeed, a few years later Price published *Christianity and Social Problems* (1928), a survey of "Christian sociology," based on his courses at the seminary. Maston read the manuscript and offered suggestions for improvement.[19] Meanwhile, in the School of Theology Maston encountered Walter T. Conner, who had done some work under Walter Rauschenbusch

[16] Ibid., p. 41.

[17] Oral Memoirs, Maston, pp. 10–13.

[18] Ibid., pp. 23, 108; Maston to author, May 25, 1981.

[19] John Milburn Price, *Christianity and Social Problems* (Nashville: Sunday School Board of the Southern Baptist Convention, 1928), p. 7.

at Rochester Theological Seminary from 1908 to 1910. Maston later recalled that "the whole atmosphere of southern Baptists . . . was rather sympathetic" to social Christianity in the early 1920s.[20] Although an overstatement, such a conclusion is understandable in light of Maston's student experiences, for at Southwestern he became familiar with the social gospel ministers, especially Rauschenbusch.

In 1922, while still working on a master's degree in the School of Religious Education, Maston accepted an opportunity to teach a course at the seminary on applied Christianity. This was the beginning of a distinguished teaching career. By 1925 the new instructor had obtained master's and doctoral degrees from Southwestern. However, his pursuit of formal education had not ended. In 1927 he obtained a Master of Arts in Sociology from Texas Christian University, and in 1928 and 1929 he took summer courses at the University of North Carolina and the University of Chicago, respectively. Howard W. Odum, a respected authority on southern culture, was one of Maston's professors at North Carolina.[21] Such training broadened his social vision in several areas, though race was already a matter of special concern. In 1927 he wrote "Racial Revelations," a pamphlet published by the Woman's Missionary Union of the Southern Baptist Convention. This was the first of a long series of observations by Maston on race and the Bible.[22]

In 1932, at the depth of the Great Depression, Maston entered Yale University. He later explained that he had chosen Yale in order "to expand my view, . . . to broaden my perspective." Actually, Maston's social thinking was refined rather than altered by the New Haven experience. He studied under H. Richard Niebuhr and examined the works of Reinhold Niebuhr, Karl

[20] Oral Memoirs, Maston, pp. 24–25.

[21] Ibid., pp. 15–20. For an account of Odum's racial thought, which changed significantly, see I. A. Newby, ed., *The Development of Segregationist Thought* (Homewood, Ill.: Dorsey Press, 1968), pp. 63–69; and George B. Tindall, *The Ethnic Southerners* (Baton Rouge: Louisiana State University Press, 1976), pp. 88–115. See also Fred C. Hobson, Jr., *Serpent in Eden: H. L. Mencken and the South* (Baton Rouge: Louisiana State University Press, 1974), pp. 84–88, 90–98.

[22] W. T. Moore, *His Heart Is Black* (Atlanta: Home Mission Board, Southern Baptist Convention, 1978), p. 61.

Barth, and Emil Brunner. Although acknowledging the influence of Richard Niebuhr, Maston believed "the overall impact of Yale" was more important than association with any one scholar.[23] Maston actually spent only two academic years at New Haven, 1932–33 and 1936–37, returning to Fort Worth after each occasion to resume teaching and to labor on a dissertation. In 1939 he obtained the coveted Yale Ph.D. Meanwhile, the range of his social concerns was indicated in a series of lessons he had written for the Southern Baptist Sunday School Board in 1933. Topic headings included "The Young Christian and Social Problems," "Christianizing Economic Life," "Improving Society through Legislation," and "The Christian Attitude toward Other Races."[24]

Maston's social consciousness, then, was kindled by humble family origins and refined by educational experiences. But how did he exert influence among fellow Texas Baptists, churchmen whose intense concern for personal evangelism caused him at times some uneasiness? President Lee Rutland Scarborough gave so much attention to soul winning, for instance, that Maston felt uncomfortable, but he managed to resolve this anxiety. Maston never thought "of personal evangelism and ethics as being two separate things." Rather, they were "just two ways of looking at the same coin." Neither aspect should be neglected, but Maston knew that other churchmen would always stress personal evangelism and missions. Hence, he chose to stress social ethics, believing his "primary emphasis ought to be on discipleship, the kind of life lived *after* one has been converted."[25] And the foundation of his influence was the seminary.

Maston spent his early years as a seminary professor preparing lectures and writing lessons on social problems for Sunday school and training union quarterlies. As commendable as these endeavors were, they failed to bring the kind of academic respect Maston desired. Consequently, he increasingly felt the need to attend a prestigious institution. "I wanted to go to a big university," he said, "because all my previous experience had

[23] Maston, interview with author, p. 11.
[24] Oral Memoirs, Maston, pp. 27–28, 71–72.
[25] Maston, interview with author, pp. 6, 8, 12, 29.

been in these smaller institutions."[26] Moreover, Maston's training in the School of Religious Education was suspect to some colleagues, particularly among "the old-timers in the School of Theology," whose ranks Maston joined when ethics was moved from Education to Theology in 1937.[27] Although it was never verbalized, Maston sensed some resistance in the School of Theology, primarily from Dr. Walter T. Conner. "I had a little problem coming from Religious Education over to Theology," Maston admitted. "I don't know of any formal resistance," but, he said, "I do know it took a little while to win . . . respect, from the viewpoint of scholarship and publishing."[28]

An Ivy League diploma was helpful, but ultimate academic acceptance, even from Conner, who was chairman of the Committee on Graduate Study, came as many of the better graduate students at Southwestern went into Christian ethics. When "these students began to specialize in ethics," declared Maston, "my colleagues were more or less forced to increase their respect for the [Ethics] Department."[29] And in the 1940s and 1950s Maston, despite his being a demanding teacher, did draw many of the better students.[30] Numerous factors accounted for this. Maston was always prepared for class; he stayed abreast of current literature in his field; he synthesized material from diverse sources; and he had time for students, undergraduates as well as graduates, outside the classroom. He was not a dynamic lecturer. His classroom style was "quiet, conversational, [and] folksy."[31] Former students held him in lofty esteem.[32]

Steadily, Maston increased course offerings in ethics and increasingly emphasized race. And President Scarborough, de-

[26] Ibid., p. 11.

[27] Oral Memoirs of Ralph A. Phelps, Jr., Waco, 1972, Baylor University Program of Oral History, p. 25.

[28] Maston, interview with author, p. 12.

[29] Ibid., p. 31.

[30] Oral Memoirs, Phelps, p. 25; James M. Dunn, interview with author, Dallas, May 23, 1979, p. 14. All citations from this interview are taken from a transcript of tape-recorded conversations. Foy Valentine to author, Aug. 20, 1979.

[31] Dunn, interview with author, pp. 11–15.

[32] Pinson, Approach to Christian Ethics, is a tribute to Maston, consisting of brief articles written by twenty-three of his former students.

spite his primary concern for evangelism, gave Maston encouragement and support.[33] In 1938, one year after the teaching of ethics was moved to the School of Theology, Maston introduced a new course, "Social Problems in the South," concentrating largely on racial conditions. And in 1944 in the midst of a global conflict fueled in part by Nazi racism, he offered "The Church and the Race Problem." For this class Fort Worth became a laboratory. Students went on field trips through black neighborhoods; they investigated specific aspects of the city's race problem, such as public schooling; and prominent blacks were invited to address the class. Meanwhile, since 1942 Maston had been teaching ethics full time, no longer dividing his attention among other fields.[34]

Maston, however, was more than a devoted classroom teacher. He was a prolific author as well. Indeed, as Maston recognized, his influence beyond the classroom stemmed largely from his writings.[35] Along with innumerable Sunday school and training union lessons, pamphlets, articles, and columns in Baptist weeklies, notably the *Baptist Standard*, Maston wrote nineteen books, ten published after his retirement.[36] His literary endeavors were twofold. He wanted to do "something that would be reasonably accepted from the viewpoint of college and seminary teachers, something more or less scholarly." *Christianity and World Issues* (Macmillan, 1957) and *Biblical Ethics: A Biblical Survey* (Word, 1967), which Maston considered his most scholarly efforts, grew out of this desire. Another reason Maston went to Yale was to enhance general academic acceptance of his scholarly works. He did not want to be ignored just because he "was a Southern Baptist . . . teaching way out here in the Southwest."[37]

That Maston sought academic respectability and recognition was apparent. Nonetheless, instead of addressing himself

[33] Maston to author, May 21, 1981.
[34] Pinson, *Approach to Christian Ethics*, p. 62.
[35] Maston, interview with author, p. 9.
[36] Pinson, *Approach to Christian Ethics*, pp. 83–85.
[37] Oral Memoirs, Maston, pp. 141, 145.

"generally to the Christian community," he devoted his attention primarily to Southern Baptists.[38] So in addition to learned studies, Maston wrote "these simpler books for the masses." Publications such as *Right or Wrong?* (Broadman, 1955) and *God's Will and Your Life* (Broadman, 1964), both directed at young people, were of this type.[39] Practically all of Maston's writings for the rank and file arose from a sense of need. Certainly this was the case with race. In an effort to help Southern Baptists understand this "major issue," Maston wrote *Of One* (1946), a reasoned plea for racial justice, almost a decade before the 1954 *Brown* decision. Though perhaps the most controversial, this was not the only work in which he dealt with this sensitive topic. *The Bible and Race* (1959), which Broadman Press, an agency of the Southern Baptist Convention, finally published after Maston toned it down some, and *Segregation and Desegregation* (1959), written upon request by Macmillan, offered calm advice for Christians grappling with racial issues in the late 1950s and early 1960s.[40]

And the impact of Maston's writings "for the masses," including articles in the *Baptist Standard*, pamphlets, and the aforementioned books, was considerable. To be sure, many readers dismissed the seminarian with the usual epithets. He was a "Negro lover," a dupe of the Communists, a troublemaker, unfit to teach in a Baptist institution, an amalgamationist, and just plain ignorant. A Baptist pastor from Greenville, South Carolina, considered *Of One* "the most dangerous unbiblical book that has been presented to our denomination in many decades."[41] After a lengthy denunication of Maston for writing *Of One*, another critic declared: "I for one are proud of the K.K.K. [I] hope they will live for ever to protect people from such a person as you, [you] negro lover." In 1956 a speech by Maston on "Southern Baptists and the Negro" to the Southern Baptist Convention in Kansas City evoked a similar reaction. A respondent from Little Rock, Arkansas, who wondered "how much the

---

[38] Maston, interview with author, p. 12.
[39] Oral Memoirs, Maston, pp. 145–46.
[40] Maston to author, Aug. 17, 1979; and Oral Memoirs, Maston, pp. 139–40.
[41] Letter to T. B. Maston, Feb. 27, 1946, Maston Collection.

negroes of this country [were] paying Maston," exclaimed: "If I were you I'd shut my mouth. If you want to live with negroes, go live with them, but don't try to make other people do it." Likewise, Buford C. Stockard, pastor of the Morningside Baptist Church, Graham, Texas, reacting to a series of Sunday school lessons written in 1958, accused Maston of "either purposely or ignorantly" propagating "the Pro-Communist line for Social Justice." And after reading *Segregation and Desegregation*, Kenneth G. Ansley, a businessman from East Chicago, Indiana, sent Maston a lengthy diatribe filled with racial slurs. "I think you are doing the whites a distinct disservice by advocating integration," he said. "Are we to be dragged down to a savage level and be a mongrel group [?]" Ansley, moreover, had an easy solution for Baptists who fretted over the effects of domestic racial practices on foreign missions—he believed all missionaries should be recalled. "We need them at home," Ansley claimed. Furthermore, "by introduction of sanitation we have increased the menace of communism by increasing the population which as soon as they outgrow our aid will be in as bad condition as formerly."[42] Patiently and kindly, Maston replied to such letters.

All respondents, however, were not critical. Many readers praised the Baptist leader. With perhaps a slight air of condescension, the Reverend Ronald Cloward of the Council on Christian Social Progress of the Northern Baptist Convention, New York, commended *Of One*. "Northerners are sometimes surprised to find how much real insight our Southern leaders have into the Race problem," he wrote. "This proves how provincial we are. More power to you." In Belton, South Carolina, the pastor of the Second Baptist Church, Lewis G. Prince, stated that he "heartily" agreed with "every premise" of *Of One*. "I had been thinking for some time that the time had come for someone to attack [segregation] with vigor and without compromise," he wrote. "You have done it." And from Chester, Virginia, a high school senior wrote that *Segregation and Desegregation* had been very helpful in a recent school debate on integration.

---

[42] Letter to Maston, undated and unsigned; letter to Maston, June 1, 1956, unsigned; Stockard to Maston, Feb. 22, 1961; Ansley to Maston, Oct. 6, 1969.

"We as Christians must not continue discrimination of the races by segregation," she asserted.[43] Overall, letters favorable and unfavorable to Maston's writings on race balanced out fairly evenly.

The classroom and the pen were the major sources of his influence, but Maston did not confine himself to those endeavors. An ordained deacon in the Gambrell Avenue Baptist Church, Fort Worth, he worked with his pastor to achieve desegregation of the local congregation. This was accomplished without incident.[44] And the admission of blacks in 1951 to day classes at Southwestern was the culmination of an effort begun within the seminary by Maston, other faculty members, and President Scarborough. Maston insisted the faculty would have admitted blacks even earlier, but resistance came from the trustees and rank-and-file Southern Baptists.[45] Maston also accepted many speaking engagements. In February, 1961, for instance, when the Dallas School Board was under court order to begin desegregation the coming September, Maston addressed the Dallas Baptist Pastors' Conference on "The Pastor's Role in a Community Facing School Desegregation." He encouraged pastors, as community leaders, to prepare their congregations to accept desegregation. They could do this by appealing to law and order, good citizenship, and civic pride, stressing that Dallas would not want to be linked to Little Rock and New Orleans. Maston also urged the ministers to confront the moral issues inherent in the quest for racial justice. It was not enough to exhort "thus saith the law." Pastors, Maston explained, should always "undergird" their position "with basic Christian principles." To the Baptist ethicist, this essentially meant that God was no respecter of persons and that Christ had died for all people. Because the *Dallas Morning News* covered the meeting, Maston's remarks had an impact throughout the area. He re-

[43] Cloward to Maston, Mar. 9, 1946; Prince to Maston, Mar. 20, 1946; Susan Bock to Maston, Oct. 30, 1960.

[44] Maston, interview with author, pp. 26–29.

[45] Blacks had been attending night classes at Southwestern for several years prior to 1951. Maston, interview with author, pp. 25–26.

ceived more than twenty letters, most of them "very critical."[46]
A Weatherford Baptist, after reading the *Dallas Morning News*
account, "was ashamed that a Baptist preacher would so express
himself." She concluded, "I hope people are not so ignorant that
they believe what you are teaching." At least a few readers, however, thought Maston's comments were "well said and so very
needful. How I hope and pray your advice will be heeded."[47]

Although his career demonstrates that individual effort can
be significant, Maston nevertheless believed that long-standing
social ills, particularly in the area of race, required group effort.
Individuals had to cooperate through organizations and institutions to accomplish needed change. In 1946, for instance, Maston urged pastors and lay persons alike to work closely with such
organizations as the Southern Regional Council, the National
Association for the Advancement of Colored People, and the Urban League to reduce prejudice.[48] But Maston did more than
encourage others—he set an example. Although not too active,[49]
he belonged to all three of these interracial agencies, and he
served for several years on the executive board of the Fort
Worth branch of the Urban League. And the Baptist teacher
fended off charges that such groups were pro-communist.[50] Indeed, in a 1947 address entitled "The Urban League and the
American Way of Life" at the third annual meeting of the Fort
Worth Urban League, Maston told the audience that the league
rested upon basic American ideals such as democracy and concern for the needy.[51]

Of course, as a devoted advocate of applied Christianity,

[46] *Dallas Morning News*, Feb. 21, 1961, sec. 4, p. 1; Maston to Mrs. Travis Carrington, Mar. 27, 1961. See also *Baptist Standard*, July 19, 1961, p. 8.

[47] The assumption that Maston was a Baptist preacher was common, but errone-
ous. Maston was a layman, never having been ordained as a minister. Mrs. Mattie Buck-
ley to Maston, Feb. 23, 1961; Mrs. Travis Carrington to Maston, Mar. 20, 1961.

[48] "The Christian Strategy in Regard to Race Relations," Aug. 26, 1946, 1950, Maston collection, Miscellaneous Articles.

[49] Maston, interview with author, p. 8.

[50] *Baptist Standard*, Aug. 10, 1950, p. 15.

[51] "The Urban League and the American Way of Life," Nov. 21, 1947, Maston
Collection, Miscellaneous Articles, 1945–1946, 1950.

Maston believed the church should be the institution to lead the quest for social justice.[52] It was this conviction which set in motion shortly after World War II a sequence of events culminating in the creation in 1950 of the Christian Life Commission of Texas, an agency dedicated to a social application of the "good news." In 1948 Maston corresponded with a small group of Texas Baptists, including Dr. J. Howard Williams, whose support Maston considered essential, about the possibility of a Christian Action Conference in Fort Worth.[53] In 1936 Williams had relinquished his position as executive secretary of the Baptist General Convention to accept the pastorate at the First Baptist Church, Amarillo. In late 1940, after concluding a one-year term as president of the General Convention, Williams left Amarillo to become minister of the First Baptist Church, Oklahoma City. After a successful five-year ministry in Oklahoma,[54] this indefatigable Baptist worker returned to Texas, serving a second time as executive secretary from 1946 to 1953. In 1948 Williams suffered a heart attack, and so the conference proposed by Maston never materialized.

At the 1949 General Convention in El Paso, however, Williams secured the appointment of a three-man committee consisting of Maston, Acker C. Miller, and William R. White, president of Baylor University, to study ways in which Texas Baptists could most effectively confront social ills. "It is my conviction that this convention should initiate some plan," Williams explained, "by which we can help our people to understand the grave issues of our day in terms of Christian faith and practice." Maston, White, and Miller accepted this charge, and after a few preliminary meetings the trio evolved into the Committee of Seven, with Maston as chairman. Arthur B. Rutledge, Maston's former student who was then pastor of the First Baptist Church, Marshall, was one of the seven. Another Maston protégé, Ralph

[52] See Thomas B. Maston, *Of One* (Atlanta: Home Mission Board, Southern Baptist Convention, 1946), p. 8; Thomas B. Maston, *Christianity and World Issues* (New York: Macmillan, 1957), p. 79.

[53] Maston, interview with author, pp. 14–15.

[54] *Baptist Standard*, Jan. 3, 1946, p. 1.

Phelps, soon joined the committee when one of the original seven became ill.[55]

In November, 1950, when Texas Baptists assembled in Fort Worth, Maston's committee, which had held three long meetings during the year, recommended the establishment of an agency designed to focus denominational attention on social concerns. As the committee explained, "the major need of our day is an effective working combination of a conservative theology, an aggressive, constructive evangelism and a progressive application of the spirit and teachings of Jesus to every area of life."[56] The Christian Life Commission of Texas was to be the vehicle through which these worthy objectives would be implemented.

Although this new organization was expected to grapple with social issues, Maston and his colleagues wisely avoided the word *social* in the selection of a name. "One reason for" this, Maston disclosed later, "was the prejudice of many Southern Baptists toward the so-called 'social gospel.'"[57] And the Committee of Seven had reason to be cautious. David M. Gardner, editor of the influential *Baptist Standard*, favored the abolition of the Social Service Commission of the Southern Baptist Convention, having been offended by its social activism, and W. A. Criswell, the prominent Dallas pastor, in September, 1949, had traced at length the shortcomings of the social gospel and had forcefully reasserted the traditional view that "our main business is everlastingly one of evangelism."[58] Given such sentiment, Maston and his associates did not want to create unnecessary problems for the Christian Life Commission by choosing an appellation that would alarm some churchmen. Consequently, in his report to the Fort Worth convention, Maston had origi-

[55] Baptist General Convention of Texas, *Proceedings*, 1949, pp. 25, 174; 1950, p. 181 (cited hereafter as BGCT, *Proceedings*). See also *Baptist Standard*, June 15, 1950, p. 3; Dec. 28, 1950, p. 3.

[56] BGCT, *Proceedings*, 1950, p. 181.

[57] Maston to author, June 11, 1981.

[58] Oral Memoirs of Acker C. Miller, Waco, 1973, Baylor University Program of Oral History, pp. 118–19; *Baptist Standard*, Sept. 22, 1949, pp. 1, 6, 12; Apr. 22, 1948, p. 4.

nally referred to the new body as the Commission on Problems in Christian Living.[59]

It was Acker C. Miller who suggested the title "Christian Life Commission," and, ironically, he was inspired by an evangelist who had misgivings about this planned venture into social Christianity. The night following Maston's report, a speaker from the Evangelistic Department, fearful that any emphasis on social involvement would detract from evangelism, "warned [the convention] against the appointment of a 'commission on the Christian life.'" Miller immediately turned to Maston, who was seated next to him in the audience, and whispered: "That's our name. . . . Why not call it the Christian Life Commission?"[60]

Maston and other prominent churchmen later insisted that the Christian Life Commission was primarily the work of J. Howard Williams.[61] Admittedly, the support of Williams was crucial. He was a respected and tireless worker whose friendships encompassed people of widely differing views. As executive secretary of the General Convention from 1946 to 1953, for instance, Williams was a member of the First Baptist Church, Dallas, and a close friend of the intensely evangelistic Dr. W. A. Criswell.[62] Later, as president of Southwestern Seminary from 1953 until his death in 1958, he and Maston enjoyed a warm friendship.[63] So Williams clearly was a denominational leader who could count on a broad base of support for his plans. According to Miller, if Williams supported something, Texas Baptists invariably went along.[64] His endorsement of the Christian Life Commission, therefore, was essential.

In other ways, however, Maston and Miller were just as important. Through his writings on numerous social issues, Maston had helped educate Texas Baptists on the need for a practical application of the scriptures. Moreover, he had schooled an

[59] BGCT, *Proceedings*, 1950, p. 188.

[60] Oral Memoirs, Miller, pp. 70–71, 87–88.

[61] Oral Memoirs, Maston, p. 100; Oral Memoirs, Miller, pp. 67, 71, 82; Oral Memoirs, Phelps, p. 44; and Valentine to author, Aug. 20, 1979.

[62] H. C. Brown, Jr., and Charles P. Johnson, eds., *J. Howard Williams: Prophet of God and Friend of Man* (San Antonio: Naylor, 1963), pp. 48, 57, 123.

[63] Maston, interview with author, pp. 15, 20.

[64] Miller to author, June 30, 1982.

army of students who were ideally suited to work through an agency such as the Christian Life Commission. Miller, as director of the Department of Interracial Cooperation, was already in the field working to improve race relations in Texas. Consequently, he was sympathetic with the purpose of the Christian Life Commission and was the logical choice as director when his department was absorbed by the new agency.[65]

Initially, there was no expressed opposition to the Christian Life Commission, but criticism soon surfaced.[66] There was speculation that the commission, fashioned by leaders who were ahead of their constituents on social issues, was basically out of step with the sentiments of rank-and-file Baptists in Texas. Dr. Ralph Phelps, who taught ethics with Maston at Southwestern before assuming the presidency of Ouachita Baptist College in Arkansas, insisted that if most Texas Baptists had realized how active the new agency was going to be, they would never have supported it. "Texas Baptists didn't have the foggiest idea that the Christian Life Commission would ever amount to anything," he argued.[67] Though Maston would not go that far, he nevertheless agreed that the Christian Life Commission was primarily the result of constructive Baptist leadership. "But . . . that's not only true of the Christian Life Commission," added he, "but almost everything else."[68]

There is little doubt that the Christian Life Commission was the handiwork of capable Baptist leaders, some of whom, such as Maston, certainly were ahead of the other Texans, non-Baptists as well as Baptists, on social issues. And some important churchmen definitely were unenthusiastic about this new denominational venture. W. A. Criswell, for instance, though not openly hostile, was not supportive.[69] But the prominent Dallas cleric did not represent all Baptists in Texas. By the late 1940s and early 1950s many church leaders were prepared to support

[65] BGCT, *Proceedings*, 1950, pp. 173, 175, 181; 1951, p. 198.
[66] Oral Memoirs, Miller, p. 71; Miller to author, June 30, 1982.
[67] Oral Memoirs, Phelps, pp. 44–45.
[68] Maston, interview with author, p. 16.
[69] Oral Memoirs of Jimmy Raymond Allen, Waco, 1973, Baylor University Program of Oral History, p. 116.

an organized effort in behalf of social justice. In Austin, Blake Smith, who had become pastor of the University Baptist Church in 1943, was an articulate spokesman for applied Christianity. Since the 1920s, when he first encountered the social gospel at Columbia and Yale universities, Smith had preached on social responsibility. In 1946, as the racial issue increasingly tested the faith and tolerance of many Christians, Smith's congregation posted a sign that read: "People of all races and nations welcome."[70] Smith did not wield much influence among fellow Baptists, however, since many churchmen considered him a theological liberal.[71]

But elsewhere across the state there were numerous pastors and laymen who were not only "sound" theologically but also progressive on social issues. Arthur B. Rutledge, whose Marshall congregation was in predominantly black Harrison county, addressed many social concerns, including race. By the late 1940s he had begun to nudge his flock toward racial justice. Shortly thereafter he became the first chairman of the new Christian Life Commission, serving from 1951 to 1955.[72] Likewise, pastors Herbert Howard, Park Cities Baptist Church, Dallas; Harold Basden, Gaston Avenue Baptist Church, Dallas; H. Strauss Atkinson, First Baptist, Canyon; Vernon O. Elmore, Baptist Temple, San Antonio; and Loren M. White, who succeeded Elmore at the Baptist Temple in 1963, recognized the social message of the gospel and applied it in their local congregations. Aside from Maston, Howard subsequently served on the Christian Life Commission longer than anyone else, and Basden was twice chairman of the agency.[73] And Atkinson, Elmore, and White, demonstrating the importance of pastoral leadership, all forthrightly confronted the racial issue, despite some opposition. Furthermore, White's San Antonio congregation provided English language classes for ethnics, developed

[70] Oral Memoirs of Blake Smith, Waco, 1972, Baylor University Program of Oral History, pp. 116–25, 149, 155–62, 197.

[71] Maston to author, July 30, 1981.

[72] Rutledge to Maston, May 9, 1946; BGCT, *Proceedings*, 1951, p. 199; *Christian Life Commission, Baptist General Convention of Texas, 1950–1970* (Dallas, Christian Life Commission of Texas, n.d.), p. 8.

[73] Oral Memoirs, Allen, pp. 112–13; *Christian Life Commission*, pp. 6–8.

day care and kindergarten programs, established a center for drug addicts based on the methadone approach, expanded recreational opportunities for neighborhood children, and initiated programs for older people.[74] So at the grass-roots level there was significant support by the early 1950s for a practical application of the scriptures. As Foy Valentine assessed the situation, the Christian Life Commission was not "an outgrowth of a particularly expanding social awareness among Texas Baptists in general," but conditions nevertheless were favorable.[75]

Advantageous circumstances also prevailed within Texas by the early 1950s. To the extent that the South's resistance to change can be attributed to its rural background and traditional values,[76] the Christian Life Commission was launched at a propitious moment. In 1950 Texas was no longer a rural state. Its populace was 62.7 percent urban. The population of Fort Worth, Maston's home since 1920, had more than tripled during the seminarian's long tenure at Southwestern, increasing from 106,482 to 356,268 in 1960. And Houston, Dallas, San Antonio, El Paso, and Beaumont–Port Arthur each experienced dramatic growth from 1940 to 1960.[77] As elsewhere, by 1950 race was perhaps the most serious social issue in these Texas cities, particularly with regard to housing, jobs, and education. However, after the 1954 *Brown* ruling, southern urban leaders often sought to ease racial tension, "less because they were committed to full racial equality than because they desired to protect their businesses and their national urban image."[78] So in terms of the urbanization of Texas and the readiness of many local Baptists to

[74]Elmore to author, Nov. 28, 1979; H. Strauss Atkinson to author, Jan. 28, 1980; and Loren M. White to author, Apr. 10, 1980.

[75]Valentine to author, Aug. 20, 1979.

[76]See Spain, *At Ease in Zion*, p. 211; John Lee Eighmy, *Churches in Cultural Captivity: A History of the Social Attitudes of Southern Baptists* (Knoxville: University of Tennessee Press, 1972), p. 55.

[77]*Dallas Morning News Texas Almanac and State Industrial Guide, 1970–1971, Tour Texas Edition* (Dallas: A. H. Belo Corp., 1969), pp. 165, 171–74.

[78]Blaine A. Brownell, *The Urban South in the Twentieth Century* (Saint Charles, Mo.: Forum Press, 1974), pp. 24–29; Numan V. Bartley, *The Rise of Massive Resistance: Race and Politics in the South During the 1950's* (Baton Rouge: Louisiana State University Press, 1969), pp. 23–24.

accept its leadership in applied Christianity, the time was auspicious for the Christian Life Commission.

Because of its position on specific issues, the Christian Life Commission would at times arouse opposition. In general, however, the new agency quickly won the confidence of fellow Texans. It did so by pursuing a basically conservative strategy. Although dramatizing for Texas Baptists the urgency of applied Christianity, and thus the desirability of social change in certain areas, the Christian Life Commission consistently counseled moderation and gradualism. As the Committee of Seven explained in 1950, "any program of social change should not only be Christian in its goals . . . but also in the methods . . . it uses to achieve those goals."[79] Again, the influence and thought of Thomas Maston were apparent.

Maston was a theological conservative in the tradition of Joseph M. Dawson. He could not have been otherwise. Like the Waco pastor, Maston could not have retained his position for so many years at Southwestern nor exercised much influence among fellow churchmen had he not shared their conservative theology. But as demonstrated by Maston's career, theological conservatism does not automatically predispose one to view social ills as consequences of human depravity and, hence, something to be endured rather than solved. Although convinced of the flawed character of human nature, Maston saw social ills as an indication of inequities within the social structure. So, like Walter Rauschenbusch, whom he admired, and Reinhold Niebuhr, whom he encountered while at Yale, Maston easily combined theological conservatism and social activism. Indeed, on social issues, the seminarian was a progressive. Perhaps Maston said it best with regard to Southern Baptists in general. What Southern Baptists have "needed for a long time," he asserted, was "a combination of what I call a basically conservative theology and a social liberalism." For Maston, there was no contradiction in this.[80]

But if theological conservatism did not obscure Maston's grasp of social maladies, it predisposed him, as it has the direc-

[79] BGCT, *Proceedings*, 1950, p. 182.
[80] Maston, interview with author, pp. 5, 34–35.

tors of the Christian Life Commission of Texas, to a cautious
political strategy. For two generations Maston advised Southwestern students to proceed cautiously when dealing with sensitive issues. If one moved too rapidly and aggressively, local
churchmen would become alienated and all chance for improvement would be lost. Clarence Jordan, the noted Southern Baptist who in 1942 founded Koinonia Farm, a racially integrated
community near Americus, Georgia, was a case in point. In
1946, during Student Week at the Ridgecrest Baptist Encampment in North Carolina, students voted overwhelming to admit
blacks. Camp officials refused, however, claiming that the time
was not right. Jordan, who was on the platform when the decision was announced, promptly rebuked Ridgecrest authorities.
The time, he retorted, was never ripe for the application of
Christian principles. Instead of being captives of their culture,
the churches should be agents of social change. Jordan had been
invited annually to Student Week from 1940 to 1946. He was not
asked to return.[81] Maston believed that Jordan's outspokenness,
although courageous, eroded his influence. The seminarian
readily conceded, however, that such people as Jordan made it
easier for moderates such as himself to gain acceptance. Still,
Maston insisted, one must "start where the people are and keep
the pressure in the right place, pointed in the right direction."
This eventually would yield desirable and lasting results.[82]

Reformers eager for quick improvement would readily find
fault with Maston's cautiousness. Even Maston recognized the
danger in his strategy of compromising too much and settling for
too little.[83] Judging by his accomplishments, however, Maston
never compromised too much. Furthermore, his vision of social
Christianity and his strategy for dealing with public concerns
were institutionalized in the Christian Life Commission, which
commenced its operations under the capable direction of
Acker C. Miller in 1950.

[81] Davis C. Hill, "Southern Baptist Thought and Action in Race Relations,
1940–1950" (Th.D. diss., Southern Baptist Theological Seminary, 1952), p. 329.

[82] Maston, interview with author, pp. 50–51.

[83] Ibid., pp. 51–52.

(*Left*) Benjamin Franklin Riley, pastor of the First Baptist Church, Houston (1900–1907); head of the Anti-Saloon League in Texas (1907–1909); and a progressive on the racial issue. (*Right*) Charles T. Alexander while pastor at the First Baptist Church, Cleburne (1902–1905). (Courtesy Southwestern Baptist Seminary)

Walter T. Conner, in his office at Southwestern Baptist Theological Seminary, 1947. (Courtesy Southwestern Baptist Theological Seminary)

Joseph M. Dawson at work in the library-study of the church parsonage, Waco. (Courtesy Texas Collection, Baylor University)

John M. Price, Sr., in his office at Southwestern Baptist Theological Seminary, 1951. (Courtesy Southwestern Baptist Seminary)

A. C. Miller chatting with Foy Valentine in the offices of the Christian Life Commission, SBC, Nashville, 1981. (Courtesy David Wilkinson, Christian Life Commission, Nashville)

Thomas B. Maston, November, 1973. (Courtesy Southwestern Baptist Seminary)

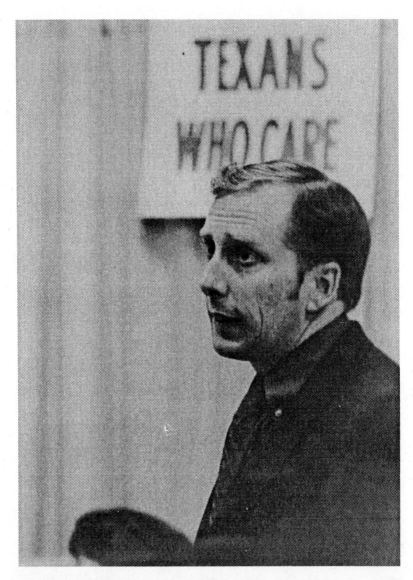

James Dunn, director of the Christian Life Commission, ca. 1970.
(Courtesy Southwestern Baptist Theological Seminary)

(*Left*) Foy Valentine, ca. 1970. (*Right*) Jimmy Allen, 1981, shortly after becoming president of the Radio and Television Commission of the Southern Baptist Convention in Fort Worth. (Courtesy Southwestern Baptist Seminary)

Foy Valentine, executive secretary of the Christian Life Commission of the Southern Baptist Convention, greets his former mentor, Dr. T. B. Maston, and Mrs. Maston, 1971. (Courtesy Southwestern Baptist Theological Seminary)

Directors of the Christian Life Commission of Texas (*left to right*): Phil Strickland, 1980–   ; James Dunn, 1968–80; Jimmy Allen, 1960–68; Foy Valentine, 1953–60; and A. C. Miller, 1950–53. (Courtesy the Christian Life Commission of Texas)

CLC publications such as these in the *Strengthening Families* series address current social issues affecting families.

CLC publication of the series *The Bible Speaks* reflects the conservative theology behind social Christianity among Southern Baptists.

6

Leadership and Institutional
Development of the CLC,
1950–1980

THE Christian Life Commission (CLC) today is securely nestled within the bureaucracy of the Baptist General Convention. As reflected in a steadily expanding budget and a growing professional staff, it has become a major agency. This was not always so. From the outset, some Texas Baptists were philosophically opposed to the new commission, while many others objected to its stand on specific issues, such as race, abortion, or political activism. Consequently, in 1959 there was a strong move to downgrade, if not destroy, the CLC. The effort, which was partially successful, offered a glimpse of intradenominational politics, as individual churchmen maneuvered for position and influence. That the CLC survived at all to become eventually an integral part of Texas Baptist life is both an indication of support within the General Convention and a tribute to the outstanding quality of its leadership.

As established in 1950, the CLC was composed of nine persons who served staggered three-year terms. A chairman was to be elected from within this group. In turn, this body, the CLC, was to be guided by a full-time director and professional staff located in Dallas. The director was responsible to both the CLC and the executive secretary of the General Convention.[1] This structure has been modified only twice. In 1952 the commission's

---

[1] Baptist General Convention of Texas, *Proceedings*, 1950, p. 188 (cited hereafter as BGCT, *Proceedings*). Originally, in addition to the nine elected commission members, the executive heads of five other departments were automatically members of the CLC. The executive secretary of the General Convention and his associate were ex officio members. Not until 1967 did the executive heads of these other departments cease meeting with the CLC. See BGCT Proceedings, 1967, pp. 28, 59; Oral Memoirs of Jimmy Raymond Allen, Waco, 1973, Baylor University Program of Oral History, p. 125.

membership was increased to twelve, and in 1967 it was expanded to fifteen, with a minimum of six members from the laity.[2]

In the early 1950s the new agency faced a formidable task. Many churchmen were suspicious, believing the commission would detract from evangelism. W. A. Criswell, for instance, was unenthusiastic.[3] Soon, many other churchmen were annoyed by the agency's stand on the racial issue, which became all the more intense after the *Brown* decision in 1954. So, while laboring to expand the social horizons of Texas Baptists and focusing denominational attention on divisive issues, the CLC was compelled to reassure fellow Baptists that a broader application of the scriptures would neither detract from nor become a substitute for personal evangelism.[4]

In 1953, seeking to assuage critics, the CLC forcefully declared that evangelism and ethics were inseparable. The present "emphasis on the practical applications of Christianity," stated the commission, was in the tradition of "astute leaders among us" who through the years had "challenged Texas Baptists, not to discontinue their faithful emphasis on the necessity of the new birth, but to proclaim with proportionate emphasis the moral responsibilities of the Christian life." And there was sound scriptural basis for ethical commitment. Practical Christianity, the commission elaborated, "did not begin in 1950, nor yet with Rauschenbusch," but was "boldly proclaimed throughout the Bible," from the Genesis declaration that Cain "was his brother's keeper" to the eighth-century prophets to Jesus' ministry. Consequently, instead of making "a novel and unnecessary innovation" in creating the Christian Life Commission, Texas Baptists merely "made a long over-due place for a doctrine" that was "an utterly vital part of the Christian religion."[5] The following year the CLC further explained that one's relationship to God was "very closely tied" to service to fellow humans, and "the Chris-

---

[2] BGCT, *Proceedings*, 1952, p. 197; 1967, pp. 28, 59.

[3] Oral Memoirs of Acker C. Miller, Waco, 1973, Baylor University Program of Oral History, pp. 87–89, 91; Oral Memoirs, Allen, p. 116.

[4] See *Baptist Standard*, June 14, 1951, p. 6.

[5] BGCT, *Proceedings*, 1953, p. 195.

tian Life Commission was established by this Convention in 1950 to give direction to our efforts at this point." Moreover, the CLC went on to rebuke those Baptists whose faith was one-dimensional, asserting that churchmen who believed "that Christianity was never meant to piddle in politics or interfere with economics, or wrestle with race relations or fool with family life or meddle with moral issues" reduced "their Christianity . . . [to] the Christianity of the vesper, the organ, the vested choir, and the dimly lighted aisles." Said the commission: "They have divorced their religion from life and in so doing have forsaken the New Testament pattern, only to be forsaken themselves by the Holy Spirit of God."[6] Similar declarations would be repeated many times.[7]

Such reproach by an upstart like the CLC no doubt rankled many of the faithful. The young commission was able to get away with it, however, because of the quality of its membership and professional staff. The CLC has attracted some of the denomination's more able and respected leaders. Members have been drawn from the ranks of not only pastors but also educators, homemakers, lawyers, state legislators, journalists, physicians, and businessmen and women. To the extent that this represents a cross-section of Texas Baptist life, it suggests that the denomination has shed its rural, humble beginnings. Thomas Maston, who was on the commission at various stages for a total of eighteen years, was the most prominent member. Despite a full teaching load at the seminary, he attended meetings, helped write pamphlets, always emphasized the necessity of a biblical basis for social involvement, and established the tradition of having an ethicist from Southwestern Seminary on the commission. Although not as well known nationally as Maston, Herbert Howard, pastor of the Park Cities Baptist Church, Dallas, and an informed and knowledgeable churchman who had studied under ethicist Jesse B. Weatherspoon at Southern Seminary, was also a valuable CLC member. Like Maston, he was on the CLC from the beginning, eventually serving fifteen years. The first chairman, Arthur Rutledge, provided excellent leadership from 1951

[6] Ibid., 1954, pp. 169–70.
[7] Ibid., 1964, p. 29; 1967, pp. 99–100; and 1975, p. 31.

to 1955. William R. White, president of Baylor University, served from 1950 to 1956. His grasp of social Christianity did not match that of Maston, Howard, or Rutledge, but his presence on the CLC during its formative years was enormously helpful. Just to have a person of White's stature on the new agency was of considerable importance.[8] Diplomacy and politics have at times figured in the selection process. Although never a member, J. Howard Williams was always supportive of the CLC, and his influence among Texas Baptists was considerable.

The positions of denominational leadership subsequently held by many members is another indication of the commission's caliber. Maston chaired the Southern Baptist Advisory Council on Work with Negroes, created by the national convention after the 1954 Supreme Court desegregation ruling. In 1958 Rutledge was elected director of the Division of Missions by the Home Mission Board of the Southern Baptist Convention.[9] Soon thereafter he became the executive secretary of the Home Mission Board.[10] Orba Lee Malone, an El Paso attorney, was on the CLC three different times and served as chairman in 1959 and again in 1970. In 1962 he was elected chairman of the Christian Life Commission of the Southern Baptist Convention in Nashville.[11] William R. Pinson, Jr., an associate director of the CLC from 1957 to 1963, later served on the fifteen-member commission from 1967 to 1972.[12] After a stint as president of Golden Gate Baptist Theological Seminary in California, Pinson in 1982 was selected to succeed James H. Landes as director of the executive board of the General Convention.

Of course, not all members of the CLC fully shared its objectives. According to James Dunn, who became director of the agency in 1968, one of two things usually occurred in these cases. Frequently, the member developed an appreciation of the social aspects of the gospel. Dunn interpreted this as intellectual

[8] Maston to author, June 11, 1981.

[9] *Baptist Standard*, Dec. 31, 1958, p. 14.

[10] *Annual* of the Southern Baptist Convention (Nashville, 1965), p. 159; *Encyclopedia of Southern Baptists* (Nashville: Broadman Press, 1982), IV, 2444.

[11] *Baptist Standard*, Mar. 14, 1962, p. 11.

[12] *Christian Life Commission, Baptist General Convention of Texas, 1950–1970* (Dallas: Christian Life Commission, n.d.), pp. 5–8.

"growth and maturation." But other members simply went along with the CLC "out of a sense of commitment to the denomination, as a duty to the denomination." In either event, the result was a high level of agreement on the commission, even on the more controversial issues. Consequently, the commission's annual report to the General Convention often reflected the unanimous judgment of the membership.[13] This was a tribute to executive leadership.

From Acker C. Miller to James Dunn, the directors of the CLC have been consistently outstanding. All four men were of relatively humble origins; they were brought up in homes in which the Baptist faith was important; they recognized the value of education; they became ordained ministers and held pastorates before joining the CLC; they were able platform speakers, although each somewhat different in style; they wrote lucidly; and each one experienced considerable ecclesiastical success in Texas and beyond. With the exception of Miller, they all earned doctorates from Southwestern Seminary, majoring in ethics and writing dissertations under Thomas Maston. They were all theological conservatives who believed in the flawed nature of humanity and the tenacity of sin. This view influenced their approach to social problems. Though recognizing the necessity of social change, they pursued it cautiously. James Dunn, in words strikingly reminiscent of Maston, said it plainly. "I'm an incrementalist, a reformer rather than a radical. I don't want to destroy institutions, but to improve them."[14] With the exception of Foy Valentine, the directors came from north central and west Texas. Two were reared in large metropolitan centers; the other two had rural backgrounds. And each except Miller was relatively young and ambitious when he became director of the CLC.

Acker C. Miller was born on a horse ranch near San Angelo in December, 1891. Three years later his family moved to Colorado City, where Miller grew to maturity. In the fall, 1917, following his graduation from Hardin-Simmons College, a Baptist school at Abilene, Miller enrolled in Southern Seminary. His

[13] James M. Dunn, interview with author, Dallas, May 23, 1979, pp. 37–38. All citations from this interview are taken from a transcript of tape-recorded conversations.
[14] Ibid., p. 43.

choice was revealing. It would have been easier to have gone to
Southwestern Seminary in Fort Worth, but the youthful Miller
was eager to leave Texas in order to broaden his vision. Besides,
he later recalled that instructors at the Fort Worth seminary
"were teaching the books that the Louisville men were writing." [15]

The young Texan's studies at Southern Seminary were inter-
rupted by World War I. In 1917 Miller enlisted in the army as a
chaplain and subsequently served eighteen months, although
never overseas. Upon returning to the Kentucky seminary in
1919, Miller met another student from Texas, J. Howard Williams, who was to become a dynamic force in Texas Baptist life.
Miller's experience at Southern fulfilled his expectations. His
perspective definitely was broadened. Before going to Louisville, Miller had no understanding of the social aspects of faith.
"I didn't have any source from which I could get it," he explained. But at Southern, Miller studied under Dr. Charles Gar-
diner, who introduced him to Walter Rauschenbusch and other
social gospel ministers. Miller especially enjoyed reading the
sermons of the noted liberal minister Harry Emerson Fosdick.
Those sermons, he said, "did me a great deal of good, . . . and I
found nothing that was so terribly upsetting as far as his statements were concerned." [16]

In 1921, with the B.D. from Southern, the Texas minister
returned home. He spent the next twenty years pastoring to
small congregations in Cleveland, Oklahoma (1921–26), Cisco,
Texas (1926–31), and Belton, Texas (1931–40). In January, 1941,
he went to work for the Baptist General Convention, directing
denominational work with soldiers during World War II. From
this, Miller went on to lead the Department of Interracial Cooperation in 1944, which in 1947 was renamed Our Ministry with
Minorities. In purpose and scope, this newly fashioned ministry
foreshadowed the Christian Life Commission. In addition to coordinating endeavors with all racial minorities in Texas, it sought
to apply the gospel in a practical way to a wide range of social
concerns. [17] Because of the nature of his responsibilities within

[15] Oral Memoirs, Miller, p. 24.
[16] Ibid., pp. 26, 29.
[17] Ibid., pp. 54, 60–65.

the General Convention, Miller was the logical person to head the new Christian Life Commission in 1950. His own grasp of social and racial issues had matured considerably since 1941; he had amply demonstrated his administrative ability in recent convention posts; he was widely respected around the state; his theology, as perceived by fellow Baptists, was sound; and he understood and appreciated the need to educate evangelistic-minded Baptists on social Christianity.

Although his tenure was brief, lasting only through 1952, Miller charted the basic course followed by the Texas commission ever since. At regularly scheduled quarterly meetings and special work sessions, his commission confronted issues and mapped strategy. Knowing that Baptists would have to be shown that applied Christianity was firmly grounded in scripture, Miller immediately embarked on an educational and organizational campaign. His commission wrote and distributed tracts, published articles in the *Baptist Standard*, and conducted seminars around the state on race, industrial relations, world order, family life, and public morals.[18] Notably, in Miller's first year the CLC developed a body of literature entitled "The Bible Speaks." Three pamphlets in this series begun before Miller resigned were "The Bible Speaks on Race," "The Bible Speaks on Economics," and "The Bible Speaks on Family."[19] Thomas Maston believed this series, quoting directly from the Bible, was largely responsible for giving "the Christian Life Commission its good start."[20] Distributed by the millions, these brief tracts certainly had an enormous impact. Placed "in churches everywhere, . . . they were used as sermon outlines by *hundreds* of preachers all over the state."[21] Always, Miller was careful to point out that this social emphasis was essential to "the full gospel," inasmuch as the Bible taught that "man's spiritual relationship to God imposes on him a moral responsibility to his fellowman."[22]

[18] Ibid., p. 91. See also *Baptist Standard*, June 14, 1951, p. 6; and June 21, 1951, p. 9.

[19] Oral Memoirs, Miller, p. 90.

[20] Maston to author, Aug. 21, 1981.

[21] Dunn, interview with author, p. 39. See also Oral Memoirs of Foy Dan Valentine, Waco, 1975–1976, Baylor University Program of Oral History, Interview 3, p. 4.

[22] *Baptist Standard*, Feb. 28, 1952, p. 3; June 5, 1952, p. 4.

This instructional drive was paralleled by an attempt to organize Christian life committees at the local associational level.[23] Miller explained that each of the associations within the state was urged to establish a standing committee through which the state commission could outline its purpose and goals and distribute ideas and literature to the rank and file. Most of the associations held monthly workers' conferences, Miller elaborated, "and we would try at these monthly conferences to have the associational Committee on the Christian Life to bring a brief report . . . followed by a speaker and discussion."[24] Thus, educational and organizational endeavors coalesced, one reinforcing the other.

In June, 1952, Miller announced his resignation. However, the sixty-one-year-old Baptist leader was not retiring from active church life. On the contrary, he was planning to move to Nashville in January, 1953, to serve as executive secretary of the Social Service Commission of the Southern Baptist Convention, a post he retained until 1960. Meanwhile, Texas Baptists, who agreed that Miller's "wise leadership and sane direction" had gotten the new CLC off to a good start,[25] faced the difficult task of finding a suitable successor. Ordinarily, the opportunity to head an organization within the General Convention would have produced several eager prospects. Such was not the case with the young CLC. Because the CLC was not yet firmly established and was still an object of some suspicion, leadership of the commission was not yet seen as a sure route to advancement among Texas Baptists. As late as 1960 Jimmy Allen feared the worst for his career when he became director.[26]

In terms of background and training, Foy Valentine was the most likely replacement for Miller. Born on July 3, 1923, he grew up in Edgewood, a small rural community in northeast Texas. His social outlook was influenced by his parents and the

---

[23] Within the Baptist General Convention, locally autonomous churches are grouped geographically into associations. There are approximately 115 such associations throughout Texas.

[24] Oral Memoirs, Miller, pp. 90–91.

[25] BGCT, *Proceedings*, 1953, pp. 195–96.

[26] Oral Memoirs, Allen, pp. 105–107.

Great Depression. His family came through the 1930s without experiencing severe hardship, but Valentine was aware of privation, and this colored his perception of government. He believed that government, as exemplified by various New Deal programs, could and should be used to ameliorate human want. Valentine asserted that east Texans, like the embattled Populists, were fiercely independent, poor people who wanted "the government not to provide welfare for the rich but to do something for everybody."[27] Valentine credited his parents for helping him "to recognize the social imperatives of the Christian faith." His father, whose formal education ended with the sixth grade, was a dirt farmer; his mother, who attended but did not graduate from Baylor University, taught school in Edgewood; both were faithful members of the local Baptist church. His parents taught him not only the virtues of the Protestant ethic but also that religion was to be applied to everyday affairs. From his father, Valentine learned that blacks were to be respected. At about the age of twelve he made a profession of faith and joined the church of his parents.[28]

By the time Valentine entered the Edgewood Independent School, he was clearly an achiever with political aspirations. He was class president his last two years in high school, president of the Future Farmers of America, and an avid debater. The senior class voted him the student most likely to become governor. Appropriately, Valentine planned to attend the University of Texas, study law, and eventually enter politics. Shortly after graduation his plans changed abruptly when he accepted a call to preach.[29]

Valentine subsequently pursued a ministerial career with the same determination evident in his previous planning for political success. East Texas Baptist College at nearby Marshall would have been more convenient, but Valentine went to Baylor. Having decided "to be a preacher of the gospel," he resolved to "go to the biggest and best Baptist school available." Valentine took Baylor in stride. Despite a part-time, off-campus job, he

---

[27] Oral Memoirs, Valentine, Interview 1, pp. 22–23.
[28] Valentine to author, Aug. 20, 1979. See also Oral Memoirs, Valentine, Interview 1, pp. 7–11.
[29] Oral Memoirs, Valentine, Interview 1, pp. 13–14, 26–27.

led an active campus life, running for every office available. More importantly, his educational experiences in Waco matured the seeds of social awareness planted by his parents. Clarence Jordan, who visited Baylor in the early 1940s, was especially influential. To Valentine, Jordan was "one of the great Christians of our time." In 1944, following graduation from Baylor, Valentine spent the summer at Koinonia Farm. Jordan had established the racially integrated community near Americus, Georgia, in 1942, and through it he sought to share agricultural knowledge with poor farmers and to demonstrate in a practical way the Christian values of brotherhood, peace, and sharing. Although genuinely impressed by the "ideals and idealism" of Jordan, the pragmatic Texan considered the Koinonia experiment unworkable. "I did not see it then as the pattern of the future," Valentine observed, but rather "as just one Christian man's witness to the world." In that respect, Koinonia Farm "had great value."[30]

After ten weeks under Jordan's tutelage, Valentine enrolled at Southwestern Seminary in the fall of 1944. Interested in Christian ethics, he quickly gravitated toward Thomas Maston. Valentine admired the visionary Jordan, but he felt more at home with the practical-minded Maston. To the Baylor graduate, Maston "was a God-called teacher" who was in touch with reality. The Southwestern ethicist, Valentine explained, "opened up . . . new vistas and new understandings of what the church ought to be doing, and what I as a minister of the gospel ought to be attempting."[31] In 1947 Valentine completed the requirements for the Th.M. and two years later obtained the Th.D., writing a dissertation entitled "A Historical Study of Southern Baptists and Race Relations, 1917–1947." The young seminary graduate then went to the First Baptist Church, Gonzales, in 1950.

By this time the able and articulate Valentine had already attracted the attention of leaders within the Dallas bureaucracy. From 1947 to 1948 he had served the convention as a special representative on race relations, and from 1949 to 1950 he had directed Baptist student activities in Houston colleges. After he

[30] Ibid., pp. 31, 32–39, 42; Interview 2, pp. 13–14.
[31] Ibid., Interview 2, pp. 16–18.

went to Gonzales, his ties to the General Convention increased. First, he was elected to serve on the important executive board of the convention and soon thereafter was appointed to the nine-member CLC. Given his training, obvious interest in applied Christianity, and close ties to prominent denominational leaders, Valentine appeared to Executive Secretary J. Howard Williams to be the obvious choice as Miller's replacement. Happy in Gonzales, Valentine turned aside Williams's initial overture. The executive secretary offered the position to at least two other men, then returned to Valentine. This time the persuasive Williams prevailed. In June, 1953, shortly before his thirtieth birthday, Valentine took the job.[32]

As director of the CLC, Valentine followed essentially the same course as his predecessor, although at an accelerated pace. An excellent speaker, the youthful minister tirelessly traveled the state, attending local associational meetings, conducting seminars, addressing college audiences, and visiting regional Baptist encampments at Palacios and elsewhere.[33] Moreover, the volume and distribution of tract literature grew enormously under Valentine. Besides "The Bible Speaks," new series entitled "Christian Answers to Family Problems," "Christian Principles Applied," and "Teen Talk" were added to the inventory. Among the issues addressed were race, political activism, war and peace, economic concerns, and a variety of family-related matters. Additionally, a booklet was prepared on "Bases for Separation of Church and State." When Valentine took the helm, the commission was distributing about 25,000 pieces of tract literature annually; when he left in 1960, the figure was in excess of 1,235,000 pieces annually.[34] Valentine persuaded the Nashville-based Broadman Press, the publishing arm of the Southern Baptist Convention, to print its first work on social ethics—*Christian Faith in Action* (1956), a compilation of sermons.[35]

[32] Ibid., pp. 24–28.
[33] Ibid., Interview 3, p. 4.
[34] BGCT, *Proceedings*, 1960, p. 104; *Christian Life Commission*, pp. 9–10.
[35] Oral Memoirs, Valentine, Interview 3, pp. 10–11.

Valentine believed the launching of an annual workshop to focus attention on social ethics was one of the more noteworthy educational programs of his tenure. Begun in 1957 and usually held at Southwestern Seminary, these yearly meetings attempted "to bring together a cross section of Baptist leadership, particularly pastors, to discuss the application of the gospel to a particular area of life."[36] Continued by his successors, the workshop has become a standard feature of the CLC program. Each of the first three workshops grappled with an assortment of issues, such as race, church and state, and politics,[37] but thereafter they were organized around one general topic. In 1960 and again in 1965 the conference theme was "Christianity and Political Action." Gov. John Connally was a featured participant in 1965. In 1962 the topic was "Christianity and Race Relations," and in 1975 it was "Unto Caesar . . . Unto God . . . ," dealing with civil religion.[38]

Valentine also enjoyed considerable organizational success at the local level. In 1956 there were only 14 associational Christian life committees. Four years later there were 110.[39] These impressive figures are probably misleading. Jimmy Allen, who succeeded Valentine in 1960, maintained that the commission had actually established associational committees only in the larger cities. Elsewhere, what often passed as a committee was no more than one person through whom the CLC disseminated information.[40] Nevertheless, whether through committees or reliable individuals, the commission under Valentine's direction forged a statewide network of local contacts.

In 1960 Valentine once again succeeded A. C. Miller, who had recently stepped down as executive secretary of the Christian Life Commission in Nashville.[41] Unlike 1953, when he had

[36] Valentine to author, Aug. 20, 1979.

[37] *Baptist Standard*, Mar. 1, 1958, p. 4; Jan. 14, 1959, p. 5; Feb. 18, 1959, pp. 12–13.

[38] Ibid., Feb. 17, 1965, p. 11 *Christian Life Commission*, p. 11; BGCT, *Proceedings*, p. 8.

[39] *Christian Life Commission*, p. 8.

[40] Oral Memoirs, Allen, pp. 108–109.

[41] In 1953, shortly after Miller arrived in Nashville, the Social Service Commission

to be coaxed by J. Howard Williams, now Valentine was eager to accept the new challenge.[42] Before going to Nashville, however, Valentine encouraged Jimmy Raymond Allen to assume leadership of the Texas CLC. Although fearful that the job would close the door to prestigious urban pulpits, Allen took charge of the commission in June, 1960.[43] Bright, dynamic, and politically oriented, Allen was an excellent choice for the turbulent 1960s.

Allen was born in Hope, Arkansas, on October 26, 1927. Not long afterward the lure of employment took the family to Detroit. Hard times had already come to the auto city, however, and Allen's father struggled at selling insurance from 1929 to 1932. He then became a preacher and ventured to Dallas. Frequently on the move, the Allen family lived in thirteen different Dallas locations. Growing up in area Baptist churches, Allen made a profession of faith at the age of seven. Ten years later he followed his father into the ministry.[44]

Allen's determination to succeed was evident by the time he entered Forest High School in south Dallas. There was no pressure from his parents to make good grades, but Allen often rose at 4:00 A.M. to study because he wanted to excel scholastically. In 1944 the sixteen-year-old youth graduated from high school and soon thereafter enrolled at Howard Payne College, a Baptist school in Brownwood. He went to Howard Payne, "a common man's school," because Baylor was too expensive. Eager to do well, he took a course in shorthand to improve his note-taking skills. Although Allen enjoyed the friendliness of Brownwood students, he was disappointed in the academic quality of the Baptist institution. The facilities were inadequate and the level of instruction poor. Consequently, Allen felt unprepared academically when he entered Southwestern Seminary in 1948.[45]

Allen's association with the seminary lasted until 1958, a ten-year period during which he also took a job for the General

---

of the Southern Baptist Convention emulated Texas Baptists, changing its name to the Christian Life Commission.

[42] Oral Memoirs, Valentine, Interview 4, pp. 2–4.
[43] Oral Memoirs, Allen, pp. 103, 105–107.
[44] Ibid., pp. 1–10.
[45] Ibid., pp. 25–26, 31, 43–45.

Convention as director of the Royal Ambassadors, a Baptist organization for young boys, and held three pastorates. It was a decade of intellectual and spiritual growth for the young minister, as classroom lessons and practical experiences converged to broaden his understanding of the Christian faith. Like so many other Baptists, Allen believed Christianity *was* evangelism, and throughout his undergraduate years in Fort Worth, 1948–51, his interests remained narrowly evangelistic. He took two courses in ethics, one on the family from Thomas Maston and another on race from Ralph Phelps, but was unimpressed by either. The youth evangelism movement, strong in Texas in the late 1940s and early 1950s, was more to his liking. The turning point came when Allen, as a graduate student, took Maston's course on the philosophy of ethics. The effect was apparent. Allen immediately turned his attention to Christian ethics, eventually completing a dissertation under Maston's guidance.[46]

But Maston was not altogether responsible for the redirection of Allen's life. During the summer of 1944, after graduation from high school, Allen had attended a Baptist encampment in Ridgecrest, North Carolina, where he encountered Clarence Jordan. The Koinonia leader ridiculed the racist attitudes Allen had learned from his parents and grandparents. Although the young Texan became "very angry," the experience set him to thinking about the racial issue. He would later thank Jordan.[47] Similarly, at Southwestern Seminary, Allen grew in his understanding of the race issue, as well as other social concerns. Practical experience, however, was equally important to the student's development. Field training reinforced academic learning. As Allen ministered to his successive congregations in north central and east Texas in the 1950s, he saw clearly that racism was a blind spot in Texas Baptist life, and he resolved to help fellow churchmen understand the ethical implications of their faith.[48] Just as experiences in the Hell's Kitchen and Detroit contributed, respectively, to the maturation of Walter Rauschenbusch

[46] Ibid., pp. 85–86, 89.
[47] Ibid., pp. 18, 32–33.
[48] Ibid., pp. 94–95, 97.

and Reinhold Niebuhr, so also was Jimmy Allen affected by his experience.

In 1958, when Allen obtained the Th.D., he made a decision that reveals the inner man. His real name is Jimmy, not James. But at this point in his life, "Dr. Jimmy Allen" somehow seemed inappropriate; "Dr. James Allen" or "Dr. J. Raymond Allen," he thought, would have been more suitable. Although tempted, Allen did not change his name. He decided he would succeed even with an ill-fitting moniker.

Allen soon faced a more serious decision—whether or not to become the director of the controversial CLC. On the surface, Allen appeared to be driven primarily by personal ambition. Career advancement was certainly important to him. Yet, when faced with a tough decision, one that could have adversely affected his career, he made the choice on the basis of conviction rather than ambition. As Allen explained, he assumed leadership of the CLC "because the convictions that seized" him were "deep" and the "vision" he had for Baptists was "real." Still, his parents, who had higher aspirations for their able son, "were aghast" upon learning of the decision.[49] Their anxiety proved groundless. The CLC would be more of a springboard than a dead end, as Allen went on to serve as president of both the Baptist General Convention (1970–71) and the Southern Baptist Convention (1978–79).

Allen's association was a turning point for the CLC. Prior to his tenure, the commission had been primarily a think tank producing educational literature. To be sure, Allen continued this function, expanding somewhat the variety of pamphlets.[50] But he significantly altered the course of the commission, making it an instrument of political activism. Actually, the commission from the outset had shown some interest in politics. On specific issues, Miller had encouraged local churchmen to engage in letter-writing campaigns,[51] and Valentine had occasionally testified before legislative committees in Austin.[52] But Allen for-

[49] Ibid., pp. 1–4, 104–107.
[50] BGCT, *Proceedings*, 1967, pp. 100–101; *Christian Life Commission*, p. 10.
[51] BGCT, *Proceedings*, 1950, pp. 201–202.
[52] Oral Memoirs, Allen, pp. 108–109.

malized the process and gave political involvement major emphasis. If this troubled other Baptists, it never disturbed Allen. In 1961 he reported to the General Convention that "the principle of church-state separation has never meant in this nation that the Christians should not seek to influence the policies of the state to reflect a higher morality."[53]

As his tenure coincided with the upsurge of national political activism during the Kennedy-Johnson presidencies, it was not surprising that the politically astute and remarkably energetic Allen would steer the CLC into politics. "We needed to do political action," he argued, "if we were going to make [an] impact in the field of ethics."[54] Consequently, the preacher became a virtual one-man lobby, spending considerable time in Austin dogging legislators. Allen challenged liquor bills, thereby placing the CLC in opposition to Gov. John Connally;[55] endorsed legislation outlawing racially discriminatory hiring practices;[56] opposed bills providing for segregated housing; supported increased funding for mental health facilities; called for penal reform; and advocated bilingual education.[57] And in 1967, just before resigning from the commission, he persuaded Phil Dowell Strickland, a young attorney (University of Texas School of Law, 1966) and Baptist layman who had one year of training at Southwestern Seminary, to join the CLC.[58]

In retrospect, Allen believed the formal involvement of the CLC in the political process was the major accomplishment of his incumbency. In his judgment, he had changed the CLC "from an academic group that created literature as its major function" to "an action oriented . . . group dealing with ethical issues."[59] But though the redirection of the CLC was important, it was not Allen's most significant accomplishment. That distinction belongs to his success in rescuing the commission from pos-

[53] BGCT, *Proceedings*, 1961, p. 82.
[54] Oral Memoirs, Allen, p. 109.
[55] *Baptist Standard*, Feb. 8, 1967, p. 3; Nov. 8, 1967, p. 4; Dec. 6, 1967, p. 3.
[56] Ibid., May 10, 1967, p. 9.
[57] Oral Memoirs, Allen, pp. 130–31, 142–53.
[58] Phil Dowell Strickland, interview with author, Dallas, Nov. 6, 1981.
[59] Oral Memoirs, Allen, p. 156.

sible obscurity and ensuring its status as a major agency by 1967.

There had always been some opposition to the CLC. To some churchmen, the socially oriented agency was philosophically offensive; to many others, its pronouncements on specific issues were irritating. Most of the dissenters probably were of the latter type, and in the 1950s the issue that angered the people most was race.[60] Clearly, sentiment to abolish, or at least to curb, the CLC was building, and in the late 1950s the opposition sensed an opportunity—an opportunity in which denominational politics coalesced with plans to restructure the Baptist General Convention.

In order to meet the anticipated needs of the coming generation, the executive board of the General Convention authorized a comprehensive assessment of its programs, institutions, and organizational structure in late 1957. This task was assigned to a Survey Committee composed of twenty-five persons. Thomas Armour Patterson, pastor of the First Baptist Church, Beaumont, was chairman. Broadly, the Survey Committee was to pinpoint the denomination's primary goals, decide how those objectives could most effectively be accomplished, and determine how the executive board, its staff, and agencies could best serve the local churches. To ensure "a clearly objective viewpoint," the Survey Committee subsequently employed the Chicago management consultant firm of Booz, Allen, and Hamilton.[61] After a thorough investigation, the professional consultants were to give their report to the Survey Committee, which would then analyze it and make recommendations to the General Convention.

In June, 1959, the Booz, Allen, and Hamilton report, a bulky five-volume tome, much of it highly technical and statistical, was turned over to Patterson. His Survey Committee examined it and offered recommendations to the General Convention when it assembled in Corpus Christi in October. Patterson told the messengers that the primary purpose of this exhaustive

[60] Dunn, interview with author, pp. 32–34.
[61] *Baptist Standard*, Sept. 9, 1959, pp. 5–6.

two-year study had been to provide a source of guidance for the future growth of the General Convention and its programs. All the proposals were general, added Patterson, except those regarding the reorganization of the General Convention and its executive board. To Patterson, reorganization was the top priority, and he urged Texas Baptists to deal first with "organizational improvements." The "more detailed findings, conclusions, and recommendations" could wait until later.[62] The influential editor of the *Baptist Standard*, E. S. James, described the Survey Committee report as "a splendid document" and asserted "that it should be accepted by the convention."[63] The messengers heeded James's advice.[64]

Implementation of Patterson's report brought about a major restructuring of the Baptist General Convention, a restructuring that was not beneficial to the CLC. Behind the scenes there had been a strong effort through the reorganization process to either scuttle the commission or reduce it to insignificance within the Dallas bureaucracy.[65] Moreover, this effort had come at an inopportune time for the agency. Death had recently claimed one of its more influential advocates, and its director had already resolved by that time to take a position in Nashville with the Southern Baptist Convention. J. Howard Williams, who had resigned as executive secretary of the General Convention to become president of Southwestern Seminary in 1953, died in April, 1958. Meanwhile, in late 1953 Forrest Chalmers Feezor, pastor of the First Baptist Church, Waco, had succeeded Williams as executive secretary. Unlike his predecessor, Feezor, according to Foy Valentine, "was never overwhelmingly committed to Christian social ethics."[66] Jimmy Allen concurred. Feezor thought the CLC was a good idea, said Allen, but he "never did

[62] Ibid., Sept. 9, 1959, p. 5. See also BGCT, *Proceedings*, 1959, "Survey Committee Report," p. 3; *Baptist Standard*, June 3, 1959, p. 2.

[63] *Baptist Standard*, Oct. 21, 1959, p. 5.

[64] BGCT, *Proceedings*, 1959, pp. 24–25.

[65] Oral Memoirs, Valentine, Interview 3, pp. 21–22; Oral Memoirs, Allen, pp. 110–11; Oral Memoirs of Thomas Armour Patterson, Waco, 1978, Baylor University Program of Oral History, pp. 180–83.

[66] Oral Memoirs, Valentine, Interview 3, p. 19.

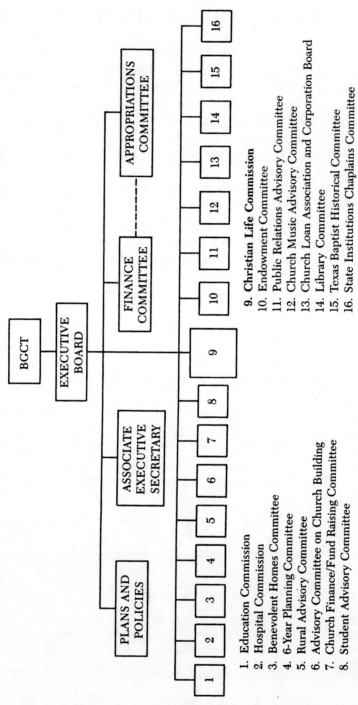

FIGURE 1   Organizational Structure of the Baptist General Convention of Texas before 1959.

1. Education Commission
2. Hospital Commission
3. Benevolent Homes Committee
4. 6-Year Planning Committee
5. Rural Advisory Committee
6. Advisory Committee on Church Building
7. Church Finance/Fund Raising Committee
8. Student Advisory Committee

9. **Christian Life Commission**
10. Endowment Committee
11. Public Relations Advisory Committee
12. Church Music Advisory Committee
13. Church Loan Association and Corporation Board
14. Library Committee
15. Texas Baptist Historical Committee
16. State Institutions Chaplains Committee

SOURCE: "Survey Committee Report," Baptist General Convention of Texas, *Proceedings*, 1959, pp. 24-25.

FIGURE 2   Organizational Structure of the Baptist General Convention of Texas after 1959.

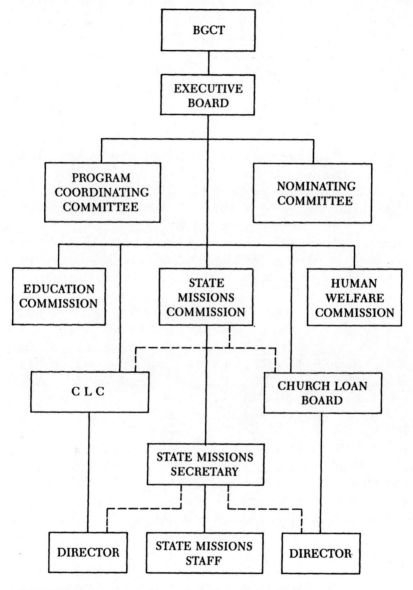

SOURCE: "Survey Committee Report," Baptist General Convention of Texas, *Proceedings*, 1959, p. 42.

NOTE: The dashed lines indicate the subordination of the CLC and its director to the newly established State Missions Commission and its secretary.

understand it very well."[67] Furthermore, in 1958, Valentine
learned that A. C. Miller was planning to retire as executive secretary of the Christian Life Commission of the Southern Baptist
Convention. Valentine wanted to succeed Miller. Consequently,
when he was offered the Nashville position, he readily accepted
it in February, 1960.[68] So as the reorganization process gained
momentum, the post of executive secretary of the convention
was no longer occupied by an ardent supporter of the CLC, and
the director of the agency was preoccupied with plans to leave.

T. A. Patterson acknowledged that the most intense debate
within the Survey Committee focused on the CLC. Some committee members wanted it abolished.[69] This was not accomplished, for the Survey Committee included several staunch
backers of the commission, notably Orba Lee Malone, who was
chairman of the CLC in 1959, and Charles Wellborn, an articulate and popular pastor from Seventh and James Baptist Church,
Waco.[70] Forrest Feezor, moreover, refused to join the commission's opponents.[71]

Unable to destroy the CLC, its detractors then attempted
to downgrade it from the status of a commission to a committee.[72] Their effort was partially successful, although the commission retained its title. The Survey Committee, upon the advice
of consultants from Booz, Allen, and Hamilton, had recommended the formation of three major commissions—one for
educational programs and institutions, one for state missions,
and one for hospitals and other human welfare services. The
CLC was still a commission, but it was clearly not equal to the
other three. It had only twelve members, whereas the others
had fifteen; it was headed by a director, whereas the chief executive officer of the others was a secretary; and its director
was subordinate to the secretary of the State Missions Com-

[67] Oral Memoirs, Allen, p. 112.
[68] Oral Memoirs, Valentine, Interview 4, pp. 2–4.
[69] Oral Memoirs, Patterson, pp. 180–83.
[70] BGCT, Proceedings, 1959, "Survey Committee Report," pp. 1–2.
[71] Oral Memoirs, Valentine, Interview 3, pp. 21–22.
[72] Oral Memoirs, Patterson, p. 180.

mission.[73] Jimmy Allen put it aptly. The CLC was now "a hybrid in the bureaucracy, . . . a commission that wasn't quite a commission."[74]

Some churchmen saw reorganization as a means of crippling the CLC, but others saw in it an opportunity for self-aggrandizement. Consequently, the CLC also fell victim to a bid for denominational power and influence by J. Woodrow Fuller. Associate executive secretary under Feezor and interim head of the Department of Stewardship and Direct Missions,[75] Fuller exercised considerable influence with the consultants from Booz, Allen, and Hamilton. As a result, the State Missions Commission, of which Fuller was the first secretary, secured "the lion's share of programs and program money" in 1959. And the CLC, according to Jimmy Allen, was one of the programs Fuller wanted to absorb under his new State Missions Commission.[76]

In mid-1960 Forrest Feezor announced plans to retire as executive secretary at the end of the year. To the distress of E. S. James, editor of the *Baptist Standard*, politicking for this important position began immediately.[77] Fuller was ambitious for the job, but he was not the only contender.[78] In September, 1960, nineteen men were nominated. The eventual victor was T. A. Patterson.[79] Chairmanship of the Survey Committee had catapulted the Beaumont pastor into the forefront of Texas Baptist life. And, importantly, his election possibly saved the CLC from being buried within the Dallas bureaucracy.

Jimmy Allen had become the director of the CLC just two months before Patterson's election. In 1960 Allen believed his most pressing task was to save the CLC from Woodrow Fuller and the State Missions Commission. The CLC director feared that absorption by Fuller's agency would be the "death knell to our commission." So Allen, an adroit denominational politician,

[73] BGCT, *Proceedings*, 1959, "Survey Committee Report," pp. 42–44.
[74] Oral Memoirs, Allen, p. 104.
[75] BGCT, *Proceedings*, 1959, p. 88.
[76] Jimmy Allen to author, Nov. 27, 1979.
[77] *Baptist Standard*, Aug. 3, 1960, p. 4.
[78] Allen to author, Nov. 27, 1979.
[79] *Baptist Standard*, Sept. 21, 1960, p. 6; Sept. 28, 1960, p. 4.

readily resorted to "politicking for the preservation of the Christian Life Commission."[80] The potential leverage was at hand. As a result of the recent executive secretary's election, the relationship between Fuller and Patterson was strained. "There was a continual stress factor in that relationship," Allen maintained, a stress factor that he exploited to the advantage of the CLC.[81]

In 1961, as soon as Patterson assumed his new duties, Allen discussed with him the status of the CLC, especially whether or not the agency, technically subordinate to the State Missions Commission, would be represented on Patterson's administrative staff.[82] Patterson's major concern had always been evangelism. Characteristically, following his recent election he had told fellow Baptists that "evangelism should pervade everything we do," for "the main business of the church is winning souls to Christ."[83] Clearly, Patterson was not philosophically in tune with the CLC, and he later advised a few men being sought by Allen against serving on the agency.[84] Nevertheless, in 1961 Patterson was eager to broaden the base of his leadership and to check the influence of Fuller,[85] and so he readily invited Allen to attend the staff meetings, thereby giving the director of the CLC a seat alongside the secretaries of the other three commissions. Allen quickly took full advantage of this opportunity "to prize pole [pry] the Christian Life Commission out of its very minor role into a more creative and functioning influence in the Baptist General Convention of Texas."[86]

Indeed, Allen's efforts were quite successful. In 1966 the General Convention established a Committee of 100, composed of an equal number of laypersons and pastors, to review, without the assistance of hired consultants, its boards, commissions, committees, and institutions. E. Hermond Westmoreland, pas-

[80] Oral Memoirs, Allen, pp. 110–11.
[81] Allen to author, Nov. 27, 1979.
[82] Ibid.
[83] *Baptist Standard*, Sept. 21, 1960, p. 7.
[84] Oral Memoirs, Allen, p. 113.
[85] In February, 1964, Woodrow Fuller resigned as head of the State Missions Commission to become associate pastor to W. A. Criswell at the First Baptist Church, Dallas. See *Baptist Standard*, Feb. 12, 1964, p. 10.
[86] Allen to author, Nov. 27, 1979.

tor of the South Main Baptist Church, Houston, and soon to become a member of the CLC, was chairman. In November, 1967, the General Convention accepted Westmoreland's recommendations, several of which dealt with the CLC. Notably, the convention increased the commission from twelve to fifteen members, ended its subordination to the State Missions Commission, and authorized the employment of additional staff members to help with research.[87] So when Allen resigned that same month in 1967 to become pastor of the First Baptist Church, San Antonio, the CLC was a full-fledged equal with the other commissions. As the departing director put it, the CLC was finally "recognized across the state as being a legitimate commission of Texas Baptist life." And this "was not accidental." It was, said Allen, the result of a lot of hard work by churchmen who believed in the CLC.[88]

Allen recommended James M. Dunn, who had been the associate director of the CLC since October, 1966, as his successor.[89] On January 1, 1968, Dunn became the agency's fourth leader. In terms of their backgrounds, there were several similarities between Dunn and his predecessor. Both men grew up in racially tense neighborhoods in the Dallas–Fort Worth metroplex; as high school youngsters, each stoutly defended segregation; and both had dramatic encounters that compelled them to rethink their racial views.

Dunn was born in Fort Worth on June 17, 1932. Because of convenience, his Baptist parents took him to a Presbyterian church for a time. Later, the family joined the Evans Avenue Baptist Church, and Dunn became a Christian at the age of eleven. The influence of his pastor at Evans Avenue, Woodrow Wilson Phelps, a Th.D. graduate in ethics under Thomas Maston, was considerable. Under Phelps's influence, Dunn began to glimpse the social aspects of faith.[90]

Race, however, remained a blind spot for Dunn, although not because of the pastor. Without being abrasive Phelps had

[87] BGCT, *Proceedings*, 1967, pp. 23, 56, 58–59.
[88] Oral Memoirs, Allen, p. 111.
[89] Ibid., p. 171.
[90] Dunn, interview with author, pp. 1–5.

begun to nudge his Fort Worth congregation toward a better understanding of race in the late 1940s and early 1950s. But Dunn was impervious, and in high school he debated against President Harry Truman's efforts in behalf of civil rights. Just as Jimmy Allen had been challenged by Clarence Jordan, however, Dunn was confronted with the discrepancy between his Christian faith and racial attitudes by a visiting speaker at Evans Avenue, Ralph Phelps, Jr., no relation to the pastor but another of Maston's Th.D. graduates. Like Allen, Dunn became angry and argued publicly with Phelps. For the next two or three years the young man struggled with the racial issue, finally resolving it by his freshman or sophomore year in college.[91] By that time Dunn had made another important decision—he had resolved to enter the ministry.

Dunn's parents were humble people. Their Christian faith was practical, something to be lived daily. The father was a milkman; neither parent had a college education, but both valued schooling and encouraged their son in his academic pursuits. Of the CLC directors, Dunn was the first to graduate from a non-Baptist institution. He attended Texas Wesleyan College, a Methodist school in Fort Worth. His educational experience at Southwestern Seminary, which began in 1953, was drawn out over thirteen years. Upon completion of the B.D., Dunn entered the doctoral program under the direction of Thomas Maston, whose emphasis upon practical religion appealed to him. Finally, in 1966 Dunn obtained the Th.D., writing a dissertation entitled "The Ethical Thought of Joseph Martin Dawson." Dunn's stay at the seminary, although extended, was not leisurely. He not only did his course work, research, and writing, but also held a variety of church-related jobs in Collin County and Weatherford from 1954 to 1961. From 1961 to 1966, when he joined the CLC, Dunn was the Baptist Student Union director and instructor of religion at West Texas State University in Canyon.[92]

If Jimmy Allen initiated the formal involvement of the CLC

[91] Ibid., pp. 6–8.
[92] Ibid., pp. 1–5, 9–10.

in politics, Dunn and his associate, Phil Strickland, broadened and refined the process. Together, they involved the CLC more deeply in the political process than Allen had ever attempted. Because the CLC staff researched a wide range of public concerns, the commission began regularly to offer informed testimony before state legislative committees. Soon, many legislators began to seek out the CLC as a knowledgeable source on public issues.[93] Between 1968 and 1980 the commission lobbied the legislature to increase welfare ceilings, which was accomplished by the passage of Constitutional Amendment Five in August, 1969, allow therapeutic abortions in some circumstances, protect consumers against advertising frauds and harassment from credit collectors, upgrade conditions among Mexican-American farm workers in the Rio Grande Valley, provide for annual legislative sessions, and improve conditions in Texas prisons.[94] Dunn was unequivocal on this last issue. "I'm for voting the Texas Department Corrections enough funds to see to it that they don't have to put four men in a one-man cell."[95] In 1970 the commission conducted a statewide voter registration drive.[96]

At the same time that Dunn and Strickland expanded the lobbying activities of the CLC, they also sought to educate and inform fellow Baptists on political matters. In 1970 the commission began printing the *CLC Legislative Report* and published *Politics: A Guidebook for Christians*, containing chapters on "How to Get into Politics," "How to Get the Church into Politics," "How a Pastor Relates to Politics," and "How to Preach on Political Issues."[97] This was followed in 1972 by the *Voting Analysis of the 62nd Legislature*, which was placed in every Baptist church in Texas, and in 1980 by *Leaven*, a monthly newsletter dealing with legislative issues.[98] Moreover, in 1976 the

[93] Strickland, interview with author.

[94] BGCT, *Proceedings*, 1969, pp. 86–89; 1971, p. 30; 1973, p. 29; 1975, p. 32; 1978, p. 73.

[95] Dunn, interview with author, p. 43.

[96] BGCT, *Proceedings*, 1970, p. 95.

[97] James M. Dunn, ed., *Politics: A Guidebook for Christians* (Dallas: *Christian Life Commission*, 1970), p. 7; BGCT, *Proceedings*, 1970, pp. 91–92.

[98] BGCT, *Proceedings*, 1972, p. 156; 1980, p. 119.

CLC organized LIGHT (Legislative Information Group Helping Texas), which was composed, ideally at least, of one person from every congregation in the state, and SALT (Special Advisors on Legislation in Texas), a statewide network of Baptists whose primary task was to contact local state representatives and senators about current political concerns.[99] During legislative years, Strickland, or another member of the CLC, would meet with representatives from SALT at various locations to review issues scheduled to come before the legislature. These grass-roots contacts enabled the commission to generate impressive letter-writing campaigns, thereby bringing considerable pressure to bear on the legislature in regard to certain issues.

To allay criticism of such political activism, Dunn never presumed to be the official spokesman of locally autonomous Baptist congregations. When offering testimony in Austin, he and Strickland always pointed out that they spoke for themselves and the CLC, not the entire Baptist General Convention.[100] Moreover, ever since the Jimmy Allen era, the commission had studiously avoided any suggestion that its stand on a particular issue was the only Christian position. "No one political movement or ideal can ever be identified as thoroughly Christian," Allen had told the General Convention in 1961, for "the Bible does not give a Christian blueprint for an economic or political order." Dunn continued in this tradition, as best exemplified in his final report to the General Convention on the eve of the 1980 presidential election. With obvious reference to such individuals and groups as the Reverend Jerry Falwell and the Moral Majority, Dunn warned against "those who come with 'packaged political agendas' which they identify as 'Christian.'" He also urged churchmen to "beware of single-issue politics," noting that in the current political swirl many Americans had "fallen into the patently unfair and immoral practice of crusading for the defeat of a candidate solely because of his views on a single issue." As "a good example," Dunn cited "the current debate on abortion."[101] Despite the circumspection of Dunn and

[99] Ibid., 1976, p. 110.

[100] Dunn, interview with author, pp. 34–35; Strickland, interview with author.

[101] BGCT, *Proceedings*, 1961, p. 83; 1980, p. 77.

Strickland, the commission's political activism still aroused the ire of many Baptists. Indeed, Dunn believed political activism was the most controversial aspect of his tenure.[102]

In 1980 Dunn left Texas to become the chief executive officer of the Baptist Joint Committee on Public Affairs in Washington, D.C. By that time, the CLC was comfortably established. No serious threat to its continuation loomed on the horizon. In contrast to the days when A. C. Miller, a part-time assistant, and an office secretary ran the agency on a budget of $24,000, the commission in 1980 was headed by a director, and it employed three associates, a research associate, and a secretarial staff; it operated on a budget of $275,000.[103] The number of educational pamphlets produced by the commission had grown from five to more than fifty, and more than a million pieces of literature were being distributed annually.[104] The CLC not only survived, it prospered. Ironically, as the commission approached middle age, institutional success was potentially its greatest threat. As with other organizations, acceptance could cause the CLC to reflect rather than challenge denominational posture, to seek consensus rather than boldly to proclaim what the church ought to do. A possible safeguard is a fairly frequent turnover in leadership, which has occurred within the CLC. Since 1950 the agency has been led by four men, who in turn have been aided by a steady flow of able associates. Consequently, the commission has had frequent access to leaders with imagination and fresh ideas, a fact made evident in the agency's response to troublesome issues.

[102] Dunn, interview with author, p. 34.
[103] Oral Memoirs, Miller, pp. 88–92; BGCT, *Proceedings*, 1953, p. 88; 1980, pp. 119, 624.
[104] *Christian Life Commission*, p. 9.

7

Responding to Issues, 1950–1980

TEXAS Baptists have always been interested in social issues, but for the most part that concern has been limited to family matters and those proverbial sins of drinking and gambling. Although it has continued to address these traditional items, the CLC has emphasized that the Good News has a vastly broader social application. The commission's range of interests was amply demonstrated in the breadth of its pamphlet literature and the varied themes of its workshops and seminars. Specifically, in 1951 the commission outlined five major areas of interest: family life; public morals, which included alcoholic consumption, pornography, and gambling; race relations; economic life, especially "issues involved in the rapid industrial growth of the South and the Southwest, the materialistic influences on the spiritual life of the Christian, [and] the stewardship of labor and management"; and international affairs.[1] In 1954 the CLC replaced international affairs with citizenship and in 1957 added church and state.[2] Under one heading or another, the CLC has devoted at least some time to almost every important issue to trouble American society since 1951. It opposed universal military training,[3] upheld the Supreme Court in desegregation and school prayer rulings, sanctioned therapeutic abortions, promoted sex education, grappled with drug abuse, urged a settlement of the Vietnam conflict, declared that people were "more important

---

[1] Baptist General Convention of Texas, *Proceedings*, 1951, p. 199 (cited hereafter as BGCT, *Proceedings*). See also 1950, pp. 182–87.

[2] *Christian Life Commission, Baptist General Convention of Texas, 1950–1970* (Dallas: Christian Life Commission of Texas, p. 12. See also BGCT, *Proceedings*, 1960, p. 104.

[3] BGCT, *Baptist Standard*, Feb. 7, 1952, p. 3; Feb. 21, 1952, p. 3. See also BGCT, *Proceedings*, 1952, p. 195.

than profit" and demanded "that businesses take the necessary steps to eliminate pollution from the air and water,"[4] condemned "raw violence" and the exploitation of sex on television, advocated bilingual education, endorsed programs to rehabilitate Texas prison inmates, warned against "Christian" political parties, encouraged energy conservation, and recommended restraint "in wage and price increases and in our own consumption habits" as a means of dealing with inflation.[5]

In arriving at its pronouncements, many of which were divisive, the CLC followed a precedent set by A. C. Miller. In 1951 subcommittees of the commission were assigned to investigate each of the major areas of concern. Miller explained that each member "had some phase of . . . work to study." Then, at the quarterly meetings, following a thorough discussion of each topic, the commission collectively drafted a statement. Rather than have the director and his staff submit completed drafts for the approval of the CLC, the entire group formulated its reports.[6] This was a wise procedure, for it made it impossible to isolate the director or an individual commission member as being the author of a specific declaration.[7] And this was something to be concerned about. In dealing with controversial subjects, the CLC was more concerned about proclaiming what appeared to be the proper course for Christians than in simply verbalizing what seemed to be prevailing Texas Baptist or national sentiment at the moment. Because of this prophetic posture, the CLC often angered those churchmen who were comfortable in Zion, especially regarding racial issues.

Reaction across the South to the *Brown* decision of May, 1954, varied widely, ranging from militant segregationists whose influence was exercised through groups such as the KKK and Citizens' Councils to liberals who, although few in number, sup-

[4] BGCT, *Proceedings*, 1967, p. 18.
[5] Ibid., 1979, p. 77. See also 1966, p. 89; 1967, p. 19; 1971, pp. 30–32; 1972, pp. 30–31; 1975, p. 34; 1976, p. 70; and 1977, p. 73.
[6] Oral Memoirs of Acker C. Miller, Waco, 1973, Baylor University Program of Oral History, p. 93; BGCT, *Proceedings*, 1951, p. 199.
[7] Oral Memoirs of Jimmy Raymond Allen, Waco, 1973, Baylor University Program of Oral History, p. 127.

ported integration to business conservatives whose concern for image often facilitated racial accommodation. Geographically, the staunchest resistance was in the deep South, where a 1956 poll by the American Institute of Public Opinion showed that 90 percent of the whites opposed the Supreme Court's recent rulings on school desegregation. Politicians such as James O. Eastland of Mississippi and Herman Talmadge of Georgia capitalized on this sentiment, decrying judicial activism and rallying the forces of white supremacy. In early 1956 Strom Thurmond of South Carolina, Harry F. Byrd of Virginia, and Richard B. Russell of Georgia took the initiative in drafting a Declaration of Constitutional Principles, popularly known as the Southern Manifesto. This document rebuked the Supreme Court, encouraged southerners to resist forced integration by any lawful means, and sought the support of nonsoutherners by hinting that they too could someday be victimized by judicial encroachments. Of the South's 128 national lawmakers 101 signed this declaration of defiance, including Sen. Price Daniel of Texas. State lawmakers behaved accordingly. Between 1954 and 1957 legislatures from the deep South variously prohibited public school desegregation, thereby making it illegal to comply with the court decision; passed measures to abolish in whole or in part their public school systems; and endorsed interposition, a presumably legal way for the "sovereign" states to subvert the court's rulings.[8]

Predictably, most of the organizational means for resisting judicial change also emanated from the deep South. About fifty organizations dedicated to white supremacy sprang up in the wake of the *Brown* case. Illustrative of these were the KKK and Citizens' Councils, which, despite a common objective, drew support from widely disparate elements of southern society. The Klan, although rejuvenated by the controversy over school desegregation, lacked efficient organizational structure, respectability, and access to the political establishment. Only in Alabama did state politicos in the 1950s court the hooded knights.

[8] Numan V. Bartley, *The Rise of Massive Resistance: Race and Politics in the South During the 1950's* (Baton Rouge: Louisiana State University Press, 1969), pp. 13–14, 67, 77, 116–17, 131.

Through violence and intimidation, the Klan wielded influence outside the law. Its members tended to be unskilled and semi-skilled laborers, lower middle-class whites in occupations of little status, and lower-class rural whites.[9] By contrast, the councils enjoyed some public esteem, recruited successful professional and middle-class business people who often belonged to the local Kiwanis, Lions, or Rotary clubs, promoted "legal" methods of negating court edicts, and wielded considerable political pressure. John Bell Williams of Mississippi, along with Thurmond and Eastland, had cordial relations with the group, and Ross R. Barnett, a longtime council member, was elected governor of Mississippi in 1960. Founded at Indianola, Mississippi, in July, 1954, the council soon had chapters in most of the former Confederate states and by early 1956, the peak of its numerical strength, claimed more than 200,000 members.[10]

The situation in Texas was significantly different. Ironically, at the moment the *Brown* decision was rendered, Foy Valentine was holding a seminar on race relations at the First Baptist Church, Marshall, where Arthur Rutledge, then chairman of the CLC, was pastor. Valentine later insisted that the racial furor ignited by the desegregation ruling was not as intense in the Lone Star State as elsewhere. Aside from east Texas, "which culturally reflected the racism of the Deep South," Valentine elaborated, there simply was not "that much of a crisis over race in Texas in those days."[11]

Valentine's recollections are essentially sound, but Texas was by no means free of racial tension. Gov. Allan Shivers was certainly unhappy with the high court, and he was not above exploiting the racial issue to his political advantage. In the 1954 gubernatorial campaign he appealed to racial prejudice against challenger Ralph Yarborough; in 1955 he created an Advisory Committee on Segregation in the Public Schools, which, having been stacked with ultraconservatives, recommended in late

[9] Ibid., pp. 201–10. See also David M. Chalmers, *Hooded Americanism: The History of the Ku Klux Klan* (New York: Franklin Watts, 1975), pp. 343–65.

[10] Bartley, *Rise of Massive Resistance*, pp. 83–107.

[11] Oral Memoirs of Foy Dan Valentine, Waco, 1975–1976, Baylor University Program of Oral History, Interview 3, pp. 5, 7–8.

1956 that Texas, among other things, restore segregation in all its public schools. In early 1956 he intervened decisively to prevent court-ordered desegregation at Texarkana Junior College and at Mansfield High School in a small community southeast of Fort Worth. The governor justified the steps taken in Texarkana and Mansfield on the dubious grounds that local hostility took priority over federal court instructions to desegregate. That substantial numbers of Texans shared the governor's sentiment was evident in the primary elections of July, 1956. By overwhelming majorities the voters expressed support for interposition and disapproval of racial intermarriage and coerced integration in the public schools.[12]

Even so, Texas was not Mississippi or Alabama, and the state's religious leaders never had to contend with the massive public resistance typical of the deep South. Approximately 75 percent of white Texans in 1956 opposed desegregation, as compared with 90 percent in the region from Louisiana to Georgia. And despite the heated rhetoric, Governor Shivers and the state legislature generally behaved moderately. State lawmakers enacted no legislation hampering voluntary compliance with school desegregation, and the state Board of Education even offered to assist school districts grappling with locally conceived desegregation plans. By the end of 1955 Texas had already achieved a greater degree of school desegregation than the rest of the South combined, as some eighty-four districts, all in or adjacent to the predominantly white western part of the state, quietly submitted. A chapter of the Citizens' Council was established at Kilgore in the summer of 1955 under the leadership of Dr. B. E. Masters, president emeritus of Kilgore Junior College, but the Texas organization was a mere shadow of its counterparts in Mississippi and Alabama. As for the Southern Manifesto, it was ignored by most of the state's federal poli-

[12] Bartley, *Rise of Massive Resistance*, pp. 73–74, 140–41, 146–47; Sam Kinch and Stuart Long, *Allan Shivers: The Pied Piper of Texas Politics* (Austin: Shoal Creek Publishers, 1973), pp. 156–61; George Norris Green, *The Establishment in Texas Politics: The Primitive Years, 1938–1957* (Westport, Conn.: Greenwood Press, 1979), pp. 151–92; *Dallas Morning News*, Feb. 24, 1956, pt. 1, p. 1; *Houston Post*, Feb. 24, 1956, sec. 1, p. 1.

ticians. Lyndon Johnson, then Senate majority leader, was not asked to sign the document, and sixteen of Texas' twenty-two House delegates refused to endorse it. In retrospect, Texans from 1954 to 1957, though agitated by the racial issue, appear to have been more interested in the tidelands oil controversy and scandals in the Shivers administration. Furthermore, in May, 1956, Shivers lost control of the state Democratic party to an unwieldy coalition headed by Lyndon Johnson and House Speaker Sam Rayburn. Later that year this coalition backed moderate Price Daniel of Liberty for governor. Governor Daniel subsequently pursued a moderate course on race. During the remainder of the decade Texas neither joined the forces of massive resistance nor advanced school desegregation.[13]

Texas Baptist leaders, meanwhile, reacted swiftly and responsibly to the court's landmark ruling. Though many denominational spokesmen questioned the wisdom of the judicial order, not one supported the establishment of private academies as a means of circumventing the decision. The sixty-seven-year-old editor of the *Baptist Standard*, David M. Gardner, who had been educated at Baylor University and Southwestern Seminary, was a case in point. Although he had previously attributed the South's racial troubles to outside "racial rabble rousers" and "ill-advised agitators" and had implied that communists were behind the *Brown* case, Gardner still acknowledged that the Supreme Court's decree, whether one liked it or not, was "now the law of the land, a fact which we must face and adjust ourselves to as good citizens and loyal Americans." Gardner believed it was now imperative for blacks and whites to work together "in the interest of saving our free public school system," for the idea of abolishing public education was "unthinkable."[14]

Perhaps the editor's calm response was due in part to the educational campaign initiated by Charles T. Alexander and continued by the CLC. Since 1936, when Alexander had gone to

[13] Bartley, *Rise of Massive Resistance*, pp. 13–14, 97–99, 116, 138; Kinch and Long, *Allan Shivers*, pp. 171–82; and Green, *Establishment*, pp. 168–78.

[14] *Baptist Standard*, Aug. 16, 1945, p. 3; Oct. 7, 1948, p. 4; June 10, 1954, p. 2. See also Feb. 21, 1952, p. 2; Nov. 13, 1952, p. 2.

work for the General Convention, interracial contact, primarily among ministers, had grown; the convention had committed itself to improving race relations; and informative literature on racial matters had been widely distributed. In 1952 the commission had printed "The Bible Speaks on Race." In 1954, moreover, Valentine and the CLC moved quickly to defend the court and to urge acceptance of its decision. At its quarterly meeting on June 22, just weeks after the ruling, the CLC chided churchmen for having to be forced by the Supreme Court to face up to what had always been essentially a moral issue. "It is high time the churches assumed the spiritual leadership which is rightfully theirs with regard to the race problem," declared Valentine, adding that continued silence "in the face of such a grave issue would be to become derelict in Christian responsibility."[15] And in October when the General Convention assembled in Fort Worth for its annual session, the CLC was unequivocal. "We cannot afford . . . to sit around and whine about what the Supreme Court has done and wait timorously and fearfully to see what they are going to do," the commission asserted. "Our God," continued the report, "is no respector [sic] of persons and He has made it abundantly clear from Peter's day to our own day that He does not want His people to be respectors [sic] of persons." The commission concluded that the time had come "for Texas Baptists not only to believe right but to do right with regard to race relations."[16]

Texas Baptists were not unique in issuing such bold pronouncements. In the summer and fall of 1954 religious bodies across the South took similar stands. Methodists, Presbyterians, and Baptists in their national meetings affirmed that the Supreme Court decision was in harmony with both constitutional principles and Christian ideals and implored their communicants, as the Southern Baptist Convention put it, "to conduct themselves in this period of adjustment in the spirit of Christ."[17]

---

[15] Ibid., July 15, 1954, p. 6.

[16] BGCT, *Proceedings*, 1954, p. 170.

[17] *Annual* of the Southern Baptist Convention (Nashville, 1960), p. 407 (cited hereafter as *Annual*, SBC); Kenneth K. Bailey, *Southern White Protestantism in the Twentieth Century* (1964; reprint, Gloucester, Mass.: Peter Smith, 1968), pp. 142–43.

Corresponding declarations emanated from many of the state conventions, conferences, and synods. Presbyterians in Virginia and Arkansas; Methodists in North Carolina, Arkansas, and north Texas; and Baptists in North Carolina and Virginia joined the chorus.[18] There were even favorable responses from the deep South. Leon Macon, editor of the *Alabama Baptist*, applauded the recent statement of the Southern Baptist Convention, declaring that it accurately reflected "the thinking of Southern Baptists on the Supreme Court decision." Rather than "become rebels again," said the Alabamian, Southern Baptists would now "work along quietly and sympathetically to carry out the Supreme Court decision in a manner that will result in happiness and peace among the people."[19]

Given the democratic polity and local autonomy of churches within the Southern Baptist Convention, it was always difficult to translate progressive convention declarations on controversial subjects into action at the congregational level. And as public opposition to school desegregation mushroomed in 1955, many southern religious leaders found this task more onerous than usual. By 1956 Leon Macon's optimistic expectation had given way to reality. "The ideal thing . . . would be to see our nation comply in an orderly manner with this decision of the Supreme Court," wrote the Alabama Baptist. "However, the ideal is not always practical."[20] Faced with tenacious opposition from the laity, other religious spokesmen in the South came to similar conclusions.[21]

In *Christians in Racial Crisis* (1959), Ernest Q. Campbell and Thomas F. Pettigrew described this situation as the "basic 'Protestant dilemma'"—that is, the problem of forcefully proclaiming Christian ideals without jeopardizing institutional growth and economic well-being. Campbell and Pettigrew be-

---

[18] Bailey, *Southern White Protestantism*, pp. 144–45.

[19] *Alabama Baptist* (Birmingham), June 17, 1954, p. 2. See also May 27, 1954, p. 3; Nov. 14, 1954, p. 3; and Dec. 9, 1954, p. 3; *Christian Index* (Georgia), Mar. 18, 1954, p. 6; Oct. 28, 1954, p. 6; June 9, 1955, p. 6; *Biblical Recorder* (North Carolina), May 29, 1954, pp. 5, 8; June 5, 1954, p. 5.

[20] *Alabama Baptist*, Mar. 8, 1956, p. 3. See also May 3, 1956, p. 3; Oct. 10, 1957, p. 3.

[21] Bailey, *Southern White Protestantism*, pp. 145–51.

lieved many churches muted their advocacy of racial justice in order to satisfy basic organizational needs.[22] There is no denying that many southern churches faced a dilemma of this sort over race by the mid-1950s. Many communicants from all the major denominations angrily cast aside their leaders' exhortations to accept the desegregation ruling.[23] The editor of the *Baptist Record* of Mississippi, for instance, dismissed the lofty 1954 Southern Baptist Convention statement on the *Brown* case as "the lowest point of the whole Convention" and served notice that no convention could "bind any Baptist church," since each was "a rule unto itself." As a result of such opposition, one scholar has concluded that the churches subsequently "buried the principle of the *Brown* decision in evasive pronouncements or drowned it in silence" and exerted virtually "no positive influence on the racial attitudes of even their most devoted laymen."[24] Though true of some churches in certain parts of the South, this harsh generalization does not apply to Texas Baptists.

Although difficult to gauge the extent of its influence, the educational campaign begun under Alexander and continued by the CLC did filter downward and affect the faithful in the local pews. The testimony of several Texas pastors suggests that the tireless efforts of the commission, as exemplified in associational programs, Sunday school lessons, church bulletins, literature, and sermons had a fairly broad impact. In 1951, for example, Jimmy Allen was pastor of the First Baptist Church, Van Alstyne, a small community approximately seventy miles north of Dallas. With two other local ministers, Allen organized a racially integrated service. The program celebrated a Boy Scout Day, he explained, but the "real purpose was to pull the people together across the racial lines." Originally, the service was scheduled to be held at the Methodist church, but unforeseen circumstances

---

[22] Ernest Q. Campbell and Thomas F. Pettigrew, *Christians in Racial Crisis: A Study of Little Rock's Ministry, Including Statements on Desegregation and Race Relations by the Leading Religious Denominations of the United States* (Washington, D.C.: Public Affairs Press, 1959), pp. 11–12, 63–84.

[23] Bailey, *Southern White Protestantism*, pp. 146–47.

[24] *The Baptist Record*, June 19, 1954, p. 3; Bartley, *Rise of Massive Resistance*, pp. 304–305.

compelled the organizers to move the meeting to First Baptist. This created a tense situation. Some of Allen's deacons objected to the use of their building for an interracial service. One man candidly voiced opposition, but went along anyway because the General Convention was on record in support of such programs. This experience taught Allen "that denominational posture really did assist a [local] congregation."[25]

In 1954 that belief was strengthened. Allen was then pastoring at Wills Point in northeast Texas, where racial prejudice ran deep. Allen believed the positive response of the Southern Baptist Convention, which met in Saint Louis, June, 1954, to the recent Supreme Court decree was epochal.[26] "I think it was one of the most significant decisions that Southern Baptists made in the decade," he claimed, "because if we had gone on record in the other direction, . . . the robbing of the local church of what I discovered in Van Alstyne, which was denominational witness, would have devastated us."[27] Allen was not unique. Numerous other ministers agreed that affirmative convention leadership, such as that exemplified by the CLC, enabled them to discuss sensitive issues more forthrightly with their churches.[28] Of course, given the autonomy of Baptist congregations, local pastors could easily ignore convention declarations. Nevertheless, positive stands by the convention reinforced the position of those pastors who wanted to lead their congregations to a better understanding of racial justice.

This does not mean that the *Brown* decision created no problems for Texas Baptists. On the contrary, signs of internal tension were soon evident. Despite his initial calm, for instance, editor David Gardner, like so many religionists of all faiths in the mid-1950s, found it difficult to adjust to the racial changes

[25] Oral Memoirs, Allen, pp. 92–93.
[26] *Annual*, SBC, 1954, pp. 56, 403–404.
[27] Oral Memoirs, Allen, p. 95.
[28] Strauss Atkinson to author, Jan. 28, 1980; Loren M. White to author, April 10, 1980; Vernon O. Elmore to author, Nov. 28, 1979. Much of the subsequent material dealing with race was first published in John W. Storey, "Texas Baptist Leadership, the Social Gospel, and Race, 1954–1968," *Southwestern Historical Quarterly* 83 (July, 1979): 29–46.

wrought by the judicial process. In a barbed editorial in October, 1954, the Baptist journalist asserted that "we have never subscribed to the absurd and antiquated theory of the infallibility of popes," and neither "do we believe in the impeccability of the Supreme court [sic] of the United States." Although conceding that "forced segregation" in tax-supported schools was unconstitutional, Gardner wondered about "voluntary separation." The "vast majority" of southern blacks, he believed, preferred separate schools, "just as they prefer separate churches." Turning from public to private institutions, the editor was unequivocal. "Church groups and denominational schools that go in for desegregation hastily will discover that they are doing a disservice to both whites and Negroes," he argued. "Hasty decisions to desegregate will not advance the interests of education, but will advance the interests and encourage the efforts of agitators."[29] Clinging to a past outdated by recent events, the aging editor of the Texas Baptist journal retired in November, 1954.

And Gardner was not the only prominent Texas Baptist to have doubts about the Warren court. Though W. A. Criswell said nothing publicly in 1954 or 1955, he was nonetheless perplexed by the *Brown* verdict. Having been reared in a west Texas community in which there were few blacks, the Dallas pastor "was not brought up with any particular racial prejudices." Prior to 1954 he had given scant attention to racial matters. Yet Criswell not only accepted but also rationalized racial separation. As a result of pastoral experiences in west Dallas, Criswell concluded that it was difficult if not impossible to unite different ethnic groups in one congregation. "When you tried to put them all together, you had a hard time, and eventually failed," he explained. But "when you divided them up and . . . had the black people with the black pastor and the Anglo people with the Anglo pastor, and the Mexican people . . . with a Latin pastor, why they just flourished over there [in west Dallas]."[30] So Criswell not only embraced the southern racial pattern, he considered it

[29] *Baptist Standard*, Oct. 14, 1954, p. 2.
[30] Oral Memoirs of W. A. Criswell, Waco, 1973, Baylor University Program of Oral History, pp. 261–63.

a pragmatic arrangement. In the churches it produced desirable results.

The more Criswell thought about the court's desegregation decision, the more irritated he became. It especially infuriated him that "the people who wanted to solve the racial problem in the South were from Harlem and South Chicago and Detroit." Convinced that the North had a more serious racial problem than the South, Criswell thought northerners should concern themselves with their own situation. "I just seethed on the inside," he explained, "when those people up there tell us how to solve the racial problem. Why don't they solve it in Harlem? Why don't they solve it in South Chicago? Why don't they solve it in Watts?" But not until February, 1956, did Criswell become publicly involved in the racial debate. In a speech to the State Evangelism Conference in Columbia, South Carolina, the Dallas minister rebuked "those people in Harlem and South Chicago" for telling southerners "how to solve our racial problem." These remarks promptly led to an invitation to address a joint session of the South Carolina legislature, where Sen. J. Strom Thurmond, who shared the Texan's sentiments, introduced Criswell "with great reverence."[31]

Speaking extemporaneously, the Dallas cleric defended segregation in such private areas as the home and church. Taking what he considered a practical approach, Criswell asserted that blacks had greater opportunities for service and self-expression in black congregations. Reflecting the view that blacks had a natural aptitude for song, he noted that his congregation in Dallas could not sing spirituals, "but they can over there at the colored folks' church." And, he added, "I've never seen a white preacher in my life that can preach like an honest-to-goodness, old-time, old-fashioned, colored preacher." Consequently, the Texan believed it was "better for them to be over there in their way, in their church, with their preacher, carrying on as they like to do," while "I'm over here with my flock and my kind . . . carrying on like we want to do."[32]

[31] Ibid., pp. 7–8.
[32] Speech by W. A. Criswell to the General Assembly of the South Carolina Legislature, Feb. 22, 1956, pp. 6–7, filed with Oral Memoirs, Criswell.

Satisfied that this was a harmonious and just arrangement, Criswell then assailed in an angry outburst "those two-by scantling, good-for-nothing fellows who are trying to upset all of the things that we love as good old southern people and as good old Southern Baptists." After raising the specter of racial intermarriage, Criswell concluded: "Don't force me by law, by statute, by Supreme Court decision . . . to cross over in those intimate things where I don't want to go. . . . Let me have my church. Let me have my school. Let me have my friends."[33] These remarks attracted national attention. The hometown *Dallas Morning News* carried the headline "Criswell Rips Integration," and over the next two days the minister shared the front page with Governor Shivers and stories on interposition.[34] In Dallas, church, state, and press were of one mind. The minister of the largest Southern Baptist congregation in the world was thereafter regarded as a staunch segregationist and racist.

Significantly, Criswell's comments did not go unchallenged. From Tokyo, evangelist Billy Graham, then a member of Criswell's Dallas congregation, mildly rebuked the Texan by announcing that "my pastor and I have never seen eye to eye on the race question."[35] But the sharpest response came from Thomas Maston of the Texas CLC, who considered Criswell's intemperate speech a tragedy. A few days afterward, Maston was in Nashville, Tennessee, for a meeting of the Southern Baptist Advisory Council on Work with Negroes, which had been formed in 1954. As chairman of this body, Maston subsequently collaborated with other Baptist leaders, including many blacks, on a statement to counteract Criswell's address, although the Dallas clergyman was not specifically mentioned in the document. Entitled "Appeal for a Christian Spirit in Race Relations," this declaration implored fellow Baptists to recognize that "prejudice against persons or mistreatment of persons on the grounds of race is contrary to the will of God." This was signed by the president of the Southern Baptist Convention, presidents of seven

[33] Ibid., pp. 7–8.
[34] *Dallas Morning News*, Feb. 23, 1956, pt. 1, pp. 1, 3; Feb. 24, 1956, pt. 1, pp. 1, 3, and pt. 2, p. 16.
[35] Ibid., Feb. 23, 1956, pt. 1, p. 1.

Southern Baptist colleges and seminaries, heads of numerous convention agencies, and others.[36]

Upon request of the Advisory Council, Maston then appeared before the 12,000 messengers at the Southern Baptist Convention in Kansas City on May 31, 1956. His brief talk, "Southern Baptists and the Negro," was picked up by the wire services and thus reached a national audience. The seminarian challenged Southern Baptists to apply Christian principles to race relations. "How tragic it would be for the churches in the South," he declared, "to place the stamp of divine approval upon social customs and traditional modes of behavior that fall far short of the spirit and teachings of Jesus."[37] The *Dallas Morning News* presented a good summary of Maston's talk, although the space allotted the professor was considerably less than that devoted to Criswell's earlier diatribe.[38]

In late 1956 the Christian Life Commission of the Southern Baptist Convention published and distributed to Baptist pastors across the South a pamphlet by Maston entitled *Integration*, which the Advisory Council had urged him to prepare. Essentially an elaboration of his Kansas City talk, Maston encouraged Christians to abide by Supreme Court decisions, help local communities adjust to new conditions, and graciously accept black children into the public schools. And in what was possibly a pointed rebuke of Criswell, Maston concluded that a Christian "should never be found in the camp of those who seek to make themselves popular with the people by appealing to their prejudices."[39] Although his pamphlets and addresses perhaps reached a wider audience and thereby had greater impact, Maston published two books on race in 1959 that also were important: *The*

---

[36] Oral Memoirs of T. B. Maston, Waco, 1973, Baylor University Program of Oral History, pp. 129–30; Thomas B. Maston, interview with author, Fort Worth, Mar. 16, 1979, pp. 27– 48. All citations from this interview are taken from a typed transcript of taped conversations; Bailey, *Southern White Protestantism*, p. 143.

[37] "Southern Baptists and the Negro," Maston Collection; *Annual*, SBC, 1956, p. 48.

[38] *Dallas Morning News*, June 1, 1956, pt. 3, p. 6. See also *Houston Post*, June 1, 1956, sec. 1, p. 16.

[39] Maston, *Integration* (Nashville: Christian Life Commission, Southern Baptist Convention, 1956), pp. 11–15.

Bible and Race and *Segregation and Desegregation*.[40] Of the two, *The Bible and Race* was probably the more influential. Broadman Press printed more than 50,000 copies, and the Woman's Missionary Union used it as a study book in 1962, thus ensuring an extensive distribution.[41]

Because Maston was a devoted churchman and nationally recognized scholar, his support of the Texas CLC on race during the late 1950s was invaluable. His words carried considerable weight with fellow Baptists. But he was not the only prominent Texan to give the new agency vital assistance. When Ewing S. James succeeded Gardner as editor of the *Baptist Standard* in late 1954, the CLC acquired another influential advocate.[42] Unlike his predecessor, who had often scoffed at social Christianity, urged the abolition of the Social Service Commission of the Southern Baptist Convention, and berated the Supreme Court,[43] the fifty-four-year-old James was more receptive, particularly to racial and social change. James Dunn's characterization of James was illuminating. The Baptist editor, said Dunn, was "parochial in culture and background and history," but "not parochial of intellect and spirit."[44] James's career as editor of the *Baptist Standard* reflects the accuracy of this assessment.

As a pastor in west Texas, James "had simply accepted the racial distinctions without much thought." Southerners, he explained in 1963, "lived in a culture where segregation was practiced, and we thought little about it until circumstances forced it upon our attention."[45] For the new editor, those "circumstances" were the court's desegregation order and recognition that southern racial practices adversely affected Baptist foreign missions.

[40] Oral Memoirs, Maston, pp. 138–39.

[41] William J. Pinson, Jr., ed., *An Approach to Christian Ethics: The Life, Contribution, and Thought of T. B. Maston* (Nashville: Broadman Press, 1979), p. 63.

[42] Maston, interview with author, pp. 43–44; Valentine to author, Aug. 20, 1979; Oral Memoirs, Allen, p. 100; James M. Dunn, interview with author, Dallas, May 23, 1979, pp. 23–24. All citations from this interview are taken from a transcript of tape-recorded conversations.

[43] See *Baptist Standard*, Apr. 22, 1948, p. 4; Oct. 14, 1954, p. 2; and Oral Memoirs, Miller, pp. 118–19.

[44] Dunn, interview with author, p. 25.

[45] Oral Memoirs of E. S. James, Waco, 1973, Baylor University Program of Oral History, pp. 89–90; *Baptist Standard*, July 24, 1963, p. 3.

These external pressures caused James to perceive more clearly the discrepancy between the ideals of his faith and Dixie's racial patterns. "I began to look the matter straight in the face," he recalled, "and I decided a person couldn't . . . be a segregation-ist and be the kind of Christian I ought to be." So the Baptist journalist threw his "influence . . . on the side of desegregation because . . . it appeared to be right in the sight of God."[46]

In the late 1950s James, who was "disturbed" by Criswell's outburst in South Carolina, did use the Baptist journal in behalf of racial accommodation. Articles of a moderate nature on racial topics frequently appeared in the *Standard*.[47] As yet, however, the editorial column disclosed a superficial if not naive position. On one occasion James lectured the NAACP on first-class citizenship. It meant more than voting, attending school, sitting in a particular place, or participating in community affairs. Regardless of color, asserted James, the person "who lives honorably, loves his nation, obeys its laws, seeks its welfare, and does his utmost to follow the will of Christ is a first-class citizen in capital letters."[48] On another occasion he recommended silence, since disagreement on race was too pronounced for society to reach a consensus.[49] In 1955 he applauded an evangelistic campaign in New Orleans in which blacks and whites, although remaining in their "own realm" with their "own people," conducted simultaneous revivals. Curiously, the results proved to James that God's favor rested "upon those big enough to forget color, circumstances, and classification in an united [revival] effort."[50] It later angered him when southerners were accused of being unchristian for resisting desegregation.[51]

During the early 1960s there was a noticeable shift in James's racial thought, and Jimmy Allen claimed a share of the credit. After Allen became director of the CLC, he and James

[46] Oral Memoirs, James, pp. 89–90.

[47] See *Baptist Standard*, Feb. 11, 1956, p. 11; Mar. 10, 1956, p. 9; Oct. 6, 1956, p. 5; Nov. 10, 1956, p. 5; Oct. 12, 1957, p. 12; Oct. 19, 1957, p. 10; Mar. 29, 1958, p. 10; Nov. 19, 1958, p. 10; and Mar. 11, 1959, p. 13.

[48] Ibid., Aug. 11, 1956, p. 2.

[49] Ibid., Jan. 11, 1958, p. 2.

[50] Ibid., Apr. 16, 1955, pp. 2, 11.

[51] Ibid., Feb. 18, 1959, pp. 2, 15.

became fast friends. For almost five years they had lunch together twice a week. Harold Basden, pastor of the Gaston Avenue Baptist Church in Dallas, frequently joined them. And
when Foy Valentine was in town, they made it a foursome.[52]
James thoroughly enjoyed the company of Allen and Valentine
and respected their work with the Texas CLC.[53] The atmosphere
at these luncheons was cordial and the exchange of views candid.
In Allen's judgment, these biweekly gatherings contributed to
the maturation of James's racial thinking.[54]

Allen is perhaps correct, but undoubtedly James was also
affected by the rush of events. Between 1955 and 1963 the civil
rights movement assumed revolutionary proportions. The fed-
eral government, albeit slowly at first, increasingly used its
might to achieve desegregation. Accordingly, in 1957 President
Dwight Eisenhower federalized the National Guard and sent in
Army paratroops to ensure integration at Central High School in
Little Rock, and in 1962 and 1963 President John Kennedy acted
similarly to have James Meredith enrolled at the University of
Mississippi, where a night of rioting left two dead, and Vivian
Malone enrolled at the University of Alabama, where Gov.
George Wallace made a defiant stand in the schoolhouse door. At
the same time, blacks themselves became more assertive. In
protest of the demeaning requirement that blacks sit in the rear
of the buses, Martin Luther King, Jr., organized a successful
boycott of the bus system in Montgomery, Alabama, in 1955.
Five years later four black college students in Greensboro,
North Carolina, staged a sit-in at the local Woolworth's segregated lunch counter. This incident, which attracted national
attention, had an electrifying effect. Similar demonstrations
spread to more than a hundred cities. Then, in May, 1961, to
challenge segregation laws and practices, the Congress of Racial
Equality sent the first wave of "freedom riders" into the South.

[52]Oral Memoirs, Allen, pp. 100, 131–32; Dunn, interview with author, pp. 23–24.
[53]Maston, interview with author, pp. 43–44.
[54]Oral Memoirs, Allen, p. 100. Although Allen's assessment is perhaps correct,
James in his Oral Memoirs, pp. 89–90, made no reference to these luncheons and acknowledged the influence of no one in particular on the racial issue. Said James, "I just
faced my own conscience on racism for the first time."

The Student Nonviolent Coordinating Committee, the Southern Christian Leadership Conference, and the Nashville Student Movement soon joined the effort, dispatching over a thousand riders across Dixie.

Such activities, of course, enraged militant segregationists. Violence erupted, most notably at Birmingham, Alabama, where in May, 1963, local police used dogs, electric cattle prods, and fire hoses against black demonstrators. Shown on national television, these graphic scenes captured the moral bankruptcy of segregationism. And in September, 1963, the nation was stunned by the killing of four black children in the bombing of a Birmingham church.[55]

By the early 1960s, moreover, editor James did not have to look beyond his hometown to be reminded of the racial crisis. Race was an inescapable topic of conversation in Dallas. On February 12, 1961, black students staged a "stand-in" at the city's segregated downtown theaters. When not allowed to purchase a ticket, the blacks returned to the end of the line and went through again and again. White students from Southern Methodist University joined the black protesters. An editorial the following day in the *Dallas Morning News* condemned both groups.[56] On February 20, 1961, the ubiquitous Thomas Maston addressed the Dallas Baptist Pastors' Conference on "The Pastor's Role in a Community Facing School Desegregation." This was timely, for Dallas was then struggling with court-ordered school desegregation. Because the seminarian's remarks were immediately picked up by the *Dallas Morning News* and later printed in the *Baptist Standard*, they had an impact throughout the area.[57] One year later Allen and the CLC devoted the sixth annual workshop to "Christianity and Race Relations," which

[55] John Hope Franklin, *From Slavery to Freedom: A History of Negro Americans* (New York: Alfred A. Knopf, 1967), pp. 623–33; Sydney E. Ahlstrom, *A Religious History of the American People* (New Haven: Yale University Press, 1972), pp. 1072–78; Harvard Sitkoff, *The Struggle for Black Equality, 1954–1980* (New York: Hill and Wang, 1981), pp. 13–20.

[56] *Dallas Morning News*, Feb. 13, 1961, sec. 4, p. 2; Feb. 14, 1961, Sec. 4, p. 1.

[57] Ibid., Feb. 21, 1961, sec. 4, p. 1; *Baptist Standard*, July 19, 1961, p. 8; Buford Stockard to Maston, Maston Collection, Feb. 22, 1961.

featured Kyle Haselden, editor of the *Christian Century*; Charles A. Wells, noted journalist and lecturer; and several persons who had lived through racial crises in Clinton, Tennessee, and in Little Rock. "We are a generation late in having a meeting of this kind," Allen told over four hundred pastors and laymen who attended the two-day session in Fort Worth, "but it could not have been held five years ago."[58] The *Baptist Standard* devoted several columns to this historic meeting.[59]

The cumulative effect of such events upon James was surely significant, but it was a meeting with President Kennedy that produced the most noticeable change in the *Standard*'s editorial pronouncements. In June, 1963, James attended a White House conference on civil rights. The results were immediate. Upon returning to Texas, the Baptist journalist expressed shame "that representatives of religion had to be reminded of their moral duty by representatives of government." He was particularly distressed by the recalcitrance of Southern Baptists. "With the exception of the courageous secretaries of the Christian Life Commission and the men who work with them," James asked, "how many of us have ever really risked our necks in defense of the Negro's rights?" Inasmuch as desegregation was "right in the sight of God," the editor wondered how much longer Southern Baptists would ignore their responsibility in this matter. "If Jesus were here in the flesh there is no doubt that He would defend the rights of the downtrodden just as He did when He was here. As His followers we can do no less," challenged James. Baptists should help implement integration rather than "hurl their epithets at the court."[60]

James thereafter consistently encouraged racial justice. In the fall, 1963, when Baylor University finally desegregated after almost a decade of foot-dragging,[61] James warmly commended

[58] *Baptist Standard*, Mar. 21, 1962, p. 8; Oral Memoirs, Allen, pp. 117–20.
[59] *Baptist Standard*, Jan. 24, 1962, p. 14; Feb. 21, 1962, p. 15; and Mar. 21, 1962, pp. 8–9.
[60] Ibid., June 26, 1963, p. 4.
[61] Protestant denominational colleges and universities in the South were much slower to desegregate than the region's state colleges and universities. Whereas 105 of 206 state institutions of higher learning were desegregated by 1957, only 55 of 188 Protestant institutions had followed suit. In May, 1963, 14 of 23 Southern Presbyterian ju-

the Baptist school.[62] And in 1964, when President Lyndon B. Johnson's far-reaching civil rights proposal became law, James, along with Jimmy Allen and Herbert Howard, voiced approval. "No Christian has a moral right to disobey any law of his nation unless it contravenes his obligation to God," James declared, "and there is nothing in this new law that in any measure prevents one's full devotion to God." The editor, furthermore, chided those Baptists who suggested that desegregation would lead to intermarriage.[63]

The shift in the editorial posture of the Baptist journal was quickly noticed. Many Baptists applauded James's forthright endorsement of civil rights and racial justice, but others were incensed. An irate Dallas Baptist announced that his church was going to drop the *Standard* from its budget until James "quit bragging on that communistic Supreme Court and quit preaching such communistic doctrines as race-mixing."[64] Especially annoying to many readers was James's refusal to publish pro-segregation articles. The editor minced no words in his explanation. James declared that racial segregation was "wrong spiritually and morally." Furthermore, as interpreted by the Supreme Court, the Constitution demanded "equal rights for everyone"; hence, it was not "proper for a Christian magazine to advocate doing something" prohibited by "the law."[65]

James's concern for racial justice was genuine, but his method was distinctly conservative. He preferred voluntary to coerced integration, especially in private facilities, and consequently considered "unreasonable and unneeded" that section of President Kennedy's proposed civil rights legislation that would force hotels, motels, restaurants, and stores to accept all people. Although agreeing that coercion was perhaps acceptable in public institutions, the Baptist editor strongly objected to

nior and senior colleges were still segregated. The pattern was similar in Texas. The University of Texas admitted black undergraduates in 1955; Southern Methodist University did not do so until 1962. See Bailey, *Southern White Protestantism*, pp. 147–48; *Dallas Morning News*, Feb. 16, 1961, sec. 6, p. 9.

[62] *Baptist Standard*, Dec. 4, 1963, pp. 4–5.
[63] Ibid., Apr. 1, 1964, p. 13; July 15, 1964, p. 4; and Jan. 15, 1964, p. 5.
[64] Ibid., July 10, 1963, p. 3. See also July 24, 1963, pp. 4–5.
[65] Ibid., Apr. 22, 1964, p. 5.

forced integration of private facilities that received no financial assistance from local, state, or federal agencies. Such an argument could easily be dismissed as a rationalization for delay, but this was not the case with James. "Desegregation of all private enterprises ought to be implemented now, once and for always," he stated, "but it should be done by volition rather than compulsion." James was a Christian of conservative leanings who believed that integration attained through "Christian love and respect for all mankind" was "a far more excellent way than integration by legislation."[66]

Accordingly, James resented aggressive behavior by blacks to achieve integration. Events of the early 1960s in Houston, culminating in the picketing of the First Baptist Church, were obviously distasteful to the Baptist journalist. In the spring, 1960, the city was beset by sit-ins, as black students from Texas Southern University struck the lunch counters at Weingarten's, Woolworth's, Grant's, and the city hall cafeteria. Segregation barriers quickly tumbled. With Foley's leading the way, downtown businesses, as well as the city hall cafeteria in 1961, quietly integrated their dining facilities. In 1962 Mayor Louis Cutrer prohibited discrimination in all city-owned buildings, and Sylvan Beach, a county park, complied with court orders to desegregate. The following year Mayor Cutrer ordered city swimming pools opened to all persons.[67] Amidst such activity, the large, prestigious, and segregated First Baptist Church was a logical target, especially given the prominence of its pastor. K. Owen White was elected president of the Baptist General Convention in November, 1962, and president of the Southern Baptist Convention in May, 1963. Shortly thereafter a young black man sought to join White's Houston congregation. Denied membership, the young man, joined by several other blacks, subsequently picketed First Baptist, carrying signs reading "Jim Crow Must Go" and "Father Forgive Them."[68] Editor James was an-

[66] Ibid., July 24, 1963, p. 3.
[67] David G. McComb, *Houston: A History* (Austin: University of Texas Press, 1981), pp. 169–70.
[68] *Baptist Standard*, June 19, 1963, p. 11; Aug. 7, 1963, p. 12; *Houston Chronicle*, Apr. 14, 1975, sec. 3, p. 24.

noyed. "Negroes have a right to seek membership in white churches, and under ordinary circumstances . . . should be received just as others," he wrote, "but when they resort to picketing they are wasting their energy and hurting the cause they seek to promote."[69]

By the same token, James considered violence by whites inexcusable. He was clearly agitated by the acts of savagery occurring in the trail of the Civil Rights Act of 1964. In July, 1964, a black educator from Washington was killed in Georgia by a shotgun blast from a moving car. That same month three young civil rights workers, two white New Yorkers and one black Mississippian, disappeared in Mississippi. Their bullet-riddled bodies were recovered weeks later. From June to October about twenty-four black churches in Mississippi were bombed or torched. In early 1965 the fury shifted to Alabama, where approximately 25,000 people from across the nation prepared to advance on Selma. Three more civil rights activists were slain.[70] Finally, in March, 1965, James unequivocally denounced the "cowardly assassins whose only motive was to show contempt for Negroes who sought the rights of citizenship." Importantly, white violence caused James to view somewhat more sympathetically the protest methods of blacks. "Some of the sit-ins, lie-ins, and other 'ins' are rather absurd and disgusting," he averred, but "we need to remember . . . that 20 million human beings had to find some method of protesting the second class status imposed on them by the white people." Moreover, observed James, "up until now" southern blacks had "seldom resorted to violence in pressing" their "claims for civil rights."[71]

In November, 1966, James retired. In retrospect, he considered the racial issue to have been the most difficult with which he had dealt. He was equally certain that many Texas Baptists had gradually modified their racial attitudes during his twelve years at the *Standard*. James believed the CLC deserved primary credit for this, but he promptly added: "I gave them

[69] *Baptist Standard*, Sept. 4, 1963, p. 4. See also Aug. 7, 1963, p. 12.

[70] Franklin, *From Slavery to Freedom*, pp. 637–38; Ahlstrom, *Religious History*, p. 1073; Sitkoff, *Struggle for Black Equality*, pp. 172–81.

[71] *Baptist Standard*, Mar. 24, 1965, p. 4.

[CLC] an opportunity to communicate with the people, [to] give their thoughts to the people." The journalist maintained that he had published more articles from the CLC "than from any other commission, by far."[72]

Regardless of who was most responsible, James was correct in sensing some progress. In 1963 almost one-third of the Baptist congregations within the General Convention responded to a statewide survey conducted by the Office of Public Relations. Of the 1,259 churches that replied, 63 percent had no policy on black attendance and 74 percent had no policy on black membership. But of the churches with a policy, 84 percent would seat black worshipers and 57 percent would accept them as members. These statistics further disclosed that the larger, urban congregations, those with more than 1,200 members located in cities of 25,000 or more, were somewhat more receptive to blacks than were the smaller churches with fewer than 300 members, a group that accounted for most of the responses.[73] These figures suggested that the General Convention was still in a state of flux. Most congregations had not resolved the racial question. Nevertheless, there were signs of positive change, albeit gradual, and James and the CLC could surely take some of the credit.

Signs of improvement were quickly overshadowed, however, as the racial crisis became decidedly more violent and assumed national dimensions in the late 1960s. The "southern problem" suddenly became a grave national concern, as western and northern blacks struggled for job opportunities and an end

[72] Oral Memoirs, James, pp. 161–63, 214–15.

[73] *Baptist Standard*, Sept. 18, 1963, p. 10. What was happening in Texas Baptist congregations perhaps reflected a softening of regional resistance to integration. A Gallup poll of January, 1961, showed that between August, 1957, just before the crisis at Little Rock, and January, 1961, the number of southern whites who expected integration eventually to become a way of life in their region increased from 45 percent to 76 percent. However, hostility toward the Supreme Court remained constant and intense. In June, 1954, 71 percent disapproved of the court's desegregation ruling, and in July, 1959, 71 percent still disapproved. See *Dallas Morning News*, Feb. 12, 1961, sec. 4, p. 3. Like many Baptist congregations at the time, First Baptist, Beaumont, allowed blacks to attend but would not allow them membership. See William R. Estep, *And God Gave the Increase: The Centennial History of the First Baptist Church of Beaumont, Texas, 1872–1972* (Fort Worth: Evans Press, 1972), p. 195.

to de facto segregation in education and housing. Fueled by poverty, frustration, and anger, ghetto rebellions erupted in the Watts area of Los Angeles (1965), in Newark (1967), and in Detroit (1967). Property damage was enormous and the number of deaths frightening.[74] Though the outbreaks were not as serious, Texas, too, experienced violence in 1967. In May there was a confrontation at Texas Southern University between students and the Houston police. For several hours a state of siege existed around one of the dormitories, as rocks and bottles were hurled and shots fired. A policeman was killed, and 488 students were arrested.[75] In October, 1967, the Texas CLC attributed these riots to "unjust laws and social conditions" and implored Baptists to work for the correction of such conditions. As Jimmy Allen exclaimed, it was "inconsistent only to hurl condemnation at the rioter and do nothing to correct the situation which created his plight."[76]

The following April, President Johnson's Commission on Civil Disorders, established in response to these urban upheavals, placed the crisis in a broader context. Ominously, the commission concluded that the nation was "moving toward two societies, one black, one white—separate and unequal."[77] The enthusiasm of many young blacks for Black Power not only seemed to confirm the report but also accentuated the fears of whites. Within the civil rights movement itself blacks were assuming the leadership roles and white moderates and liberals were being pushed into the background.[78] On April 4, 1968, Martin Luther King, Jr., an apostle of nonviolence, was slain in Memphis. Another wave of riots swept across the country. These events prompted John J. Hurt, who had succeeded James at the *Baptist Standard,* to accuse fellow Baptists of nonperfor-

[74] Franklin, *From Slavery to Freedom,* pp. 631, 636, 640–45; Ahlstrom, *Religious History,* pp. 1080–81; Sitkoff, *Struggle for Black Equality,* pp. 200–204.

[75] *Houston Post,* May 18, 1967, sec. 1, pp. 1, 12; May 19, 1967, sec. 1, p. 1; McComb, *Houston,* p. 170.

[76] BGCT, *Proceedings,* 1967, p. 17.

[77] Report of the National Advisory Commission on Civil Disorders (New York: E. P. Dutton, 1968), p. 1.

[78] See Joseph C. Hough, Jr., *Black Power and White Protestants: A Christian Response to the New Negro Pluralism* (New York: Oxford University Press, 1968).

mance. "We are attacking racial barriers in the churches with the effectiveness of a slingshot assault on Gibraltar," he declared.[79] By 1968, moreover, the anxiety was intensified by the growing disenchantment with the American effort in Vietnam. That Texas Baptists—indeed, Southern Baptists throughout the country— were deeply troubled by these events was reflected in a momentous declaration in June, 1968.

The 1968 Southern Baptist Convention had the earmarks of a Texas homecoming. Houston was the host city. More than 25 percent of the 15,071 messengers were Texans. W. A. Criswell was elected convention president. Arthur Rutledge gave the Home Mission Board report.[80] And Foy Valentine's controversial resolution, "A Statement Concerning the Crisis in Our Nation," dominated convention business. "Strike the crisis statement from the convention," editor John Hurt afterward observed, "and little is left."[81]

As Baptists from around the nation made ready for the Bayou City convention, there was a tense awareness of the impending debate over the national racial crisis. A few days prior to the meeting the *Houston Post* ran a story entitled "Racial Crisis Will Be Major Topic of Baptists" and described the anticipated declaration as "a manifesto on prejudice."[82] As the messengers arrived for the first meeting on Tuesday, June 4, they were greeted by student picketers urging them to act responsibly on social and racial issues.[83] The students were not to be disappointed. Speaking for the Christian Life Commission of the Southern Baptist Convention, Valentine challenged Baptists to match their ideals with deeds. Although the Baptist faith had always stressed the essential dignity, worth, and equality of all people, he said, the denomination had generally violated those ideals with regard to blacks. With the nation in the midst of a social and cultural upheaval, he added, churchmen must work toward the elimination of conditions within society that restrict

[79] *Baptist Standard*, Apr. 24, 1968, p. 6.
[80] *Annual*, SBC, 1968, pp. 5, 51, 89.
[81] *Baptist Standard*, June 19, 1968, p. 6.
[82] *Houston Post*, June 2, 1968, sec. 1, p. 11.
[83] *Dallas Morning News*, June 4, 1968, p. 17A.

equality of opportunity and contribute to racial prejudice and discrimination. "We rededicate ourselves to the proclamation of the gospel," the resolution affirmed, "which includes redemption of the individual and his involvement in the social issues of our day." Consuming almost a day, the resulting debate was at times angry. Some revisions were made, to Valentine's regret. But ultimately the "crisis declaration" was passed by a one-sided ballot vote of 5,687 to 2,119.[84] CBS News, overstating the case, called it "the most revolutionary statement" drafted by Southern Baptists.[85] James Dunn, the new director of the Texas CLC, turned his attention to putting the resolution into practice. In his annual report to the General Convention a few months later, he called on Texas Baptists to "help implement the Southern Baptist statement of concern for the crisis in our nation."[86]

But the 1968 meeting in the Space City had produced mixed results. The election of W. A. Criswell as president seemed in conflict with the social thrust of the crisis statement, for the Dallas pastor's main interest was "to lead our convention into a tremendous evangelistic and missionary revival."[87] However, Criswell, too, had changed somewhat. A few months before the convention his Dallas congregation had opened its doors to black members. When asked if this signaled a shift in his racial thinking, the pastor insisted that his position on race had always been misunderstood. Although he had never felt prejudice in his heart toward any racial group, he nevertheless had been branded a racist because of "a *vast* misinterpretation" of the 1956 speech to the South Carolina legislature. Circuitously, Criswell ex-

[84] *Annual*, SBC, 1968, pp. 67–69, 73; *Dallas Morning News*, June 5, 1968, p. 10A; June 6, 1968, p. 9A; *Houston Post*, June 5, 1968, sec. 1, p. 1; June 6, 1968, sec. 5, p. 5; *Baptist Standard*, June 19, 1968, p. 7. The assassination of Sen. Robert F. Kennedy occurred while the Southern Baptist Convention was in session and no doubt heightened the sense of crisis felt by many of the messengers. Kennedy was shot shortly after midnight, Wednesday, June 5. He lingered until Thursday, June 6, when he was pronounced dead at 1:44 P.M. The extent to which this tragedy affected the vote on the "crisis statement," which took place on Wednesday afternoon, June 5, can only be surmised. *Annual*, SBC, 1968, p. 63.

[85] *Baptist Standard*, June 19, 1968, p. 10.

[86] BGCT, *Proceedings*, 1968, p. 105. See also *Baptist Standard*, June 19, 1968, p. 10.

[87] *Baptist Standard*, June 12, 1968, p. 6.

plained that his "soul and attitude" had never changed, only his "public statements," and he had resolved to make "an about face" in his "public statements." More directly, the cleric conceded that his 1956 speech had been "a colossal blunder and mistake" stemming "from downright stupidity." Furthermore, Criswell flatly denied that his church's new racial policy had been calculated to enhance his chances of being elected convention president.[88]

Actually, the Dallas minister's adjustment on race was prompted by an assortment of motives. He never specifically said so, but the enormous changes in race relations from 1956 to 1968 must have had some effect. Fellow Baptists in Texas and around the nation who were sympathetic to the course of civil rights certainly made known to him their displeasure with his recalcitrance on race. Members of the academic community, both students and professors, continually criticized him. He was chagrined that his racial views were responsible for the withdrawal of an invitation to deliver a college commencement address. Criswell was sensitive to such rebuke. And he was aware of the changes abroad in the nation. The pastor, however, attributed his change of heart to other things. Concern for foreign missions was an important consideration. "I felt it was impossible to send a missionary from Baylor . . . over to Nigeria," he stated, "win them to Christ and then tell them, 'You can't come to this school.'" This indicates that Criswell recognized the difficulty of evangelizing the Third World while supporting domestic segregation. Another factor was apprehension about the possibility of blacks picketing his congregation, as they had First Baptist, Houston, after White's election as president of the Southern Baptist Convention. "A thing like that would kill me. Absolutely kill me," he confessed.[89] So image was important to Criswell, as it was to many conservative southern urbanites.

Whatever the precise reasons, Criswell's position on race

[88] Oral Memoirs, Criswell, pp. 225, 251, 257–71; *Dallas Morning News*, June 6, 1968, pp. 9A, 1D; *Houston Post*, June 6, 1968, sec. 5, p. 5; June 8, 1968, sec. 1, p. 18. See also *Baptist Standard*, July 17, 1968, p. 3, for a report of a national radio broadcast in which Criswell unequivocally denounced segregation.

[89] Oral Memoirs, Criswell, pp. 224–25, 267–69.

had moderated, as had to some extent his stand on social issues. Although he had had no part in its formulation, the new president endorsed the crisis statement and pledged to work for its implementation. Evangelism was still paramount, but Criswell agreed that faith could not be separated from works. Baptists concerned about applied Christianity were thus assured that the Dallas pastor would give attention to that aspect of faith.[90]

The sense of urgency that had produced the crisis statement soon ebbed, however. In 1969 the Texas CLC neglected race altogether in its annual report, and in 1970 there was only a general statement of concern.[91] Perhaps this deemphasis was due to indications of progress. By 1970 some evidence suggested an increased willingness of churches within the General Convention to accept black members, and local associations increasingly allowed black congregations into their affiliation. The First Baptist Church, Del Rio, had a black deacon.[92] Such developments, coupled to the toppling of legal segregation, no doubt gave many churchmen the impression that the racial issue had been settled. In fact, there remained much to do, and in many ways the issue had become more complex and subtle.[93] Desegregation itself generated additional concerns that were difficult to cast in moral terms and thereby prick the conscience. The immorality of legal segregation had finally become clear and obvious, and in 1968 Baptists had spoken with conviction in the crisis statement. But what about the morality of busing, white flight, and the proliferation of private academies? The commission began addressing these matters in 1971. It sanctioned busing to "overcome the sins of our fathers," branded white flight as "unchristian and unrealistic," and condemned private

[90] Oral Memoirs, Criswell, pp. 232–33; *Baptist Standard*, June 12, 1968, p. 6. In the closing address to the Southern Baptist Convention on Friday, June 7, evangelist Billy Graham had struck a similar pose. He told the Baptists they must give proper balance to evangelism and social action. See *Houston Post*, June 8, 1968, sec. 1, pp. 1, 9.

[91] BGCT, *Proceedings*, 1969, pp. 86–91; 1970, p. 94.

[92] *Baptist Standard*, Nov. 18, 1970, p. 5; BGCT, *Proceedings*, 1967, p. 17.

[93] By 1970 the idea that the racial issue had been settled was a common sentiment among white moderates and liberals, whether in or out of the church. See Robert Calvert, "The Civil Rights Movement in Texas," in *The Texas Heritage*, ed. Ben Procter and Archie P. McDonald (Saint Louis: Forum Press, 1980), pp. 160–61, 163.

Baptist schools, if their purpose was to maintain segregation.[94]

Although race had consumed considerable time and energy since the 1950s, it had not been the agency's only concern. Ever mindful of encroachments on religious liberty, Texas Baptists had also been alert to matters of church and state. In the early 1950s the appointment of an ambassador to the Vatican evoked concerted opposition; in 1960 the presidential campaign of a Catholic sparked emotional debate; in the mid-1960s the question of federal aid to private institutions sharply divided Texas Baptist leaders; and throughout the 1960s the discussion over public school prayers was intense. If these concerns lacked the moral urgency associated with race, they nevertheless disturbed not only Baptists but many other Americans as well. Labor unions, teachers' organizations, the United States Chamber of Commerce, the National Association of Manufacturers, the National Catholic Welfare Conference, and the National Council of Churches were all entangled at various points by specific aspects of the church-state problem.[95] And strange alliances were not unusual. To their discomfort, for instance, Baptists sometimes found themselves on the same side as "the most hated woman in America," Madalyn Murray O'Hair, an outspoken atheist.[96]

Controversy over matters of church and state was exacerbated after World War II by both the maturation of Roman Catholicism and the passing of the "Protestant era" in American history. Catholicism was no longer an "immigrant faith" drawing its membership primarily from underprivileged Europeans who in America had often lived in isolation, separated from the mainstream by language and a network of parochial schools. Showing remarkable vitality, Catholicism expanded from 22 million to 42 million adherents between 1940 and 1960,[97] and by mid-century Catholics wielded considerable power within the Democratic party, especially in the large urban centers. They were pros-

[94] BGCT, *Proceedings*, 1971, pp. 31–32.

[95] Murray S. Stedman, Jr., *Religion and Politics in America* (New York: Harcourt, Brace and World, 1964), p. 80.

[96] *Baptist Standard*, Sept. 16, 1964, p. 7.

[97] Edwin Scott Gaustad, *Historical Atlas of Religion in America* (New York: Harper and Row, 1962), p. 110.

perous and enjoyed respectability. Fulton J. Sheen, whose writings and television program attracted Protestants as well as fellow Catholics, rivaled Norman Vincent Peale and Billy Graham in popularity.[98] On the other hand, there had been an unmistakable erosion of the Protestant ethos. Though still the faith of approximately two-thirds of all Americans, Protestantism had failed to maintain a Protestant America and now faced the necessity of accommodating itself to a pluralistic society.[99] Will Herberg aptly assessed the situation in 1955. "Protestantism today no longer regards itself either as a religious movement sweeping the continent or as a national church representing the religious life of the people"; rather, it "understands itself today primarily as one of the three religious communities in which twentieth century America has come to be divided."[100]

As Protestants and Catholics confronted one another at mid-century, neither understood the other very well. A Catholic scholar remarked in 1957 that members of his faith had "only the vaguest notion" of Protestant beliefs and modes of worship. Similarly, a Protestant writer of the same period commented that Americans knew more about baseball batting averages and the marital spats of Hollywood stars than "the life and worship" of Roman Catholics.[101] Such ignorance compounded tension and made accommodation difficult.

Texas was a microcosm of sorts of the national religious scene. From a position of overwhelming predominance early

[98] See Ahlstrom, *Religious History*, pp. 998–1018; Robert T. Handy, *A History of the Churches in the United States and Canada* (New York: Oxford University Press, 1976), pp. 400– 401; Winthrop S. Hudson, *Religion in America: An Historical Account of American Religious Life* (New York: Charles Scribner's Sons, 1965), pp. 397–99, 405–408; and Jackson W. Carroll, Douglas W. Johnson, and Martin E. Marty, *Religion in America, 1950 to the Present* (New York: Harper and Row, 1979), pp. 8–9, 81–83.

[99] See Martin E. Marty, *Righteous Empire: The Protestant Experience in America* (New York: Dial Press, 1970), pp. 244– 54; and Franklin H. Littell, *From State Church to Pluralism: A Protestant Interpretation of Religion in American History* (Chicago: Aldine, 1962), pp. 144–62.

[100] Herberg, *Protestant-Catholic-Jew: An Essay in American Religious Sociology* (Garden City, N.Y.: Doubleday, 1955), pp. 139–40.

[101] John A. Hardon, *The Protestant Churches of America*, (Garden City, N.Y.: Doubleday, 1957), p. xv; Jaroslav Pelikan, *The Riddle of Roman Catholicism* (Nashville: Abingdon Press, 1959), p. 12.

in the century, the number of Texas Protestants steadily lost ground to that of Catholics. In 1906 Protestants composed approximately 75 percent of the state's churchgoers, with Baptists alone constituting about one-third. Catholics accounted for approximately 25 percent. Signs of change were evident by 1926. Although slowly, the percentage of Catholics was growing, while the number of Protestants, particularly Methodists, was ebbing somewhat. By 1971 the number of Catholics, representing 32 percent of the churchgoing population, had surged past the totals of all religious bodies in Texas except Southern Baptists, who totaled 37.5 percent. But the gap between the state's two largest religious bodies was closing. Although each group experienced a slight decline during the 1970s, only four percentage points separated the two by 1981. And for the first time, Catholics surpassed Southern Baptists in Harris County (Houston).[102] The obvious vitality of Catholicism in the Houston area, coupled to the slower growth rate of Baptists, prompted Louis Moore, religion editor of the *Houston Chronicle*, to predict that in Harris County, Catholics would outnumber all the various groups of Baptists combined by 1990.[103] If Texas Baptists yielded room to Catholicism, they nevertheless stiffly resisted what they perceived as efforts by Catholics to breach the wall separating church and state.

In 1951, for instance, Texas Baptists, like many Protestants elsewhere,[104] were incensed when President Harry Truman, a fellow Baptist, sought to appoint Gen. Mark Clark as ambassador to Vatican City. A. C. Miller and the CLC accused "the Catholic hierarchy" of seeking "to destroy the effect of the 1st amendment" and called upon "the Christian forces of our churches and communities for immediate and continuous action

[102] Edwin Scott Gaustad, *Historical Atlas of Religion in America* (New York: Harper and Row, 1962), p. 51; Albert W. Wardin, Jr., *Baptist Atlas* (Nashville: Broadman Press, 1980), p. 15; Douglas W. Johnson, Paul R. Picard, and Bernard Quinn, *Churches and Church Membership in the United States, 1971: An Enumeration by Region, State and County* (Washington, D.C.: Glenmary Research Center, 1974), p. 11; Bernard Quinn et al., *Churches and Church Membership in the United States, 1980* (Atlanta: Glenmary Research Center, 1982), pp. 25, 269.

[103] *Houston Chronicle*, Oct. 2, 1982, sec. 6, p. 7; Oct. 30, 1982, sec. 6, p. 1.

[104] Hudson, *Religion in America*, pp. 420–21; Handy, *History of Churches*, p. 402.

against this betrayal of our constitution and of our liberties."[105]
Joseph Dawson, then head of the Baptist Joint Committee on
Public Affairs, upbraided the president for playing politics. He
believed Truman, with an eye toward the upcoming presidential
race, was courting the Catholic vote in the big cities, those
"plague-spots under the rule of rotten political machines."[106]
Similar to Miller, Dawson maintained that if the Senate rati-
fied the appointment, "America's distinctive principle of separation of church and state" would be virtually lost.[107] J. Howard
Williams, the executive secretary of the General Convention,
was equally foreboding.[108] Texas Baptists stood united against the
Vatican appointment, and Catholic historian John Tracy Ellis's
characterization of the general Protestant reaction as "near hysteria" was not an exaggeration.[109] In the face of such resistance,
the nomination was withdrawn.[110]

The presidential election of 1960 likewise alarmed many
Protestants, but the reaction was not comparable to that of
1928.[111] In the earlier campaign Catholicism was still largely an
immigrant faith; the KKK was much more active, although its
influence upon the election results was minor;[112] prohibition
generated as much concern as religion; and prominent church
leaders throughout the country readily joined the fray against a
"wet" Catholic from New York City.[113] The Protestant establish-

[105] BGCT, Proceedings, 1951, pp. 200–202.
[106] Baptist Standard, Dec. 20, 1951, p. 3; July 2, 1953, p. 4.
[107] Ibid., Dec. 6, 1951, p. 3. See also Dec. 13, 1951, p. 3.
[108] Ibid., Nov. 1, 1951, p. 1.
[109] John Tracy Ellis, American Catholicism (Chicago: University of Chicago Press,
1956), p. 156.
[110] Hudson, Religion in America, p. 420.
[111] See James A. Michener, Report of the County Chairman (New York: Random
House, 1961), pp. 245–51, 267–72, for a running account of the religious factor at the
grass-roots level in Bucks County, Pennsylvania, and elsewhere, by a novelist turned
politician. Michener noted that religion was a major concern in every meeting he conducted in Bucks County. See also James A. Pike, A Roman Catholic in the White House
(Garden City, N.Y.: Doubleday, 1960), for an informed account by a noted Episcopalian;
and Littell, From State Church to Pluralism, pp. 151–53.
[112] Chalmers, Hooded Americanism, pp. 300–303; Robert Moats Miller, American
Protestantism and Social Issues, 1919– 1939 (Chapel Hill: University of North Carolina
Press, 1958), pp. 49–50.
[113] Bailey, Southern White Protestantism, pp. 92–110; Ahlstrom, Religious His-

ment in Texas mirrored the national mood, and J. Frank Norris led the attack, barnstorming the state in behalf of Herbert Hoover, "that Christian gentleman," and against Al Smith, that "wet-Catholic." Over a period of fourteen weeks the Fort Worth Baptist, now an independent and no longer affiliated with the General Convention, delivered 119 speeches in thirty cities. His anti-Catholicism was blatant. Conjuring up images of Dark Age persecutions, sinister papal authority, and the inevitable loss of religious liberty, Norris usually concluded with fervent appeals to "mother, flag, God, the Bible, and Herbert Hoover."[114]

Though not to the same degree as the Smith candidacy, the nomination in 1960 of another Catholic, John Kennedy, nevertheless agitated Texas Baptists. E. S. James and the *Baptist Standard* set the tone.[115] Even before Kennedy was nominated, the Baptist journalist sounded the alarm. He was troubled over matters of church and state, particularly federal aid to parochial schools, papal control over Catholic politicians, and the potential erosion of religious liberty.[116] Before the Massachusetts senator would be acceptable to James, he would have to renounce his "allegiance to the foreign religio-political state at the Vatican" and issue "a declaration of freedom from the domination of the clergy."[117] Kennedy, who had already made a strong statement in behalf of separation of church and state for *Life* magazine on March 3, 1959,[118] responded personally to James on May 4. "But I thought my previous expressions have made it perfectly clear that, in the conduct of my office and the fulfillment of any Constitutional oath, my undivided political allegiance is to the best interests of this country," wrote Kennedy, "and I determine

---

tory, pp. 903–904, 1006–1007; Hudson, *Religion in America*, pp. 398–99; Marty, *Righteous Empire*, pp. 212–15; and Miller, *American Protestantism*, pp. 48, 62.

[114] Quoted in Norman D. Brown, *Hood, Bonnet, and Little Brown Jug: Texas Politics, 1921–1928* (College Station: Texas A&M University Press, 1984), p. 411. See also pp. 393–422; Bailey, *Southern White Protestantism*, p. 106.

[115] See C. Gwin Morris, "E. S. James and the Election of 1960," *Journal of Texas Baptist History* 2 (1982): 25–36.

[116] *Baptist Standard*, Feb. 3, 1960, pp. 3–4; Feb. 10, 1960, pp. 3–4; Feb. 17, 1960, pp. 3–4; Apr. 30, 1960, pp. 3, 5; May 4, 1960, p. 3.

[117] Ibid., Feb. 17, 1960, p. 4.

[118] Quoted in Pike, *Roman Catholic in the White House*, p. 38.

those best interests on the basis of my best conscientious judgement, without domination from any source."[119]

James applauded this forthright assertion but added that he would not be fully satisfied until the Catholic hierarchy announced its concurrence in Kennedy's position. As on previous occasions, the Catholic press created problems for the presidential hopeful by disputing his claim to complete independence.[120] This time *L'Osservatore Romano*, the Vatican City newspaper, confirmed the Baptist editor's allegations. In late May it declared that the Catholic hierarchy had the "duty and right to guide, direct, and correct" communicants in both religious and political matters.[121] James quickly seized upon this and argued that a Catholic politician, regardless of what he said, could not be free of papal influence. James never let up on this point. He continued to the eve of the November election to warn Baptists of the potential danger of Catholic hegemony within American government if Kennedy should be the victor.[122]

There is little doubt that James reflected the sentiment of numerous Texas Baptists. W. A. Criswell believed a Kennedy victory would open the door for another Catholic later who would give "the pope his ambassador, the church schools state support, and finally recognition of one church above all others in America."[123] And when Blake Smith, the able pastor of the University Baptist Church, Austin, told his Sunday congregation on September 11 that the election of a Catholic would not endanger separation of church and state, members of the Austin Baptist Pastors' Association promptly rebuked him in a resolution passed by a vote of 25 to 3.[124] Even Kennedy's televised appearance on September 12 before the Greater Houston Ministerial Alliance, in which he vigorously proclaimed his belief in separation of church and state and forcefully reasserted his opposition

[119] *Baptist Standard*, May 4, 1960, p. 3.

[120] See Pike, *Roman Catholic in the White House*, pp. 38–39.

[121] Quoted in Morris, "James and Election of 1960," p. 29.

[122] *Baptist Standard*, June 15, 1960, p. 4; June 29, 1960, p. 4; Aug. 24, 1960, p. 4; Oct. 5, 1960, p. 4; Oct. 12, 1960, p. 3; and Oct. 19, 1960, p. 5.

[123] Ibid., July 13, 1960, p. 14.

[124] *Houston Post*, Sept. 12, 1960, sec. 1, p. 6; *Dallas Morning News*, Sept. 13, 1960, sec. 1, p. 11; Sept. 14, 1960, sec. 1, p. 8.

to a Vatican appointment and to federal aid for parochial schools, failed to assure Baptist leaders.[125] If the Democratic standard-bearer's confrontation with the ministers had "knocked religion out of the campaign as an intellectually respectable issue," as Arthur Schlesinger, Jr., thought,[126] it had not overcome Baptist suspicions. Pastor Criswell retorted that the senator was "either a poor Catholic" or just "stringing the people along." Editor James regarded the Houston address as "a splendid statement" of Kennedy's personal beliefs and declared once more that if the Catholic hierarchy would be equally forthright "the real controversy will suddenly come to an end."[127] Baptists elsewhere in the state had similar misgivings.[128]

The Southern Baptist Convention reflected a comparable mood. At its annual meeting in May in Miami, Florida, the national body had all but directed its followers to vote against Kennedy. The messengers affirmed their historical commitment to separation of church and state, and they insisted that "personal religious faith" should "not be a test" of one's "qualifications for public office." Then they immediately turned around and made a test of religion. A candidate who belonged to a church known to be "in open conflict with our established and constituted American pattern of life," declared the Baptist assembly, could not be expected to "make independent decisions consistent with the rights and privileges of all citizens."[129] Kennedy was not mentioned by name, but the inference was plain enough. The CLC of Texas assumed a more moderate posture. It regarded religion to be a legitimate campaign issue and urged Texas Baptists to scrutinize the position of every candidate on church-state separation, but it carefully avoided any suggestion of anti-Catholicism.[130]

Following Kennedy's subsequent victory over Richard

[125] *Houston Post*, Sept. 13, 1960, sec. 1, pp. 1, 9; Stedman, *Religion and Politics*, pp. 115–16.

[126] Schlesinger, *A Thousand Days: John F. Kennedy in the White House* (Boston: Houghton Mifflin, 1965), p. 68.

[127] *Dallas Morning News*, Sept. 14, 1960, sec. 4, p. 1.

[128] Ibid., Sept. 15, 1960, sec. 1, p. 24.

[129] *Annual*, SBC, 1960, p. 71.

[130] BGCT, *Proceedings*, 1960, pp. 107–108.

Nixon, Texas Baptist leaders, notably E. S. James, called upon
churchmen to support the new chief executive. "As good American citizens," James wrote, "Baptists and all other believers in
Christ should give their best support to the new administration
so long as he is in the right. He is entitled to our prayers daily
and to the best encouragement we can give him." James followed
his own advice and before long came to view Kennedy as not
only "sound" on church and state but also as a friend.[131]

Federal aid to parochial schools, a matter that had concerned James during the presidential campaign, was another
area of tension between Protestants and Catholics. Although
Protestants and Jews operated schools, they did so on a much
smaller scale than did Catholics. In 1960 approximately 3.5 million Catholics attended elementary church schools, as compared
with approximately 225,000 Protestants and 22,000 Jews. Given
the important contribution they were making toward educating
the nation's young, Catholics believed they were justified in
seeking federal assistance to help offset escalating costs. To many
Catholics, such aid seemed fair and reasonable. But Protestants
viewed the situation differently. The constitutional question
aside, they pointed to the awesome burden of maintaining mul-
tiple school systems if each religious group were to be treated
equally. Although the Supreme Court in *Everson* v. *Board of
Education* (1947) had ruled that direct aid to religious schools
was unconstitutional, the issue was far from settled. Still un-
resolved was the matter of federal help for transportation,
nonreligious textbooks, lunches, and health care. Local school
districts, in grappling with these issues, quickly became aware
of both the complexity and divisiveness of the church-state
controversy.[132]

[131] *Baptist Standard*, Nov. 11, 1960, p. 4; Morris, "James and Election of 1960,"
p. 32.

[132] Hudson, *Religion in America*, p. 421; Edwin Scott Gaustad, *A Religious History
of America* (New York: Harper and Row, 1974), pp. 378–79; Handy, *History of Churches*,
p. 402; John C. Murray, *We Hold These Truths: Catholic Reflections on the American
Proposition* (New York: Sheed and Word, 1960), pp. 143–54; Robert F. Drinan, "The
Constitutionality of Public Aid to Parochial Schools," in *The Wall between Church and
State*, ed. Dallin H. Oaks (Chicago: University of Chicago Press, 1963), pp. 55–72; Murray A. Gordon, "The Unconstitutionality of Public Aid to Parochial Schools," in *Wall
between Church and State*, ed. Oaks, pp. 73–94.

Texas Baptists were kept abreast of Catholic attempts to secure federal funds by the Baptist Joint Committee on Public Affairs, located in Washington and presided over by Texan Joseph Dawson until 1953, and by Protestants and Other Americans United for Separation of Church and State (POAU), a nonsectarian body Dawson was instrumental in forming in 1947. Dawson in 1955 alerted Texans to the usage of public buses for parochial schools, employment at regular salaries of nuns in church garb to teach in public schools, efforts to obtain grants for sectarian school construction, and actions of Catholic-controlled public school boards adverse to public schooling. Three years later amendments to the Hill-Burton bill to allow low-interest government loans to private hospitals attracted attention.[133]

In the early 1960s, despite President Kennedy's assurances that federal aid to parochial schools would be unconstitutional,[134] Texas Baptists nevertheless worried about education bills that permitted tax funds for private institutions.[135] Specifically, they regarded the Higher Education Facilities Act (1963) and the Elementary and Secondary Education Act (1965) as victories for the proponents of federal aid. The latter measure, a component of President Lyndon Johnson's Great Society, provided substantial assistance for the first time for elementary and secondary schools, especially those in economically depressed areas. It allowed the use of tax money for both public and private libraries, remedial programs, adult education, and the construction of educational centers.[136] Despite its obvious benefits for the underprivileged, this law alarmed many Baptists. E. S. James lamented that "little by little the wall of separation between church and state" was "being ground to powder."[137] Jimmy Al-

[133] *Baptist Standard*, July 23, 1955, pp. 6–7; July 30, 1958, p. 10.

[134] Stedman, *Religion and Politics*, p. 78. See also Schlesinger, *Thousand Days*, p. 662.

[135] *Baptist Standard*, Jan. 25, 1961, p. 4; Apr. 5, 1961, p. 4; Apr. 12, 1961, p. 5; BGCT, *Proceedings*, 1961, p. 82.

[136] Paul K. Conkin and David Burner, *A History of Recent America* (New York: Hill and Wang, 1981), pp. 578–79. See also Wilber G. Katz and Harold P. Southerland, "Religious Pluralism and the Supreme Court," in *Religion in America*, ed. William G. McLoughlin and Robert N. Bella (Boston: Houghton Mifflin, 1968), pp. 277–80.

[137] *Baptist Standard*, Jan. 8, 1964, p. 4. See also Feb. 17, 1965, p. 4; Mar. 31, 1965, p. 4; and June 9, 1965, p. 4.

len, like other Americans throughout the nation who saw in this legislation the possibility of a federal takeover of the local schools, believed "the entire nature of our society" would be affected by recent measures.[138] Similarly, in 1964 President Johnson's Economic Opportunity Act, popularly known as the War on Poverty, caused concern, inasmuch as public tax money often went to sectarian groups that administered various aspects of the program. Project Headstart, an education program for underprivileged preschoolers, was often cited.[139] Significantly, in 1964 the CLC and the *Baptist Standard* collaborated on a survey of every candidate for the U.S. Congress "on the important issue of aid to parochial schools," and the annual Christian Life Workshop that year examined church-state relations.[140]

Meanwhile, a school case in Bremond, which came to a climax in 1961–62, epitomized what Texas Baptists usually had in mind when they thought of violations of separation of church and state. A small, rural, and largely Catholic community in central east Texas, Bremond came to the attention of Foy Valentine and the CLC in 1958. At issue was Saint Mary's Elementary, a parochial school operated by the Catholic church until 1948. At that point the Bremond school board, composed of three Catholics, two Methodists, and two Baptists, leased the facility for one dollar a year and operated it at public expense. For the next twelve years Saint Mary's was a parochial school funded with public money. All the students, who were transported in public buses, were from Catholic homes; all the teachers were nuns in religious garb; Catholic insignia remained on the walls; the local priest visited the school at will; religious instruction was provided the students; and one section of the library was devoted exclusively to Catholic literature. In January, 1959, shortly after Valentine and the CLC became involved, the Citizens Association for Free Public Schools was formed. Legal proceedings were initiated, and in August, 1962, the matter ended without going to court when the Bremond school board discontinued the

---

[138] Ibid., Jan. 20, 1965, p. 13.

[139] Ibid., Mar. 25, 1964, p. 9; July 22, 1964, p. 11; Aug. 11, 1965, p. 4; Apr. 20, 1966, p. 4.

[140] BGCT, *Proceedings*, 1964, p. 111; *Baptist Standard*, Mar. 18, 1964, p. 9.

lease. To Valentine, Jimmy Allen, E. S. James, and other Baptists, the Bremond case was a clear and flagrant violation of the separation principle.[141] Baptist vigilance seemed vindicated.

By this time, however, Texas Baptists were discovering that church-state entanglements were far more bedeviling than they had imagined. To their chagrin they learned that Baptists, too, often committed transgressions. The complexities and subtleties of the issue came into sharper focus as financially strapped Baptist colleges looked longingly upon federal aid in the late 1950s and early 1960s. Consequently, in 1959 the General Convention formed a Special Committee on Church-State Relations to analyze the various facets of federal assistance and to recommend guidelines for Texas Baptist institutions. Harold G. Basden was chairman; Jimmy Allen was a member. In its report of November, 1961, the Basden committee unequivocally opposed "all direct aid" and long-term, low-interest government loans to Baptist facilities in Texas. But tax exemptions for religious establishments, loans to students under the National Defense Education Act, and research grants from the government to educational institutions were permissible. Mailing privileges for nonprofit organizations were "a technical violation," however, since this amounted to a government subsidy. Nevertheless, the committee's recommendation was not only interesting but also beneficial to the *Baptist Standard*. There was "no realistic way to approach the problem of adequately compensating the government," read the report, inasmuch as "the entire postal system" operated at a deficit. The General Convention adopted these guidelines, and the CLC was in accord with them.[142] Repeatedly, whether under Allen or Dunn, the commission implored Baptists to resist the allure of direct federal aid.[143]

Despite acceptance of the Basden report, the debate persisted. Faced with rising operational and construction costs, Texas Baptist colleges faced a crisis. Spiraling expenses had al-

[141] *Baptist Standard*, May 20, 1954, pp. 3–5; Feb. 15, 1961, p. 4; Feb. 28, 1962, p. 11; Sept. 19, 1962, p. 4; Apr. 20, 1966, p. 4.

[142] BGCT, *Proceedings*, 1961, pp. 16, 81–82, 85–93.

[143] Ibid., 1961, p. 82; 1965, p. 19; 1971, p. 30; 1978, p. 74.

ready forced Hardin-Simmons to discontinue intercollegiate football.[144] The Higher Education Facilities Act, which offered loans to sectarian institutions for building construction, appealed to many Baptists. Aware of this, the CLC in November, 1964, voiced "regret . . . that some Baptist groups" were "succumbing to this temptation" for "easy [federal] money."[145] Indeed they were. The presidents of such esteemed Baptist schools as Furman University in Greenville, South Carolina; Mercer University in Macon, Georgia; and Wake Forest College in North Carolina were forthright advocates of federal aid. In Texas, the pro-aid cause was led by President Abner McCall of Baylor University, who was elected president of the General Convention in 1964.

The issue reached a climax in 1965–66. In the spring issue of the *Baylor Line* (1965), a publication for former students, McCall offered a rationale for the acceptance of federal loans by Baptist colleges. He maintained that religious liberty was a principle "of supreme importance," whereas separation of church and state was "a political device calculated to support the principle of religious liberty, but not indispensable to religious liberty." The Baylor executive argued that the wall of separation could be breached without endangering religious liberty, whereas the suppression of liberty would render the separation principle meaningless. As for those Baptists who claimed that federal aid would lead to government regulations, McCall retorted: "I have news for them: our institutions are already licensed and regulated by the governments." Turning to the Basden report, McCall found it interesting that the committee had proscribed "only federal financial aid to the *church-related* institutions," while approving "all instances of direct or indirect governmental subsidies to the *churches* themselves," such as tax exemptions. Moreover, he noted that the financial saving to the *Baptist Standard* emanating from its nonprofit mailing privileges was "*by far the largest governmental subsidy taken by a Southern Baptist Agency.*" These factors prompted McCall

[144] *Baptist Standard*, Feb. 12, 1964, p. 8.
[145] BGCT, *Proceedings*, 1964, p. 30.

to charge that the Basden report "was based more on Baptist intra-denominational politics than on principle."[146]

E. S. James immediately joined the fray. McCall's charge of intradenominational politics "cut to the soul," and his figures regarding the *Standard*'s mailing costs were miscalculated. Even so, the journalist admitted that the Baptist paper saved more than $100,000 a year as a result of its nonprofit status. James did not approve of this, but it was up to the convention, not the *Standard*, to change the policy. And McCall, James wryly observed, was currently president of the General Convention.[147]

In October, 1965, at the General Convention in Houston, McCall's presidential address focused on the issue of church and state. He cited numerous transgressions by Texas Baptists since the 1930s. He mildly chided editor James, suggesting that other Baptist institutions should be lucky enough to receive subsidies while protesting against them.[148] But Texas Baptists were not in tune with the Baylor leader. In the convention sermon, Herbert R. Howard countered McCall. "We cannot, we dare not, we shall not forsake our Christian, our Baptist position," he exclaimed, "regardless of the consequences to our institutions." The CLC joined the chorus, declaring that "the preservation of our institutions through the use of tax money may increase the difficulty in preserving religious liberty through separation of church and state."[149] In 1965 the General Convention took no official action on federal aid, but in 1966 it specifically prohibited the acceptance of government loans by Baptist institutions and reaffirmed its commitment to the Basden report.[150] There has been little change in this position. Similarly, the CLC has consistently opposed government aid. In 1978, for instance, it even questioned the wisdom of the tuition equalization grants for students in Texas Baptist schools, explaining that this prac-

[146]"Baptist Institutions and Government Aid and Regulations," *Baylor Line*, reprinted in *Baptist Standard*, May 26, 1965, pp. 6–8.

[147] *Baptist Standard*, May 26, 1965, pp. 4–5. See also July 14, 1965, pp. 6–7; Aug. 4, 1965, pp. 6–8.

[148] Ibid., Nov. 17, 1965, pp. 6–10.

[149] Ibid., Nov. 3, 1965, p. 6; BGCT, *Proceedings*, 1965, p. 19.

[150] BGCT, *Proceedings*, 1966, pp. 21–27.

tice had weakened the denomination's traditional stand against aid to parochial schools.[151]

Whereas other church-state disputes had tended to align Protestants against Catholics, the Supreme Court's decision on prescribed prayers and Bible reading in public schools arrayed Protestants against Protestants. As Martin Marty said, these decisions exposed "the battle lines within Protestantism."[152] In *Engel* v. *Vitale* (1962), popularly known as the "Regents Prayer Case," and *Abington* v. *Schempp* (1963), the court declared that prescribed prayers and Bible reading in public schools were unconstitutional.[153] A furor erupted. "With the possible exception of its ruling on racial integration," E. S. James wrote, "nothing has so stirred the citizens of this country."[154] That Americans of varied religious and political persuasions opposed these judicial decrees was shown in numerous attempts to amend the Constitution. Evangelist Billy Graham, who finally decided that the 1962 prayer decision was proper, concluded that some sort of amendment should nevertheless be adopted to guarantee that American institutions did not become totally void of religious influences.[155] Letters to the *Baptist Standard* disclosed conflicting views among the laity. While many churchmen considered the decisions consistent with the principle of separation of church and state, others were perplexed. As a Victoria woman wrote: "We Baptists are trying so hard to keep church and state separated that we are literally joining the atheists."[156]

Generally, Texas Baptist leadership agreed with the justices and sought to explain the prayer decisions to the rank and file. This annoyed an Amarillo Baptist, who accused the *Baptist Standard* of trying to elevate "the Supreme Court to sainthood."[157] To be sure, editor James was untroubled by the judicial action and insisted that God had not "been driven from the pub-

---

[151] Ibid., 1978, pp. 70–72, 74.

[152] Marty, *Righteous Empire*, p. 249.

[153] Gaustad, *Religious History*, pp. 383–86.

[154] *Baptist Standard*, July 4, 1962, p. 5.

[155] Ibid., Aug. 8, 1962, p. 4. See also Marty, *Righteous Empire*, pp. 249–50; Katz and Southerland, "Religious Pluralism," pp. 271–75.

[156] *Baptist Standard*, July 24, 1963, p. 5. See also July 10, 1963, p. 3.

[157] Ibid., July 24, 1963, p. 5.

lic school room by the U.S. Supreme Court." The justices had not opposed religion as such, he elaborated, but had "simply ruled that prescribed and controlled religion shall not be forced upon students by the power of government." To James, this was "moral, fair, American, and best for the preservation and the progress of the nation."[158] When the Baptist journalist subsequently was asked to join the campaign An Amendment for God, he spurned the invitation. "This country doesn't need an amendment for God," he retorted. "God was not brought into American life by the adoption of the constitution, and His tenure here will not be determined by acts of Congress nor by ballots of the people."[159] James's position was unswerving. In 1964 he warned that current efforts to amend the Constitution were "an unparalleled threat to religious liberty." James believed the First Amendment was sufficient protection and should not be modified.[160] The CLC and Jimmy Allen, who as early as August, 1958, had vigorously opposed the usage of public school facilities for even voluntary religious functions, heartily concurred.[161]

But Executive Secretary T. A. Patterson was not as comfortable with the judicial action as were James and Allen. He feared that the 1962 decision foreshadowed "a further paganization of American life," inasmuch as it was a victory not only for Baptists but also for atheists. Somewhat prophetically, Patterson suggested that atheists would pressure "our schools to eliminate everything that pertains to religion." Editor James and the CLC had always explained that the justices in 1962 and 1963 had prohibited prescribed, not voluntary, prayers.[162] Indeed, the Supreme Court did not specifically ban voluntary devotionals in public institutions, but the trend in the lower courts was definitely in that direction. In 1966 a circuit court upheld a public school principal in New York who had forbidden voluntary

---

[158] Ibid., July 4, 1962, p. 5. See also *Dallas Morning News*, June 18, 1963, sec. 4, p. 1.

[159] *Baptist Standard*, Aug. 8, 1962, p. 2.

[160] Ibid., Apr. 8, 1964, p. 4. See also June 10, 1964, p. 4; Aug. 12, 1964, p. 5.

[161] Ibid., Aug. 6, 1958, p. 7; July 4, 1962, p. 12; BGCT, *Proceedings*, 1962, p. 29.

[162] *Baptist Standard*, Sept. 26, 1962, p. 9. See BGCT, *Proceedings*, 1980, p. 78.

prayers. The Supreme Court refused to review the case.[163] And in 1971, when voluntary devotionals were banned in public institutions in Massachusetts and New Jersey, the Supreme Court again declined to hear the cases.[164] So Patterson was close to the mark.

Not surprisingly, these lower court decisions sparked another drive to amend the Constitution. Until his death in 1969, the powerful Republican senator from Illinois, Everett Dirksen, gave momentum to the movement. The Prayer Amendment, as it was popularly known, came before the U.S. House in November, 1971. Consistently, the CLC urged its defeat. "The right to pray is safe now," asserted James Dunn in the commission's annual report. "The best thing that government can do for religion is to let it alone." Although still disturbed by the judicial trend, Patterson did not endorse the amendment.[165] As a body, Texas Baptists never joined fundamentalist evangelicals in the quest for a prayer amendment.

After nineteen years of uncertainty and countless efforts to alter the Constitution, the Supreme Court finally rendered a decision on voluntary prayer in December, 1981. The debate is not likely to end, however, for the court did not act decisively. In an 8–1 verdict the justices set aside a University of Missouri rule that denied religious groups access to campus facilities. According to the court, such a policy violated the right of Christian students to free speech. But the court refused to hear a similar case involving high school students in Guilderland, New York, who were denied permission to hold prayer meetings each day before school. Although the court made an important distinction between high school and college students, the matter is not over. A federal judge, whose decision is under appeal at this writing, approved the policy of a Lubbock, Texas, school board allowing voluntary religious meetings during free periods.[166]

[163] *Baptist Standard*, Jan. 5, 1966, p. 4.
[164] Ibid., Nov. 24, 1971, pp. 7, 10–11.
[165] BGCT, *Proceedings*, 1971, p. 30; *Baptist Standard*, Nov. 24, 1971, p. 7.
[166] *Newsweek*, Dec. 28, 1981, p. 49. In Mar., 1982, the Fifth Circuit Court of Appeals in New Orleans overturned the ruling of the federal district judge in Lubbock, and

Another concern of the Texas CLC, especially in recent years, has been the condition of Mexican-Americans in the Rio Grande Valley. In the early 1960s T. A. Patterson, as executive secretary of the convention, initiated the River Ministry, largely an evangelistic movement aimed at the predominantly Catholic population along the border with Mexico.[167] This missionary movement, which coincided with a period of renewed assertiveness by Tejanos, contributed to an understanding of the appalling poverty in south Texas, the plight of migrant farm laborers, and the issue of undocumented aliens. In turn, the CLC attempted to inform and educate Texas churchmen on the needs of this region.

In June, 1966, when migrant laborers, inspired by the recent success of Cesar Chavez and his United Farm Workers Association in California, went on strike against local melon growers for higher wages, they kindled a movement of considerable proportions. In an effort to involve Hispanic youths in state politics, José Angel Gutiérrez and others formed the Mexican American Youth Organization (MAYO), members of which soon established La Raza Unida Party (RUP). Using the word *Chicano* as a unifying symbol, Mexican-Americans then set out to gain political control of those Texas counties in which they constituted a majority.[168] In the meantime, Weston W. Ware, a former associate director of the CLC who was then associated with the U.S. Peace Corps, journeyed south in the summer of 1966. He subsequently described the poverty of the region and observed that farm laborers had "been excluded systematically

on Jan. 17, 1983, the Supreme Court, without comment, refused to review the Fifth Court's ruling. Meanwhile, in June, 1982, the Southern Baptist Convention became the first major denomination to endorse President Ronald Reagan's call for a constitutional amendment on prayer in public schools. In November, 1982, however, the General Convention of Texas refused to go along with the Southern Baptist Convention, voting overwhelmingly against "legislatively prescribed prayer." See *Baptist Standard*, Jan. 26, 1983, p. 6; Feb. 2, 1983, p. 9; July 27, 1983, pp. 3, 6; and *Houston Chronicle*, Nov. 12, 1982, sec. 1, p. 13.

[167] Oral Memoirs of Thomas Armour Patterson, Waco, 1978, Baylor University Program of Oral History, pp. 220–24.

[168] Rodolfo Rocha, "The Tejanos of Texas," in *Texas: A Sesquicentennial Celebration*, ed. Donald W. Whisenhunt (Austin: Eakin Press, 1984), pp. 350–52; Arnoldo De Leon, "Los Tejanos: An Overview of Their History," in *Texas Heritage*, pp. 142–43.

from almost every piece of social and welfare legislation for the last 30 years," the minimum wage being an example. Although Ware suggested no specific course of action, he insisted that the "churches certainly should not be silent." The following year Jimmy Allen observed that migrant workers had a right within the American system "to public protest and to organize for bargaining." He added that the churches, among other things, should support efforts to upgrade general adult education and to provide technical and vocational training.[169]

In 1972 the CLC chastised the state of Texas for its "abysmal failure to meet the needs of the Mexican-American quarter of the population." Citing Texas Education Agency figures that 80 percent of the Mexican-Americans who entered public school failed to graduate, the commission declared: "We can no longer tolerate a system that perpetuates ignorance at so great a cost to the state." Hence, the CLC forthrightly endorsed bilingual education. In 1978 the commission informed churchmen that the three poorest areas in the nation were "found in Texas amid the palm trees and the lush farmland of the lower Rio Grande Valley." Following a detailed description of poverty, illiteracy, and sickness, the commission called on Texas churchmen to develop day care programs and medical clinics and to support legislation giving "farmworkers power to improve their own working conditions." The need for a statutory guarantee for collective bargaining for migratory farm labor was overdue in Texas. By 1980 Texas Baptists had an extensive system of medical-dental clinics along the border and had employed the half-time services of an El Paso doctor to oversee the facilities.[170]

Intertwined with growing concern about Mexican-Americans was the issue of illegal aliens, especially public schooling for the children. Although the CLC sanctioned "efforts to decrease the flow of undocumented aliens into this country," the agency realized that the matter was not that simple. In 1975 the Texas legislature allowed local school districts either to charge tuition to children illegally in the state or to refuse them public school-

[169] *Baptist Standard*, Sept. 14, 1966, pp. 6–7; Aug. 2, 1967, p. 9.
[170] BGCT, *Proceedings*, 1972, p. 31; 1978, p. 73. See also 1977, pp. 71–72; 1980, p. 147.

ing altogether. The commitment of the CLC to public education was unquestioned. Time and again it defended the public system. Church-state considerations aside, its long-standing opposition to parochial aid, whether for Catholic or Baptist schools, stemmed from the belief that tax dollars for private institutions would jeopardize the quality of public schooling. But what about the children of undocumented aliens? Would they not place a burden upon an already overtaxed public system? In 1979 the CLC observed that the children of illegal aliens would likely become lifelong residents of Texas. Consequently, the commission believed it would be wiser and cheaper to educate the children now than to pay for the "added social services in the future" that would accompany illiteracy and poverty. Furthermore, Texas was the only state that forbade free education to such children.[171] Finally, in 1982 the CLC unequivocally urged the Texas legislature to "correct this error of the past by repealing the prohibition against the education of undocumented children and joining the other 49 states in allowing the education of all children."[172]

Its response to undocumented aliens indicates that the CLC has faced the concerns of modern American society. It has endeavored to show that the Good News was aimed not only at the individual believer but at society as well. Personal regeneration entailed ethical responsibility, and ethical behavior involved vastly more than support of prohibition and campaigns against parimutuel gambling. In applying the gospel message to a myriad of contemporary issues, the CLC demonstrated for fellow churchmen the breadth of the Christian faith. To the extent that Texas Baptists today understand the broader ethical implications of their religion, the Christian Life Commission can properly claim a large share of the credit.

[171] Ibid., 1977, p. 72; 1972, p. 31; 1975, pp. 33–34; 1979, p. 77.
[172] Baptist Standard, Feb. 3, 1982, p. 7.

8

Continuity and Change

IN a discerning analysis of southern Protestantism, church historian Samuel S. Hill, Jr., harshly criticized southern Protestantism for overemphasizing piety and evangelism and neglecting serious theological discussion and ethical responsibility. As a result, Hill believed the southern churches, notably Southern Baptists, had insulated themselves against the intellectual ferment spawned by Charles Darwin and Sigmund Freud and had ignored the social dimensions of their faith. "Having been bypassed by much of 'early modern religion,' completely out of touch with 'modern religion,'" he wrote, southern Protestantism "languishes in a patently obsolete semimedievalism, calling it 'timeless.'"[1] Specifically, Hill charged that Southern Baptists had no rationalizations for social involvement, showed no genuine respect for academic freedom, were deaf to prophetic voices, and were ignorant of the historical forces, past and present, affecting Christianity.[2]

Unfortunately, there is some validity in Hill's argument. In recent developments within the General Convention one sees the ghost of J. Frank Norris and hears an echo of the 1920s. In 1979–80, for instance, the quarrel over inerrancy, the idea that the Bible in its original manuscripts was without error, surfaced in yet another textbook controversy at Baylor University and in another intradenominational struggle for power and influence. Reminiscent of the Grove Samuel Dow affair, Jimmy Draper, pastor of the First Baptist Church, Euless, and a member of the Baylor Board of Trustees, challenged the veracity of a textbook, *People of the Covenant*, coauthored by H. J. Flanders, chairman of the Department of Religion at Baylor. Draper rebuked Flanders for interpreting symbolically rather than taking literally

---

[1] Samuel S. Hill, Jr., *Southern Churches in Crisis* (New York: Holt, Rinehart and Winston, 1966), p. 181.

[2] Ibid., pp. 171–72, 190, 200, 207.

such figures as Adam and Eve and such stories as Jonah and the big fish.[3] Flanders retained his position at Baylor, but his book was discontinued as a text for survey courses in religion and the Baptist university was advised "to use . . . diligence and caution in securing professors who believe the divine inspiration of the whole Bible."[4]

Meanwhile, Paige Patterson, the son of former Executive Secretary T. A. Patterson and head of the Criswell Bible Institute in Dallas, which is owned by the First Baptist Church, seized upon the issue of inerrancy to direct the General Convention along more fundamentalist lines and to gain control of Baptist institutions. In 1979, convinced that denominational leaders were out of step with the rank and file, Patterson hinted that he would take the Baylor textbook matter to the Southern Baptist Convention floor in Lubbock if the Baylor administration showed "no sensitivity to the feelings of individual grassroots Baptists in Texas." Furthermore, Patterson, in concert with Paul Pressler, a Texas Court of Appeals judge and Houston Baptist lawyer, urged churchmen of his persuasion to attend the upcoming Lubbock meeting in order "to see to it that the officers elected . . . believe in the inerrancy of the Bible."[5] After the fashion of J. Frank Norris, Patterson soon thereafter raised doubts about several prominent churchmen, suggesting they were not true to historic Baptist beliefs.[6]

Although W. A. Criswell shared Patterson's theological outlook, as well as his desire to purify Baptist institutions, the political tactics of the younger man disturbed him. Consequently, Patterson was instructed by his employer to forego political

---

[3] *Houston Chronicle*, Oct. 20, 1979, sec. 5, p. 1.

[4] Baptist General Convention of Texas, *Proceedings*, 1980, p. 80 (cited hereafter as BGCT, *Proceedings*).

[5] *Houston Chronicle*, Oct. 20, 1979, sec. 5, p. 1.

[6] *Baptist Standard*, May 14, 1980, pp. 4–5. In 1984, while attending the Southern Baptist Convention in Kansas City, Patterson again raised the question of scriptural fidelity, announcing that he was keeping a "heresy file" on professors and pastors whose views departed from traditional Baptist beliefs. See *Beaumont Enterprise*, June 14, 1984, p. 10C. For a good overview of the struggle within the Southern Baptist Convention, see James C. Hefly, "The Historic Shift in America's Largest Protestant Denomination," *Christianity Today*, Aug. 5, 1983. pp. 38–41.

efforts to gain control of key convention posts.[7] To Criswell, the
need of the hour was for more evangelistically oriented pastors.
In June, 1980, sounding more like a nineteenth-century anach-
ronism than a minister searching for answers to modern concerns, the Dallas minister exhorted the faithful at the Southern
Baptist Convention in Saint Louis. "We must," he declared,
"have men of God who preach not sociology but salvation, not
economics but evangelism, not culture but conversion, not reformation but regeneration, not renovation but revival, not revolution but redemption, not progress but pardon, not the new
social order but the new birth."[8]

Criswell's peroration suggests that the way to achieve harmony among Baptists is to eschew divisive social issues, stressing instead those traditional endeavors of evangelism and missions. Even T. B. Maston recently confirmed this point of view,
acknowledging that missions unified the denomination.[9] And the
budget of the General Convention is a graphic reminder that
missions will always be paramount. Whereas the CLC was allocated $275,000 in 1980, the State Missions Commission re-
ceived $4,612,484.[10] Such a division of resources is understand-
able, for an aggressive evangelism in the Criswell manner serves
a dual function—it drowns out conflict over troublesome social
matters and ensures continued institutional growth. From the

[7] *Baptist Standard*, May 14, 1980, p. 4. Despite Criswell's directive, Patterson not
only remained politically active but was also quite successful. See *Houston Chronicle*,
Mar. 31, 1984, sec. 2, p. 13; May 26, 1984, sec. 1, p. 35; June 16, 1984, sec. 6, p. 1.
James J. Thompson, Jr., *Tried as by Fire: Southern Baptists and the Religious Controversies of the 1920s* (Macon, Ga.: Mercer University Press, 1982), pp. 212–14, under-
estimates the intensity of the debate, which has been going on for the last five years
within the Southern Baptist Convention. If the heated rhetoric has recently cooled, it
has done so only because the heirs of J. Frank Norris have generally prevailed over
convention moderates. The extent to which this rightward shift within the national convention will affect Texas Baptists is difficult to gauge. The Baptist General Convention,
which owns Baylor University, is an independent body. The Southern Baptist Convention has no authority over it; yet, many of the fundamentalists who have recently influenced the direction of the national organization are Texans—Draper, Patterson, and
Pressler. If these men are as successful in Texas as they have been at the national level,
they could then affect such institutions as Baylor and the CLC.

[8] *Houston Chronicle*, June 10, 1980, sec. 1, p. 3.
[9] *Baptist Standard*, Dec. 23, 1981, p. 2.
[10] BGCT, *Proceedings*, 1980, pp. 622–24.

local pastor to the upper levels of the bureaucracy in Dallas, promotional and institutional concerns—budgets, building programs, and the enlistment of new members—continue to take precedence over social involvement.

Still, Hill's assessment is too severe, although understandable. Writing in the mid-1960s, when racial violence in the South and upheavals in black ghettos of the North reached an alarming level, Hill obviously saw little cause for optimism. The southern churches, instead of striving to ease the crisis, seemed woefully derelict. Indeed, many southern churches were recalcitrant in confronting the racial crisis and, in general, socially myopic. John Lee Eighmy's observation concerning Southern Baptists was applicable to southern churches in general—they were "in cultural captivity."[11] Even so, there were clear signs of progress among Texas Baptists. From Joseph Dawson to Maston to James Dunn, there had always been individuals within the General Convention who grappled with social issues, chided other churchmen for the one-dimensional, exclusively evangelistic nature of their faith, and accepted the challenges generated by the intellectual movements of the nineteenth and twentieth centuries. Since 1915, moreover, the General Convention had provided these individuals with institutional forums. As a result, from the Civic Righteousness and Social Service committees to the Department of Interracial Cooperation to Our Ministry with Minorities to the Christian Life Commission, there had been a continuous and growing concern within the convention about social Christianity.

Moreover, this commitment to practical religion has been genuine, especially since the launching of the CLC in 1950. The new commission was never envisioned by its founders as merely another means of winning lost souls. It was not intended to be an adjunct of evangelism. Rather, the CLC was fashioned to focus denominational attention on serious social concerns and to declare forcefully what Texas Baptists ought to be doing. Instead of searching for denominational consensus, the CLC was to be a

[11] Eighmy, *Churches in Cultural Captivity: A History of the Social Attitudes of Southern Baptists* (Knoxville: University of Tennessee Press, 1972), pp. xii–xiii.

prophet. And since the 1960s it has often suggested legislative remedies to social injustices. This does not mean that the CLC has strayed from its Baptist roots. Indeed, the agency has consistently striven for balance between evangelism and social activism. In 1967 the commission stated its position concisely. It was equally "disturbed by the tendency . . . of some advocates of . . . social action to shrug off evangelism as if it were of secondary importance" and "by the attitudes of some evangelistically minded men who treat the ethical demands of the gospel as handicaps to making converts." The following year the commission added that "personal redemption and Christian social action belong together," for "the Christian ethic is indissolubly joined with Christian conversion."[12]

Such declarations were far more than a matter of diplomacy. That is, they were not issued merely to appease evangelistically oriented Texas Baptists. The leaders of the CLC were genuinely committed to evangelism. After all, they *were* Southern Baptists. They shared the missionary interests of the multitudes. Their theology was conservative—they believed in the flawed nature of humanity, the tenacity of sin, and the transcendence of God. But like Walter Rauschenbusch, those Baptists associated with the CLC had no difficulty combining evangelism, theological conservatism, and social activism.

Among Texas Baptists, it could not have been otherwise. Churchmen such as J. M. Dawson, T. B. Maston, A. C. Miller, Foy Valentine, Jimmy Allen, and James Dunn could not have nudged the General Convention to address social problems if they had been perceived as unsound theologically. Blake Smith, the progressive and erudite pastor of the University Baptist Church, Austin, illustrates the point. His influence was sharply curbed because many fellow Baptists considered him a theological liberal. Because he was theologically suspect, his social pronouncements could be conveniently ignored. By contrast, the leaders of the CLC could not be so easily disregarded. Assiduously building upon a tradition dating back to the early 1900s,

[12] BGCT, *Proceedings*, 1967, p. 19; 1968, p. 107.

they labored from within the General Convention to teach fellow churchmen about the dual nature of faith. Evangelism was important to them, but equally so was ethical responsibility. Consequently, because of the CLC and its supporters, Texas Baptists today understand more clearly the ethical imperatives of faith than did their parents or grandparents a generation or two ago.

A Bibliographical Note

Since the footnotes indicate the sources upon which this study is based, a long bibliography citing each item once again seems unnecessary. Still, a comment regarding primary materials is in order.

The *Baptist Standard* was indispensable. This weekly newspaper was first printed in Dallas in 1889 as the *Western Baptist*. In 1892 new owners moved the paper to Waco and rechristened it the *Texas Baptist Standard*. Six years later the publication was returned to Dallas, where it remains, and renamed the *Baptist Standard*. Ownership of the paper changed hands several times between 1898 and 1909, when it was purchased by a group headed by George W. Truett and James B. Gambrell. In 1914 this group gave the journal to the Baptist General Convention, and ever since it has been the official voice of Texas Baptists. The paper is invaluable to the historian, for its reflects not only the views of top convention leadership but also discloses the issues that are of concern to the state's Baptists at a particular time. I have thoroughly examined the *Baptist Standard* from 1900 to 1980.

The *Proceedings* of the Baptist General Convention, published annually, are a record of the yearly meeting of Texas Baptists, which usually is held in October or November. The resolutions passed by this body are not binding and cannot be imposed upon member churches. Baptist congregations are locally autonomous; the General Convention has no control over them. This is reflected even in the terminology used by Texas Baptists to describe the individuals who attend the annual confab: they are not "delegates" empowered by the various congregations to represent them but, rather, "messengers" sent from the local flocks. Local autonomy does not mean, however, that convention statements are insignificant. On the contrary, given the democratic nature of Baptist ecclesiology, convention resolutions probably reflect the prevailing mood of Texas Baptists at a given moment. Furthermore, the resolutions carry the weight of moral suasion. Hence, these *Proceedings*, which I have examined from the mid-1880s to 1980, have been of considerable help in gauging denominational trends and sentiment.

In addition to annual convention records, I have studied the minutes of a selected group of local Baptist associations. Within the General convention, churches in reasonably close proximity are joined together in associations. The number of associations in the General Convention has ranged from about 100 in 1900 to about 120 in 1980. The associations meet annually, and their deliberations provide an index to Baptist opinion at the local level. Moreover, these documents indicate, to some extent, whether, or to what degree, local communicants shared the concerns of state leaders. I have examined the records for a limited number of associations, selected according to geography. That is, I attempted to get a sampling from different parts of the state. In alphabetical order, the associations studied were: Austin, Dallas County, El Paso, Limestone County (Groesbeck-Kosse area), Nacogdoches, San Antonio, San Marcos, Southeast Texas (Beaumont-Port Arthur area), Tarrant County (Fort Worth–Arlington area), Union (Houston-Galveston-Conroe area), Van Zandt County (Edgewood-Corinth area), and Waco.

Scholars at Baylor University, under the auspices of the Texas Baptist Oral History Consortium, have conducted interviews with numerous denominational leaders. The bound transcriptions of these interviews are housed in the Texas Collection at Baylor. I have read the Oral Memoirs of the following, listed alphabetically: Jimmy Raymond Allen (1973), Philip Dale Browne (1973), W. A. Criswell (1973), Joseph M. Dawson (1972), E. S. James (1973), E. N. Jones (1973), John Jeter Hurt, Jr. (1978), T. B. Maston (1973), Acker C. Miller (1973), Thomas Armour Patterson (1978), Ralph A. Phelps (unbound), Blake Smith (1972), R. A. Springer (1971), and Foy Dan Valentine (unbound). One of the values of this material is that it provides insights to denominational affairs by the participants themselves.

Additionally, I interviewed at some length James M. Dunn (Baptist Building, Dallas, May 23, 1979), a former director of the Christian Life Commission; T. B. Maston (Southwestern Baptist Seminary, Fort Worth, March 16, 1979); and Phil D. Strickland (Baptist Building, Dallas, November 6, 1981), the current director of the CLC. These discussions, like the Oral Memoirs, offered an assessment of events from an insider's point of view. I also corresponded with Jimmy Allen, T. B. Maston, A. C. Miller, Foy Valentine, and numerous local pastors.

The Personal Papers of Professor Maston, housed in the Treasure Room at the Fleming Library at Southwestern Seminary, were essential in tracing the development of his social thought, as well as assessing the reaction of other Baptists to his views. Also located at the Fleming

Library are the papers of George Washington Baines, B. H. Carroll, James M. Carroll, Walter Conner, J. Frank Norris, and Lee Rutland Scarborough. Consisting primarily of sermons, letters, and articles, much of this material was of limited use.

J. Frank Norris's newspaper, on the other hand, was quite helpful. The Fleming Library has a complete file on microfilm of this weekly, which was originally called the *Searchlight*. In April, 1927, Norris changed the name to the *Fundamentalist*. I read only selected issues, primarily from the 1920s, of this newspaper.

Index